ACTING FOR OTHERS

Hau
BOOKS

Editors
Giovanni da Col
Sasha Newell

Editorial Office
Faun Rice
Sheehan Moore
Michael Chladek
Michelle Beckett
Justin Dyer
Ian Tuttle

www.haubooks.com

ACTING FOR OTHERS
RELATIONAL TRANSFORMATIONS
IN PAPUA NEW GUINEA

By Pascale Bonnemère

Translated by Nora Scott

Hau Books
Chicago

Cover and layout design: Sheehan Moore

Typesetting: Prepress Plus (www.prepressplus.in)

ISBN: 978-0-9973675-8-4
LCCN: 2017917361

Hᴀᴜ Books
Chicago Distribution Center
11030 S. Langley
Chicago, IL 60628
www.haubooks.com

Hᴀᴜ Books is printed, marketed, and distributed by The University of Chicago Press.
www.press.uchicago.edu

In memory of Tenawi, who died in bringing life into the world in 1992. And Ikundi beri and Onorwae, my two cherished companions, who died in 2004. And to Matrena, without whom my work among the Ankave would have been very different.

Table of Contents

List of Illustrations

Table

Foreword

Marilyn Strathern

Acting for others is a book to stir the anthropological imagination. It breathes new life into debates over relationality and agency, both through a vivacious and lucid style and through the considerable assistance of the Ankave-Anga of Papua New Guinea. These people furnish Pascale Bonnemère with a beautifully orchestrated demonstration of just what is lost in overlooking women's participation in social processes, here specifically and pointedly in the stages through which men achieve fatherhood. She opens out their demonstration/her observation into a splendid critique of ritual action, and beyond that to the significance of Ankave ideas about agency. In their eyes, it is the exercise of a specific capacity that divides men from women: for the former it takes a ritual sequence to gain the vantage point from which the latter already and inevitably are actors, namely the capacity to act on behalf of—on and for—others. At the end, the author suggests just why she is writing on these matters for a broad readership, and why there are debates still to be renewed here.

  This close focus on some of the major preoccupations of Ankave people, and the anthropological controversies concerning gender and personhood to which it leads, will bring to an English-reading audience a much broader sense of Bonnemère's extensive and to some extent audacious—at once daring and courageous—exploration of ethnographic purpose than her articles already in English can convey. More than that, the present work transforms some of her own earlier emphases, as her experiences in Ankave over time were also transformative. As to the courage, the conclusion here holds a little surprise.

CAPACITY

The rewards are manifold. I am torn between wanting to engage with the intriguing perspective that Ankave have afforded Bonnemère (alongside the analytical vocabulary they have inspired) and not wishing to give too much away. For the argument unfolds rather like a drama, and although she states her central problematic clearly at the outset, the course of ethnographic description builds up in a revelatory manner. It would be a shame, for example, to anticipate the outcome of the considerable analytical finesse by which she shows how the presence of women is crucial to the capacities a man acquires.

Ankave say their rites make men, but what are men? They are not only fathers but also mother's brothers, the principal roles in which they act for others. This in turn has consequences for the identity of other participants in "the construction of the male person." As the reader will find, Ankave women's presence in these rites is not the suspended presence of absence; on the contrary, they appear as active participants in what is going on. Boys are not transformed by men's actions alone, and ritual efficacy depends on the comportment of both sexes. Indeed, women are at once crucial to registering the transformations entailed and the recipients of men's capacity to act.

Participation does not imply symmetry, and this is not a book concerned with adjudications about social equality. Bonnemère had to make several actual returns to the Anga area before being in an ethnographic position to write this account; at the same time, she is also reexamining and thus conceptually returning to a much older stratum of theorizing about gender relations in Papua New Guinea, which took literally the exclusion of women from men's rites, and which dominated early accounts of other Anga societies in particular. With as much diplomacy as determination she shows that exclusion from certain rites is not the same as exclusion from the whole sequence of events by which men find their destinies. While always being careful to note what is specific to Ankave—and there is much variation among Anga peoples, as Pierre Lemonnier (2004) underlines—she inevitably raises a question about the systematic "invisibility" of women from other anthropological visions. The process by which she pursues this question is a model of what can be gained by opening up the scope of material to be drawn into analysis; she repeatedly comes back to the need to see practices in relation to one another. If this seems an obvious anthropological strategy, the capacity of the analysis depends on just where and how that scope is defined. Bonnemère consistently draws attention to the relation between what men and what women are doing. And if I stress the analytical work, and it is superb, that is precisely to draw attention to the fact that ethnographic insight is not just there for the looking.

Many of the issues that the author raises resonate with preoccupations found across the anthropological spectrum. Women's invisibility has of course been treated from many perspectives; from being attributed to the bias of the anthropologist or being taken as a psychic insight into a fundamental human predicament, to being understood as a record of power relations. Each produces its own delineation of just what is invisible, of what it is imperative to hide and from and by whom. It is therefore important to note that, as with her edited collection on *Women as unseen characters: Male ritual in Papua New Guinea* (2004), in this book Bonnemère's principal material arises from ritual action and its mythic counterparts. So, we are dealing above all with statements about efficacy, and with actions to encourage or prevent other things coming about. We may say that such preoccupations pervade social life, but we can also say that such preoccupations are likely to emphasize aspects of it. Then again, perhaps her focus points to a pervasive ritualization of relations, where efficacy is like an ever-elusive goal; in the men's case, in particular, they have to find the "others" who will show them how efficacious they are.

While fatherhood—realized at the birth of a man's first child—is a prime stage in the making of men, Bonnemère aligns that procreative capacity with the nurturing of sister's children. The significance of the brother-sister relationship has struck Melanesian ethnographers time and again. However, the situating of the relationship—and the details the author affords us—leads to a fresh perspective on an old issue in the interpretation of cults and rites in Papua New Guinea. This is their seeming preoccupation with fertility. Consider the answer to the question of what a man is. If an anthropologist is first inclined to give it in kinship terms (a man is at once a father and a mother's brother), then it is to point to him as procreator-nurturer (of children and sister's children). The author's exegesis invites the further thought—and here I borrow from her criticism of substance-focused interpretations—that *fertility* is too literal a metaphor for Ankave, and ties their actions too closely to birth as though that were the beginning and not also the end of processes of growth. Rather, reproductive states and processes, including procreation and nurture, appear bracketed together as examples of a more general phenomenon, namely men's and women's capacity to act on and for others. The author refers to it as a positively held value. The orientation here is toward what one does (being the one who has to do the doing, so to speak) when it is on behalf of other persons' growth and well-being. A footnote: at least in English, *on behalf of* gives an unintended distance to the effects of acting, and the author and her as ever punctilious translator tend to capture the immediacy in the preposition *for* or *on and for*.

This sense of capacity that Bonnemère sees in Ankave, what it is to act for others, becomes her theoretical prism. It glints on a whole other way of thinking about that classic figure, "the mother's brother." Through it, the couvade appears in fresh colors, as do food taboos, and indeed as do what we take as significant about gender relations. And for those for whom *gender* seems a restrictive rather than expansive category, we may expand that to what we take from the ethnographic record as significant about kinship, regeneration, and the states of being that people see all around themselves.

INSIGHT

The principal field observations recorded here date from the late 1980s onward. This was at a time when initial theorizing about the significance of male "initiation" among certain Angan peoples was getting underway, and would become something of a preoccupation of the anthropological research that subsequently burgeoned in the region. Bonnemère is writing in relation to a large body of existing work, including her own ethnography, and perhaps too against an excess of interpretation, of the meaning read into things, as James Weiner (1995) once put it. If at times male ritual has been the recipient of too much interpretive attention, it makes sense that one of Bonnemère's hopes is that a return to practices as they are enacted may be the starting point for reappraisal. It is at just such a juncture that a foregrounding of "ethnographic" realities can bring "theoretical" insight anew.

Bonnemère is careful to situate aspects of the material that she holds up for scrutiny within their antecedent conceptual worlds (the problems that certain explanations were intended to overcome), and she also gestures to something of the antecedent concerns in her own trajectory. An English reader needs to know that the present volume grows out of some quite intense intellectual interchanges over the last two decades in French anthropology. Here, influential works include Cécile Barraud's *Sexe relatif ou sexe absolu: De la distinction de sexe dans les sociétés* (Alès and Barraud 2001) and Irène Théry's *La distinction de sexe: Une nouvelle approche de l'égalité* (2007); Bonnemère also edited a collection of essays with Théry (*Ce que le genre fait aux personnes*) in 2008. Although not a specific focus of the present book, mention is made of diverse Anglo-American controversies in the evolution of *gender* as an organizational concept in feminist anthropology, applied as it was to early Melanesian accounts (successively) of the position of women, constructions of identity, male-female antagonism, and cross-sex and same-sex relations. Apropos the latter, one of these older works, *The gender of the gift* (M. Strathern 1988) appears at both the beginning and end of Bonnemère's exposition, which makes its author an interested party to her arguments. This is not, of course, the place to dwell on further possible lines of debate arising therefrom. However, she herself notes something of its driver in issues and arguments of the day, and I can at least endorse her surmise apropos its conceptual focus—ethnographic description to my mind demands no less—in that among its targets were contemporary conceptualizations that seemed prevalent in existing (largely Anglo-American) critiques of gender relations.

Given her own endorsement of what was subsequently seen as the "relational" tenor of that work, and in the spirit of her own interest in intellectual history, I might add that its relational vocabulary was there in part as a corrective or supplement to an entity long since eclipsed, mid-twentieth-century depictions of society (of cosmic proportions in those days), implying overarching organization and compartmentalized or individualized domains of social life (from another perspective, also relations, of course). A fresh question that the reader might well take away from Bonnemère's stimulating exegesis of Ankave practices is what these days—and the question is widely relevant to much current debate—is entailed in insisting on a relational view. From what perspective is it a significant emphasis? What other states are implied in the term (what is not relational)? One might not think to ask but for the clarity of Bonnemère's own analysis. For that builds up to a particularly clear modeling of relations in one respect, in that her account involves a formulation of personhood that rests on the roles persons play with respect to one another, concretely demonstrable through attention to interactions between people. The conceptual rewards of this approach are very evident. Anyone who equivocates should look at her stunning relational account of food taboos: it makes a lot of older material and the arguments they generated simply fall into place. The point to stay with is that *relational* carries a specific freight here.

One of the most interesting outcomes of her relational analysis in her insistence, apropos male initiation, that ritual does not act only on the person of the novice but on the relations in which he is enmeshed. To return to her opening quotation from Meyer Fortes, something Julian Pitt-Rivers (1973: 101) observed long ago would be grist to her mill. Society, he declared, imposes its rules not on the individual (who remains the same person) but on his or her (changing) relationships. Bonnemère's advance on this position gives her insights it would be hard to match otherwise. The reader will discover this not least through the way she develops, creatively, uniquely, the concept of relation as a totality.

***

Bonnemère's new book is a leap forward from earlier anthropological concerns, not just with what it is that rituals make when they seem to be making gender but also with how they do so. She sidesteps much misleading (under the guise of commonsense) speculation, and I refer again to the work of analysis that informs her writing—indeed, there is almost a kind of analogue to her effort in the considerable labor Ankave undertake in making fathers/mothers' brothers. Finally, brilliantly, *Acting for others* underlines the asymmetry that Ankave posit between men's and women's capacities for action; in the way she follows their lead, the asymmetry renders her analysis more inclusive of the sexes than many efforts to find equivalences between them.

Marilyn Strathern
University of Cambridge

Preface to the English translation

The present translation is the revised and slightly augmented version of a work published in French in 2015 at the Presses Universitaires de Provence, entitled *Agir pour un autre: La construction de la personne masculine en Papouasie Nouvelle-Guinée*. The book grew out of a major reworking of the unpublished manuscript submitted in the context of the "Habilitation à Diriger des Recherches," formerly "Thèse d'Etat," a form of postdoctoral thesis. I was therefore able to take into account the criticisms offered by the jury on various points, which I included in the French version in view of its publication. I would like to thank the members of the jury once again here, if only to say that I remember the defense as one of the most pleasurable moments in my professional life. I do not know what Michael Houseman, André Iteanu, Denis Monnerie, Anne-Christine Taylor, and Irène Théry thought of the version published four years later, but I am most grateful to them for having taken the time to read the work and having contributed elements that enabled me to take my reflection further.

I must say that rereading Nora Scott's fine translation provided yet another occasion not only to correct the few errors that remained in the French edition but also to develop more fully the comparison with the ethnographic material collected among the Kapau-Kamea by Beatrice Blackwood and Sandra Bamford in the late 1930s and the early 1990s respectively. These additions emend a habit acquired, no doubt, in 1985 when I spent a few weeks with the Baruya, and which I did not really break when I started work on my doctoral thesis in 1987, among the Ankave. My initial points of reference were the Baruya and the Sambia, both northern Anga peoples; this time I think I have measured the need to pay more attention to the ethnography produced on this group living, like the Ankave, in the southern part of the Anga territory.[1] The present book is longer by a dozen or so pages than the original French version. Working with Nora has also been an invaluable opportunity to clarify many points and I am very grateful to her for having not hesitated to ask me questions when things remained obscure and overall for her commitment to making this work better.

Translation of the book was possible thanks to the Centre National du Livre (CNL), the Institut du genre (GIS Genre), the Centre de Recherche et de Documentation sur l'Océanie (CREDO) and the Maison Asie-Pacifique (MAP). I would like to express my great appreciation to the four subsidizing institutions (Ministère de la Culture, CNRS, Aix-Marseille Université and the EHESS) for allowing this work to be made available to English-speaking students and scholars, who represent the majority of those working in Pacific studies.

***

The ethnographic material collected by the anthropologist is never analyzed in a context devoid of reflection, and the debts I have accumulated in the course of writing this book are too many to be cited individually, but they will become evident as the book unfolds.

In the way of all field anthropologists, my first expression of gratitude goes to the people I worked with, the Ankave of the Suowi Valley, and more specifically the inhabitants of Ayakupna'wa, for whom I would like to reiterate my friendship and affection. We have often laughed together, sometimes cried, and all, or nearly all, followed our ethnographic study. I would like to assure them of the close ties that have grown up between us, including some that go beyond our respective lives. Our daughters—whom we took with us several times—know, because the people told us as much, that they will always be welcome in the villages they visited and roamed through when they were small. There they discovered another way of living and thinking, as well as a second family. Today, the children they once played with have become fathers and mothers. But the

---

1. I must say I am somewhat reassured by the fact that Sandra Bamford did the same thing, no doubt because much more work, written or translated in English, has been done on the northern Angans.

story of the ties of affection and friendship that bind us continues, even though some of our early friends are no longer with us.

Finally, heartfelt thanks to Pierre Lemonnier, with whom I have shared the joys and difficulties of fieldwork in the Suowi Valley, and whose reading of the two versions of the original manuscript in French were invaluable.

Note on the pronunciation of Ankave terms

Ankave, an as yet unwritten language, has seven vowels and fifteen consonants, some of which are difficult to transcribe using the Latin alphabet. The spelling used in the English translation is that found in the French version of the book.

Long vowels (*a* and *e*) are written twice—doubled. The glottal stop—a frequent consonant in Ankave language, not linked to any kind of special accent as in English—is written like an apostrophe, as in *a'ki'*.

The curious reader can consult the glossary at the end of the book for the pronunciation of terms used, which have been transcribed using the International Phonetic Alphabet.

Note on transcription

Ankave terms are written in italics whereas words in Tok Pisin are underlined.

Introduction

We know that, regarded from the outside,
a person can be seen as an "assemblage of statuses"
—Meyer Fortes, "Totem and taboo"

Fatherhood is important in all cultures, but the way it is approached differs from one society to the next. Some consider it a private matter, while others place it within a broader social framework and, sometimes, accompany accession to this relational position with a sophisticated dramaturgy. This is the case of the Ankave of Papua New Guinea, for whom becoming a father is not self-evident; they accompany the long construction of the male person with a series of rituals ending with the birth of a man's first child.

Among these inhabitants of a remote valley at the heart of the country, the whole community takes part in these rites, as though the paternity of each man concerned everyone. This small population is surrounded by larger neighboring groups, and over the course of their history was periodically obliged to move to the lowlands when defeated in intertribal warfare. Given this historical context, the Ankave often express the sentiment that having a large number of offspring is vital to their survival. Being a parent, then, is not only an individual matter, as it has become in the West; it is also a duty each person owes all others in order to perpetuate the group.

In the present book, I try to understand the practices and thinking surrounding access to fatherhood. None of the ethnographic material presented and analyzed here (essentially ideas about the relative roles of men and women in producing and raising a new human being, the rituals that mark the men's lives and the exchanges of goods between families allied through marriage) will be familiar to readers who have grown up in the West, nor will it remind them of the world of ideas and social conventions in which they live. And yet, even if the asymmetry between fatherhood and motherhood tends to shrink when technical reproductive procedures come into the picture, it seems to me that the ethnographic material presented here, which reveals just such an asymmetry, cannot fail to touch the reader. For he or she knows full well that men and women the world over have a special relationship with their children, and that this specificity may be linked in some way with the physiological realities and emotional experiences of gestation and birth.

As everywhere, Ankave children come out of women's bodies. But the members of this society have developed a system of representations according to which children grow in the womb through the action of the mother's blood alone. Furthermore, since there are no substitutes, mother's milk is the only food available to babies, and therefore for the first two years of their life, children owe their growth to their mother's milk, together with a few other foods (banana, sugarcane, sweet potato) gradually introduced into their diet. The father's role in the reproduction of human beings is thus diminished, and consequently participating in this human adventure of perpetuating the group as well as themselves becomes something of a wager.

Passage from the position of son to that of father, in this context where the mother is believed to be at the origin of the child's body and where the maternal kin are credited with a power of life and death over their nephews and nieces (see chapter 7), requires an elaborate ritualistic work that is often termed *initiatory*. It is the aim of the present book to analyze the different steps in this process. Comparison, if only through the reading of other representations, allows us to show just how deeply culture is imbedded in what would appear to be physiological facts characteristic of the species. I take the view, therefore, that in both Western and non-Western societies, every human group constructs its own view of how each gender is involved in making children. And even though we all reproduce in the same way, we do not do it with the same ideas in mind or with the same views of gender, of gendered functions and practices. As Esther Goody showed in 1982, based on her West African fieldwork (see also Godelier [2004] 2011), child-raising can be split into several roles, which can in turn be performed by different individuals. This way of thinking, which seeks to divide up the reality of the accompaniment of children by adults into a multiplicity of functions and agents bearing educational messages and practices, sometimes comes into effect even before the birth, particularly outside the West.

Were someone to take the most recent publications on Oceania as an indication of the present state of the anthropology of this vast region, they would immediately realize that studies on male rituals are not as common and plentiful as they used to be. In the immense majority of the populations anthropologists encounter here, Christian religious ceremonies are now a regular feature of daily life, the schools educate the children, and the AIDS epidemic has arrived. In those populations where male rituals existed, today they are organized only occasionally or, significantly, when they have not been completely abandoned in the wake of the concrete changes that have transformed people's ways of living and thinking (Bonnemère forthcoming). These upheavals occurred at very different points in time, depending on whether the population lives on an island in the Tongan archipelago, where the London Missionary Society first sent pastors in the nineteenth century, or in a remote valley in the New Guinea Highlands. But on the whole, places where globalization has not made itself felt, if only in minor ways, are extremely rare. In other words, there is no society in Oceania whose members live as their precolonial ancestors did and where their conceptions of the world have not been altered, if only very superficially.

Before New Guinea won its independence from Australia, on September 16, 1975, it was not unusual for labor recruiters to travel to remote areas looking for sturdy men to work on the country's coastal plantations. In the 1960s, several Ankave men thus came to know the outside world. They returned to their villages with a little money, machetes, a cigarette lighter, and some items of clothing their families would be seeing for the first time. It was only through these few utilitarian objects brought back by their husbands or brothers, sometimes after several years of labor on distant plantations, that the women learned about life outside their valley. The experiences of this handful of men did not revolutionize either the Ankave's way of living or the ideas about the world they had developed over the centuries; it was for this reason that, in 1994 at the time of my fourth stay there, the Ankave were organizing what is known among specialists as male initiations. Because the emphasis in these rituals is not so much on acquiring knowledge as on graduating to a new status, the term *initiation* may not be the most apt for designating Anga male rituals (see p. 21), but insofar as it is the term chosen by the specialists, I will keep it, even though

I believe the expression "collective male rites of passage" would better suit the reality of these large-scale events involving an entire local community.

What I observed at that time did not fit the descriptions I had read, and the existing analyses of such collective events did not interpret them in an altogether satisfactory manner. Yet they are still held to be the authoritative version. In this context, it seemed necessary to revisit this apparently closed subject and to show that a complementary analysis of certain male rituals in New Guinea is possible, essentially by taking into consideration new ethnographic material.

This material concerns the involvement of other actors in the ritual than those usually written up—women in this case—and the analysis pays attention to their gestures and to the behaviors required of them.[1] By adopting this point of view, I hope to provide some elements that will contribute to an anthropology of personhood in which gender is a central concern. Gender studies have evolved along similar lines since the 1960s in the English-speaking academic world and in France from the 1980s. Initially focused on the social dimensions of gender relations (sexual division of labor, female domestic spaces and male public spaces, forms of male domination), researchers subsequently turned to the symbolic aspects of these relations, looking at representations of what it is to be female or male.[2] At the same time, after having long taken gender relations expressed in the conjugal couple as an object of study—while forgetting that men and women are far from being only husbands and wives—research began to include the fact that gender comes into play in all relationships, including same-sex relations. As Catherine Alès writes, we need to "understand sex distinction outside a binary opposition of genders . . . [and] as always operating in the context of established social relations" (2001: 9). In other words, a man or a woman is never simply that; he or she cannot be entirely and only defined by belonging to a gendered group. A kinship position, a social status, a difference of generation, et cetera always inform any given relationship, of which gender can therefore never be considered as the sole feature. Such is my take on gender

---

1.   There are a few populations where the involvement of women in male initiations has been recognized: the Bedamini in Western Province (Sørum 1982, 2017), the Chambri in the Sepik area (Errington and Gewertz 1989: 49; Gewertz and Errington 1991: 58, 74), and the Kamea, an Anga southern group (Bamford 2007). I will come back later to this last work, which challenges the existing ones in proposing a new interpretation of an Anga male ritual.

2.   Françoise Héritier, the main French theoretician of male domination, has analyzed the symbolic foundations explaining its universality (1996, 2002).

in this book, as one dimension of social relations that can only be conceived of as intertwined with others, which are just as relevant both in daily life and in ritualized moments.

Among the Anga, gender is at the very heart of the succession of Ankave rituals that mark the male life cycle for, in order eventually to become a father, a young boy must begin by undergoing a number of ordeals little girls have no need to endure to accede to the status of mother, since it is considered that they become fertile spontaneously by the simple fact of growing up and reaching maturity. To try to understand how a boy grows up to become a father therefore means addressing the question of the fundamental asymmetry between men and women in matters of reproduction and parenthood. Our Western societies sometimes forget this, since access to birth control now enables women to avoid becoming mothers. For those who have opted for motherhood, the possibility of using infant formula has partially masked their essential role in the survival of the newborn baby. But in societies that have access to neither contraception nor formula, every woman is a potential mother.[3]

The question of parenthood, in other words of access to the social roles of father and mother, has hardly been touched on by the anthropologists working in other Anga groups.[4] The Anga specialists—Beatrice Blackwood, Hans Fischer, Maurice Godelier, Gilbert Herdt, Jadran Mimica, Pierre Lemonnier, and Sandra Bamford (by chronological order of their fieldwork)—have studied essentially the collective phases of the rituals in which all boys around ten years of age are subjected to a set of physical and mental ordeals designed to separate them from their mothers and the female world in which they were, until then, immersed, and to toughen them up and prepare them to defend the group from the enemy attacks that were the daily lot of these populations until the 1960s. Even Blackwood, the first anthropologist to work in an Anga group, the Kapau-Kamea,[5] who, despite her gender, was allowed to witness the secret activities

---

3. Despite the Ankave's emphasis on motherhood, barren woman are not stigmatized. Some even act as midwives (see p. 67n6).

4. There are twelve groups, whose linguistic features, oral history, and genetic profile point to a common past, related languages and social organizations that share a number of features.

5. At the time of Blackwood's fieldwork, the Kapau, whose language "is the most widely distributed of all Angan languages, with speakers in both Gulf and Morobe Provinces" (Bamford 1997: 13n5), differentiated according to the tribe they belong to. In the thirties, Blackwood worked among the Nauti (Kapau-speakers living east

of men in the forest during the first stage of the rituals, was strictly prohibited from going "on top" during the second and last stage[6] and thus from seeing the boys eating <u>marita</u> because that was strictly <u>tambu</u> for women (1978: 131). She therefore had to stay "below" with the women, and her description became the first ever of the activities of Anga women in a public phase of male initiations (1978: 129–31).[7] Some sixty years later, Bamford faced a similar although milder situation when the Kamea men "debated whether or not [she] should remain with women during the penultimate moments of the <u>marita</u> ceremony" (2007: 186n12). She decided to bring the discussion to an end by saying that she preferred to stay with the women so as to focus on their particular role in the ritual. The description she offers is very similar to that given by Blackwood, to both of which may be added the narratives that were provided to them by male informants (Blackwood 1978: 132–33; Bamford 2007: 108–9).

The other Anga specialists focused solely on the ritual actions men performed in the forest and reported only the men's discourse. This in turn led them to assert that the initiations were based on the exclusion of women and were aimed primarily at reproducing and maintaining male domination. The main goal of these rituals and an indispensable prerequisite to becoming great warriors was, it was said, "for the masculine (the men) to contain the power of the feminine, and to do so, it must first seize that power by expropriating it from the women in whom it originally resides" (Godelier [1982] 1986: 94). But while this dimension of the rituals is clearly present, it by no means exhausts their interpretation.[8]

---

    of the Upper Watut River) and the Langimar (located between the Upper Watut and the Bulolo rivers) who spoke another Anga language. Bamford explains in the note just mentioned that Kapau-speakers are now called Kapau in the Morobe Province and Kamea in the Gulf Province.

6.   It should be noted that the two phases of the initiation described by Blackwood took place in different villages and that the second was organized before the first. Even if her interpreter said, "the Manki people [Langimar] would have let me come, but that these 'bush kanakas' [Nauti, thus Kapau] were different," the negative answer she received might have been due to this specific situation as well.

7.   This should be checked more closely, but I think we could go so far as to say that her description is the first ever on women's activities in Melanesian male initiations.

8.   Other New Guinea specialists have challenged the idea that the initiations reproduce men's general domination of women. Orokaiva boys and girls are initiated during the same ritual, and the "initiation secret, for there is a secret involved, does not stand between two genders but between initiates and non-initiates of both genders"

The Ankave ethnographic material shows that the women are not excluded from the male ceremonies. To be sure they are absent from spaces[9] where the men learn what they are meant to do in their adult life: control their fear, defend the community, follow the moral rules of the society; but they are by no means sidelined from the process by which their sons become men. Systematically taking into consideration the women's involvement in the male rituals has serious consequences for the anthropological analysis of these large-scale, collective events. First of all, the idea that the men grow the boys far away from the women is compromised; second, we can no longer consider that the boys are transformed solely by the men's action. On the contrary, analysis of the gestures performed by certain categories of women (essentially the novices' mothers and sisters) and the prohibitions imposed on them shows that only acting on the relations that connect them to these women can bring about the boys' transformation. It is therefore not only by acting directly on the individual that a transformation to his status, to his person even, is brought about but also by acting at the same time on his relationship with certain close female relatives, in their presence, whatever form this presence may take.[10]

Such practices reveal a specific conception of the person, in which others play an essential role in the unfolding. Men and women here are placed in different positions since, as we will see, the capacity to act for someone else is "womanly" in the sense that women have it spontaneously,[11] whereas it takes a very long process of ritual work for men to acquire and be able to make use of it.

(Iteanu 2001: 348–49). My criticism stems from the analysis of a context similar to that on which the analysis of initiations as an institution reproducing male domination was based, where only boys undergo initiation.

9. Note that in the North Pentecost Island of Vanuatu (J. Taylor 2008: 159), "women of high rank were able to take part in the male system of grades. Such women could also take their place at the corresponding *matan gabi* [sacred fires or hearths] of the *gamali*." *Gamali*, or men's houses, should not be seen as entirely male, the author adds.

10. The word *relation* as it is used here does not designate a tie between just any two individuals but a relation between people "particularized by their respective statuses," who are complementary with one another, who depend on one another, who together form a totality (Descombes [1996] 2014: 306).

11. As will be seen throughout the book, using the word *spontaneously* does not mean that this capacity is a given that would be encountered everywhere in women. As Roy Wagner wrote 40 years ago, "all kin relations and all kinds of relatives are basically alike, and it is a human responsibility to differentiate them" (1977: 623). I take the opportunity here to recall the relevance of this article to the study of kinship relationships.

The debate over whether or not there is a specifically Melanesian conception of the person was opened at the end of the 1940s by Maurice Leenhardt, and was continued by Marilyn Strathern in *The gender of the gift*, published in 1988. In this difficult book, M. Strathern details what she considers to be the characteristics of the Melanesian view, which are different from those underpinning the Western idea of personhood. Comparison is made possible by the supposedly sufficient homogeneity of the conceptions found within each region. For instance, she criticizes the notion of men's appropriation of female reproductive powers in the rituals insofar as it implies the notion of dispossession: women possess something that men appropriate for themselves; furthermore, according to the analyses of the male rituals produced between the 1960s and the 1980s (Herdt 1981; Godelier [1982] 1986), this dispossession is related in the myths. For M. Strathern, this way of talking is tantamount to considering that femaleness is a state marked by characteristics with which each woman is endowed but which someone else can appropriate. It is a construct that perceives identity, gendered identity in the event, as a set of attributes.[12] It would lead to saying, for instance, and at the risk of caricaturing, that women are physically weak, talkative, emotional, that they show a great capacity for listening, and are caring (see p. 11n17), while men have a high pain threshold and are aggressive, strong, and brave.

For M. Strathern, men and women do not differ with regard to attributes but because of distinct and culturally specific capacities for acting. A number of years before the appearance of *The gender of the gift*, she had challenged the idea that women were universally regarded as being tied to the reproduction of human beings. She began her fieldwork in the mid-sixties, in collaboration with Andrew Strathern. Their work among the Melpa (formerly Mbowamb, and now Hagen) in the Mount Hagen region of New Guinea had enabled her to show that, in this society where large-scale, competitive exchanges of pigs and shells were a regular feature of ceremonial life, the position of women was characterized by their status as producers of valuables and as intermediaries between groups vying with each other in these exchanges (1972). Men, on the other hand, were responsible for the transactions involving these goods and were therefore associated with exchange.

In adopting this perspective, M. Strathern distanced herself from an anthropological stance that asserted that women are associated with the domestic and

---

12. For a critical discussion of this predominant approach in gender studies, see Théry (2010).

men with the public sphere; that women are on the side of nature because they bring children into the world, while men are on the side of culture. In several articles published in the 1980s based on her fieldwork, she developed the idea that representations of women and womanliness vary, and she disagreed with the tendency to act as if women the world over are characterized primarily by their physiological attributes that enable them to bear children. Without denying that this is a fundamental fact, she showed in an article responding to an American colleague, Annette Weiner (1976: 13), that in two New Guinea groups—the Melpa and the Wiru—the representations associated with women are very different.

The Wiru emphasize women's reproductive powers, and the so-called gifts "for the skin" mark and reassert a person's maternal origins, for the mother's contribution to the production of individuals is the skin (M. Strathern 1981: 676). What they value in femaleness is a reproductive capacity that manifests itself in its own products, children (M. Strathern 1981: 680). Furthermore, women in this society reproduce only themselves, unlike women in the Trobriand Islands (studied by A. Weiner), who, equally associated with the reproduction of children, ensured, in the mortuary exchanges for which they were responsible, the reproduction of both the society and the cosmos (1976). Things are different in Hagen because femaleness is not the foundation of either society itself or of the reproduction of the cosmos, but of particular exchange networks, of domestic production and connections with the outside world. The characteristic associated with women is that of "in-between" (M. Strathern 1981: 678):[13] what all women share is not the fact of being placed on the side of reproduction of life but of being endowed with "in-betweenness," of being placed between their original group and the group into which they marry, which are partners in the institution of large-scale ceremonial exchanges.

Having demonstrated that two New Guinea Highland societies, the Wiru and the Melpa, construct femaleness along different lines, M. Strathern showed that gender cannot be universalized and that each local context must be studied in order to reveal the particular representations associated with women and womanhood.

---

13. Hence the title of her first published book: *Women in-between: Female roles in a male world* (M. Strathern 1972).

MOTHERS ARE BORN, FATHERS ARE MADE

The perspective I have chosen here refuses to express the asymmetry between men and women in terms of attributes. Instead, I interpret the fact that a woman becomes a mother without the need for the community to intervene, whereas, in order to become a father, a man must undergo a long series of rituals because of their different capacity to become a parent. Initiations are not merely an institution designed to reproduce male domination and prepare men for combat in a context of intertribal feuding; as I see them, initiations are also designed to turn a young boy into a potential father. But it is not enough that a man's wife be pregnant for him to attain this status. The nature of his relationship with his mother must have changed beforehand; it must have gone from a symbiotic relationship to one in which exchange, in this case the exchange of food, has become possible. This transformation is the aim of the collective phases of the initiations and takes place in two stages: the first (*itsema'a*), when the boy is between ten and twelve years old, during which the initial state of the relationship is reiterated, or presented again; and the second (*semayi'ne*), organized a few weeks or months later, in which the new form taken by the relationship is enacted. Later, when the young man is about to become a father for the first time, it is his relationship with his sister—ideally a childless, older sister—that is transformed following the same pattern. These successive reconfigurations of relationships, orchestrated at the time of the different phases in the initiation ritual, are a prerequisite for attaining fatherhood. But it is not until he is a maternal uncle, in other words when his sister has become a mother, that he is fully endowed with the capacity to "act for others." It is as if women were endowed with this capacity by the simple fact of being born female, while men need to acquire it in the course of a gradual process of status transformation, which comes about through ritualized action on relationships in the presence of those involved.[14]

At this point, I must pause for a moment and review the recent evolution in the anthropological use of the term "agency." As Laura Ahearn writes in an article devoted to the ways social scientists conceptualize this notion, "one of the most common tendencies in discussions of agency is the treatment of it as a synonym

---

14. John Taylor writes for Raga (North Pentecost, Vanuatu): "[Men] become more 'complete' as persons by beginning to take on female qualities, themselves eventually becoming, each at the same time, 'chiefs' and 'mothers,' or *ratahigi*" (2008: 169, see also 61).

for free will [however...] such an approach ignores or only gives lip service to the social nature of agency and the pervasive influence of culture on human intentions, beliefs, and actions" (2001: 114). The Ankave situation is a good illustration of the deeply cultural character of the notion of "agency," since what they value here is not the possibility to act as an independent individual but to act for others.[15] This capacity to act for others that this culture places at the heart of its conception of social relations is reminiscent of another concept recently developed in the field of psychology, by Carol Gilligan, and which has since spread to other social sciences. This is the notion of "care." In his recent review (on the site *nonfiction.fr*) of Marie Garrau and Alice Le Goff's book, *Care, justice, dépendance: Introduction aux théories du care*, Florian Cova analyzes the notion of dependence, the subject of the book's first chapter, which wavers between the two meanings, one potentially positive and the other with negative connotations, tending to identify dependence with domination.[16] Cova goes on to quote the authors: "The first meaning . . . refers to the de facto solidarity between two or several elements: something is dependent when it cannot be realized without the action or intervention of another element. Dependence refers to a necessary and productive relationship that joins a passive element and an active element and through which the first is realized. . . . The paradigm of the first conception is 'the child's dependence,' while the paradigm of the second would 'be rather the dependence of the slave'" (2010).

How can we not see in the Ankave situation a culturally organized and staged manifestation of the first conception, which defines dependence as a relation in which the "passive element" is realized through the action of the "active element"? Even more remarkably, and as the analysis of the male ritual cycle will show, this culture combines the two notions of "agency" and "care" within the same system of thought and practices that places particular value on acting for others, to the extent even of making it a capacity acquired through the ritual cycle, at least when one is a man, since, as I have said, women have it spontaneously.[17]

---

15. M. Strathern defines "agent" in similar terms when she writes: "an agent is one who acts with another in mind" (1988: 272).

16. In a recent paper entirely devoted to the analysis of the changing ideas about care that the inhabitants of Daiden, a village of the Lower Sepik-Ramu divide area of Papua New Guinea, are developing, Anita von Poser takes over the words of Tronto in *Moral Boundaries* (1993: 134): "by its nature, care is concerned with conditions of vulnerability and inequality" (von Poser 2017: 215).

17. Note in passing that the association of "care" with women is an important theme in work on the care ethic; it has been criticized by certain feminists for its potentially

In any event, it is not by acting on the person of the young Ankave man but on the relations he entertains with certain close kin that he becomes first a father and then a maternal uncle. To be sure, he acquires these statuses *thanks to his relations* with others or *because he is in relation* with others, his wife, child, sister, and sister's children. But that is not what the Ankave rituals stage and present. They consider that, within a person, certain relational states are incompatible with others, which makes it necessary to effect these transformations in the content of his relationship with certain close kin. In other words, it is impossible for a man to become a father and at the same time remain the son he was before the birth of his own child.

It would be tempting to talk here of "kinship positions" with reference to these relational states. Yet this expression is not appropriate because it adopts a categorizing and fixist perspective that backgrounds the behaviors, experiences, and emotions that constitute what can be described as the experienced content of a relationship. Nor does this viewpoint sufficiently take into account the temporal dimension inevitably contained in these relationships owing to their multiplication over the individual's lifetime, and in particular when they become parents (see also Wagner 1977: 638). Furthermore, even a ritualized transformation of relations clearly does not change each person's respective kinship position. It simply modifies its content by making certain formerly common practices unwelcome, such as a mother giving her son food once he has become a father or the two of them taking a meal together. Vice versa, certain practices that were not until then part of the mother-son relationship now become possible: for instance, the mother can eat an animal caught by her son.

A question inevitably arises then in the context of Melanesian anthropology: Is the fact of asserting that individuals go through life and become parents while undergoing rituals that modify the content of their relations with certain close kin equivalent to M. Strathern's idea that the Melanesian person is a "microcosm of relations" (1988: 131), in other words is a composite of paternal and maternal contributions? Or, is her proposition that persons are subjected to modifications in their internal relational state or composition over time, in particular so as to engage in a reproductive relationship, similar to the proposition defended here? For this major New Guinea specialist, the person can be said to be "relational," or as she terms it "dividual," from two standpoints: insofar as

essentialist view of gender. For a discussion of these criticisms, see Sandra Laugier (2010) and Emmanuelle Lenel (2009). Similar discussions have been raised around the notion of empathy (Strauss 2004, von Poser 2017: 219).

they are a condensation of the relations that led to their birth, first and second, because these relations are constantly elaborated, reduced, or amplified in order to inscribe the person in the temporality of their existence and the social events that punctuate it. In his book *Beyond nature and culture*, Philippe Descola offers a minimum version of this position that everyone could probably subscribe to: "Marilyn Strathern has suggested that, in this region of the world, we should describe a person not as an individuality but as a 'dividuality,' that is to say, a being primarily defined by his or her position and relations within some network" ([2005] 2013: 117). But M. Strathern's theory goes much further.

If we follow her propositions, children who have been conceived by a man and a woman are "cross-sex" (her term). But when they reach adulthood, they must become reproductive persons, which supposes, in order to accede to the procreative function, becoming persons whose "internal parts are in a *same-sex* relation with one another" (M. Strathern 1988: 183; original emphasis). Rituals thus help symbolically to extract from a person those parts that do not correspond to their anatomic sex. Forced ritualized bleeding (from the nose, tongue, or penis), found in certain groups in the New Guinea Highlands, and those practices, found in other groups, that were for a time called ritualized homosexuality before being renamed "boy-inseminating practices" (Herdt 1993: ix) fulfill this role.[18] At given times in a person's life, these ritually orchestrated practices make it possible, according to M. Strathern, to detach substances from or to add substances to the body and thereby temporarily change a person's internal composition, transforming their "cross-sex," infertile state into a "same-sex," fertile one.

The present book addresses such questions concerning these rituals and the accession to parenthood, but proposes a version of Melanesian personhood that is somewhat different from M. Strathern's. My reflection is part of the ongoing debate within the community of researchers about whether it is legitimate to contrast two conceptions of the person. To put it very succinctly, it is customary to oppose an individualist conception, supposedly found in Western societies, which emphasizes personal autonomy and independence, to a socio-centric or relational view, which is purportedly characteristic of non-Western societies and values social relations over the individual.

---

18. As I showed in a comparative article, the groups that practiced ritualized bleeding were not on the whole the same as those that induced boys to ingest semen, for reasons linked to ideas on the characteristics of the bodily substances concerned as well as on pollution (Bonnemère 1990).

At the heart of the debate are the implications of these two different conceptions for persons' perception of themselves as individuals. For despite Marcel Mauss' caveats in his article on the notion of the person, in which he writes that "there has never existed a human being who has not been aware, not only of his body, but also at the same time of his individuality, both spiritual and physical" ([1938] 1985: 3), the ideal normative construction found in each society has often been confused with the concrete individual, "the agent of human acts, the one who says I/me" (Théry 2007: 448), which one encounters everywhere and in all periods of history. Descola expresses the same idea when he writes: "it is safe to accept as a universal fact the form of individuation that an indexical consciousness of the self renders manifest and that is reinforced by the intersubjective differentiation that stems from the use of 'you'" (2014: 118). But, as Irène Théry reminds us, the "concept of personhood has . . . *two very different meanings*. On the one hand it designates the individual as the agent of the specifically human act, which is universal; and on the other, a certain normative, moral and legal ideality, which varies with the society" (2007: 416).

An anthropology of the person obviously seeks to clarify these variable but a priori mutually intelligible constructions independently of whether the investigation is conducted by Africanists who, at the instigation of Geneviève Dieterlen, began reflecting in 1971 on the notion of the person, considering it from the standpoint of an organized accumulation of different components each with their own specific properties (*La notion de personne en Afrique noire* [1973] 1993); or, as it was approached more recently, in the context of a comparative study resulting in the identification of roughly two sets of societies. M. Strathern thus came to contrast a Melanesian view, which she strongly formalized, with our own Western view, which she presented in an equally conceptual manner. I would submit that the fairly abstract nature of this author's model stems from the fact that her aim was not so much to identify a Melanesian view of sociality and the person, as is generally believed, as to challenge the existing anthropological approaches to Melanesian thinking. As she indicated at the beginning of her book, she wanted to show that the presuppositions with which anthropologists set out to understand the Melanesian peoples were conditioned by a Western mind set and were valid only for Western societies. The model of Melanesian "sociality" she proposed (M. Strathern 1988: 357n20) might therefore have been developed in reaction to these concepts as much as constructed from concrete social situations.

Whereas her first studies were based on the analysis of material she had gathered among either the Melpa or the Wiru, in *The gender of the gift*, the identification of ethnographic differences in representations of femaleness, for instance, took a back seat to a theory of Melanesian social action. As she writes: "I am concerned . . . not to elucidate specific local contexts for events or behavior, but to elucidate a general context for those contexts themselves: the distinctive nature of Melanesian sociality" (1988: 10). And so, rather than picking up on cultural microdifferences between Melanesian groups the better to reveal the ethno-centric and nonuniversal character of Western representations, as she did for instance in her 1981 article already mentioned, this time M. Strathern produced a theory that systematically opposes the feminist, or "prefeminist," anthropological conceptualizations (1988: 58) of her colleagues, the result of which may then appear as the lowest common denominator of all Melanesian representations. *The gender of the gift* therefore provides not so much a description of Melanesian sociality as an image of what is produced by the systematic, abstract questioning of the foundations on which the analyses of this sociality rest. In other words, M. Strathern's Melanesian world may essentially be a world of ideas, as suggested by Alfred Gell when, at the end of his "Strathernograms" article devoted to presenting the model of the author of *The gender of the gift*, he called the system "M" and added: "which you can take to stand for Melanesian or Marilyn, as you wish" (1999: 34).

I hope to show that the analysis of ethnographic material gathered among the Ankave of the Suowi Valley will contribute to the debate on the relational conceptions of the person that, since the publication of *The gender of the gift* in 1988, have been regarded as characteristic of Melanesian peoples, even if some authors have pointed out that elements of individuality always exist side-by-side with such conceptions. Among such voices is that of Descola, for whom "without denying the existence of a theory of a 'dividual' person in Melanesia, we should bear in mind, along with Maurice Leenhardt years ago and Edward LiPuma more recently, that that theory co-exists alongside—or is in some situations supplanted by—a more egocentric conception of a subject; and there is no evidence to suggest that this theory is a product solely of European colonization" ([2005] 2013: 117). In the same vein, Andrew Strathern and Pamela Stewart have proposed the concept of "relational-individual" to designate a "form of personhood in which elements of relationality and elements of individuality coexist" (2000: 63). According to these two authors, we can expect to find relational conceptions of the person the world over, and that goes as much for Melanesia and the South Pacific as elsewhere. It would therefore be other notions, also discovered by M. Strathern, such as "permeability" and even "partibility," that would be specific to a vision encountered in this part of the world.

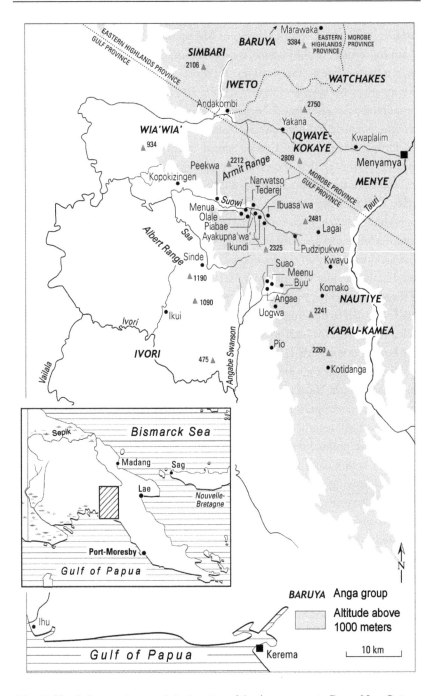

Map 1. The Ankave territory and the location of the Anga groups in Papua New Guinea.

As we will see in the course of the present study, the Ankave ethnography enables us to take part in the discussion of all these questions, in particular thanks to the analysis of the life cycle rituals that are the occasion in this society to accompany individuals at these stages, which involve them in ever-more numerous relations and gradually place them in new relational positions. As André Iteanu writes of the Orokaiva, another New Guinea society, "a person's relational sexual identity is essentially constructed through rituals" (2001: 333).

WE ARRIVE IN THE SUOWI VALLEY

The three hundred and fifty people who occupied the Suowi Valley at the time of our arrival in May 1987 (see map 1) received Pierre Lemonnier and me in a forest setting where villages built high on steep slopes stretch as far as the eye can see toward the Gulf of Papua. This is how the story began. During the fifth month of the year, as they would say, I first set foot on this forgotten territory in the foothills of the mountain chain that bisects the island of New Guinea from east to west. Our plane landed on the only airstrip in the region, located in another Ankave valley, occupied by the Angae village, along the floor of which runs the Ankave-Swanson River. We then spent a long day walking. The tiny Angae airstrip had been cleared a few years earlier by Richard Speece, an American missionary and linguist who had been living there since 1978. He had built a wooden house, introducing materials and objects hitherto unknown in the valley (saws, corrugated metal sheets, nails). Richard had quickly organized his linguistic work, for the Summer Institute of Linguistics (SIL), of which he was a member, knowing that conversion to the Lutheran Church is effective only on condition of fluency in the native language. He painstakingly inquired into local beliefs about the supernatural in order to translate the New Testament as accurately as possible. To everyone's delight, he even built a school and then attracted the young (and less young) people from the surrounding hamlets. Actively aided by Peter,[19] a young Ankave man who had become his friend, he soon began designing six textbooks for learning to read and write the

---

19. Some, the men in particular, received a Christian name during the passing visit or temporary stay of a church representative, usually Lutheran but sometimes Seventh Day Adventist (SDA). Used by few people when we first visited, their use has become increasingly frequent.

vernacular, which turned out to be very useful to the young anthropologist that I was at the time.

But on this day in May, Richard, his wife, and their three small children were not there to greet us as we descended from the familiar Missionary Aviation Fellowship's (MAF) little Cessna. They had gone to spend two months in their house in Ukarumpa, a modest American-style village where the some 300 current members of the "Papua New Guinea branch" of the organization had each bought a wooden house surrounded by a small garden. This allowed them to advance the development of the textbooks for learning the various languages of New Guinea by working in the purpose-built laboratories and sharing what they knew of these very ancient languages, which predate the famous Austronesian migration by several tens of thousands of years.[20] No fewer than eight hundred languages are still spoken in Papua New Guinea and, since 1956 when the Summer Institute of Linguistics began working in the country, nearly 50 percent of them have been described and two hundred are being studied by these fervent specialists who regularly congregate in this little town in the east.

Peter was the only one to meet us that day, with the energy and cheekiness that we would subsequently come to appreciate. Each time he came to the Suowi Valley, he would stop by to chat about insignificant things as well as others that mattered to him: survival in the valley during the 1997 drought, his desire to stand as a local counselor, his first—frightening—encounter with white people or his distress when the American missionary-linguist family with whom he had long worked decided to leave the country definitively, in 1992. He became great friends with Pierre, my partner in life and work.

Always ready to pitch in and to share his knowledge and feelings, Peter offered us a bed and a meal, then woke us after a short night. The following day he conducted us to the valley we had overflown the day before without realizing it, obscured as it had been by thick clouds and rain. Because he was familiar with the area, having spent the early 1980s there, Pierre had spotted from the window of the Cessna the powerful river that wends its way from east to west through this vast portion of the Ankave territory. Ill prepared for a difficult hike over steep muddy trails, I had struggled until we came within view of an inhabited space: first of all the gardens, which looked chaotic to eyes accustomed to

---

20. At least most of them, since certain languages spoken along the coasts are of Austronesian origin.

neat European rural plots with their straight rows, and then a zone of savannah, indicating a longstanding human presence.

I learned from an in-depth study of first contacts I did fifteen years later that, on this fine day in 1987, a woman from Ayakupna'wa had taken fright upon seeing this white woman with Pierre. She laughed when she told me she had jumped off the trail and tried to hide. For my part, I only remember a young boy, Michael, who popped up proudly in front of us with that expression of delight and willingness we would see on the faces of all of our hosts each time we arrived.

The Ankave of the Suowi Valley had been contacted for the first time in 1938, which is to say yesterday on the scale of great discoveries in the South Pacific, but in the same period as the wide valleys in the western part of the country. These highlands contain several regional capitals served by "the Highland Highway," the country's only highway. Early in the year 1938, an Australian geologist, together with Patrol Officer A. Timperley and nine policemen, walked from the Upper Vailala River to the Tauri (along the Mbwei River that flows between the Staniforth and Armit ranges; see map 1) on an exploratory patrol for Oil Search Limited Company. Timperley departed from Kerema on the southern coast on October 27, 1937, and came back on January 14, 1938, after having gone through the Mbwei Valley between December 8 and 21, 1937. This was a long and very difficult trip during which it is reported that first contact was made.[21] Next, Australian administrators accompanied by policemen and carriers visited the region, first in 1951 and then twice in the mid- and late 1960s. The first trip, led by Patrol Officer K. G. O'Brien, is well remembered because its arrival in Ayakupna'wa in October 1965 was followed by the circling of a plane that dropped a few patrol boxes and big bags of rice, small cowrie shells (girigiri), tins, sugar, et cetera (Bonnemère and Lemonnier 2009: 309–10).

Nearly twenty years later, people from the Suowi Valley hosted Pierre for a few weeks, having refused to allow a white missionary to settle in one of their hamlets, as their brothers and neighbors in Angae had done four years earlier. All that was before we had decided to undertake long-term fieldwork. In the space of twenty years, and since this short nine-month stay in 1987–88, we have spent a total of over two years in the Suowi Valley.

---

21. Several violent conflicts occurred between the population and members of the prospecting expedition, which ended with casualties on both sides as well as repeated desertions by exhausted and frightened carriers (Bonnemère and Lemonnier 2009).

The imprint of the outside world on the valley's inhabitants is rather original. It defies any generalization about the history of the colonization of the
island of New Guinea, for it is more the scarcity of visits received over nearly
seventy years than the exact date of first contact that explains the isolation of
this population, which today numbers some five hundred and twenty persons.
With the exception of the two Australian exploratory missions in 1965 and
1967, and until the 1970s, the interval between encounters has always been at
least fourteen years. And since girls are married at a very young age, this lapse
of time without visits from the outside often corresponds—give or take three or
four years—to what here is called a generation.

The other reason for their marginalization is simply an unfortunate drawing
of administrative boundaries. The Suowi Valley is located in the northernmost
part of Gulf Province, the capital of which, Kerema, is the second largest town
on the south coast, after Port Moresby (see map 1). Only a handful of Ankave
have ever been to Kerema, but all or nearly all are familiar with the administrative center of Menyamya (Morobe Province), which is reached by a long
day's walk for someone fit, or two if they are in a weakened state. Although a
2,800-meter-high mountain lies between the two places, as well as the territory
of former enemies, today the men no longer hesitate to set aside their apprehen-
sions in order to report to the police some conflict that has become unmanage-
able by means available on the spot. In this event, one or two agents come to
Ikundi or Ayakupna'wa to settle the affair, by force if necessary. If we add that
the valley is located precisely at the intersection of two other provincial boundaries, Morobe and Eastern Highlands, everything is explained. For decades, the
likelihood of ever having an airstrip, an aid post, and a school was next to zero.[22]

It was therefore not any sense of folklore that prompted the immense majority of Ankave men to still wear, in 1990, their pulpul, a voluminous short "apron"
made of rows and rows of reeds that have been pounded and then dried and
assembled. Diagonally across their chest they wore a braid to which they added
a wide belt. Both were woven from the yellow stems of a wild mountain orchid.
The short cape made from beaten ficus bark, attached by a neckstring passed
through the belt, covered their buttocks and completed their proud allure. The

---

22. In January 2011 the first plane finally landed on the Ikundi strip, but in 2017 the
building dedicated to an aid-post/clinic was still empty, and the few young women
who had been brought to town a couple of years earlier to be trained as midwives
still could not help women having difficulty giving birth.

women went bare-breasted but hid the lower part of their bodies by a skirt of pressed reeds or beaten bark. The long cape, also made of bark, which they still wear on their shoulders or their head, depending on the weather and the load they are carrying back from the garden, makes them easily recognizable.

That is why, one day in January 1988, when I saw Timiès coming toward me under the beating sun, something seemed strange about him. Why had this young man hung a long bark cape from the crown of his head? Why, above all, did he seem so idle? He was alone and carried neither bow nor arrows. Something was wrong with his male appearance. Then I learned the truth of it; a young man wearing a bark cape on his head means only one thing to all members of the valley and beyond, to each of the twelve hundred Ankave of the territory: Timiès was to become the father of his first child. This situation had a few advantages—it meant a rest, but above all it meant duties toward his wife, his in-laws, and the baby to come.

It also meant that he would soon go through the third and final stage of the initiation ritual, at the end of which his person and the nature, form, and content of his previous relations with others will have changed.

We can say that, when it is that of a man, this silhouette, created by a long bark cape the upper part of which covers the head, condenses and expresses several realities at once: a state (waiting for a first child); a position in a particular relational situation (husband of a pregnant wife); and a transitional stage in life (between not having a child and having one). As soon as his baby is born, these realities will evolve, and his silhouette will change at the same time; he will become a fully fledged man, having come to the end of the series of life cycle rituals organized for him (at least as a living person). These rituals form a mandatory sequence for every Ankave boy, at the close of which he is considered to be an adult man, but not yet someone capable of acting on others, a status that will be acquired only at the close of the final stage in the process of his personal construction and which he will be able to exercise once his sister has her own children.

Because the *suwangain* ritual celebrating the moment when a young man becomes a father for the first time ends the cycle of rituals he must undergo in his lifetime, its analysis, together with that of the collective stages experienced a few years earlier, offers a privileged position to understanding how the local population conceives the gradual process of constructing the male person. And because they foreground the role of others in the construction of the person in a particular way that I have never seen described in the literature, characterized

Photo 1. For a man, wearing a bark cape on his head is the sign he is about to become a first-time father. He will have to wear this cape for the duration of his wife's pregnancy and respect a certain number of prohibitions that will place him on the margin of the activities of other men but in relation with his sister and the future mother of his child. © Pierre Lemonnier (July 2002)

specifically by respecting food taboos for someone else, Ankave ritual practices and their underlying mental representations bring new elements to bear on this question that may help us understand how the person and their development over their lifetime are conceived in non-Western societies. The first step in such an approach implies immersing oneself in the daily life of this little population living deep in the heart of New Guinea.

CHAPTER I

An out-of-the-way situation
Prohibitions and relations

Inhabitants of the Suowi Valley are happy to remain on the fringes of village life and the neighborly relations this demands. Several times a year, and for weeks on end, each family thus retreats to the surrounding forest that carpets the better part of their territory, ranging from 600 to 2,300 meters in altitude and giving them access to a great variety of materials and foods. Harvesting the breadfruits that ripen in June at the lowest altitudes, stripping ficus bark to make items of clothing, preparing lime by burning the bark of certain trees, picking areca nuts and gathering the pandanus fruits in the highlands in November are all good excuses to get away. Several weeks or months can go by like this, living uncomfortably in leaf-covered lean-tos, set close together when the motive for leaving the village requires the cooperation of several families from the same lineage or a single clan and the space between the boulders along the river is only a few dozens of square meters (Bonnemère and Lemonnier 2007: 69, 71).

This life in the great outdoors is uncomfortable and not always easy to put up with on a daily basis, so it is with great pleasure that they finally return to their homes in the hamlet when news comes of a meal of red pandanus sauce or someone selling pieces of domestic pig killed to fuel the network of social obligations. Such reunions put everyone in a good mood, and the adults catch up on news and gossip, while the children run around until dusk. Tensions are suspended and the pleasure of eating good food together and sharing the fruits of one's labor tops all other considerations.

Listening to the conversations and observing what is done, the gestures and attitudes of those gathered around a collectively prepared meal, one discovers a whole range of interactions, which, when understood, lend insight into the way the Ankave imagine the relations an individual entertains with the other inhabitants of the valley. With "kin" first of all, for it would be no exaggeration to say that everyone is related, though to varying degrees and with no less varied consequences. The inhabitants of the Suowi Valley are members of a small population that has lived for generations on the same territory and whose ancestors lived in a hostile human environment. The great majority of the five hundred and twenty people living in the valley in 2011 were connected in a close-knit network of interrelations, made all the tighter because they were divided among six demographically very unequal clans, of which one, the Idzadze, accounts for a little over half the total population. Of course women from neighboring groups, in particular the Iqwaye,[1] regularly marry Ankave men, but the percentage of close cousins is still high.

Behaviors are therefore dictated for the most part by the gestures, words, prohibitions, and obligations that each person is supposed to observe and use in their relations with various categories of kin: with their own parents, grandparents and children; with brothers and sisters; with parents' siblings including mother's kin, who occupy a very important place in their systems of thought and social practices; and with their own in-laws or those of close family members.

Beginning in September, most villagers gather two or three times a week at someone's house to enjoy the thick sauce made from the fruits of the red pandanus (marita),[2] which, as we will see, occupies an important place in the representations of people's good health and growth. Sharing this food, as is also

---

1. The Iqwaye are an Anga group and former enemies of the Ankave. They occupy the valleys lying two days' walk to the north (these the Ankave call Iweto) and a day and a half to the east (these they call the Yarwelye). The Iqwaye have been known since the late 1970s thanks to the work of Jadran Mimica.

2. A good portion of those men who are now fifty, one day or another left to work on the coastal plantations, where they learned to speak the country's principal vehicular language, known as Tok Pisin or Melanesian Pidgin. The younger men, of course, continue the adventure and learn this language in turn. The women learn the rudiments of the language from hearing it spoken when they go to Menyamya or even sometimes around the village.

Photo 2. On the bank of one of the rivers flowing through the Suowi Valley, two families have constructed leafy shelters in which they will live for a few weeks, far from their village house. © Pierre Lemonnier (1990)

Photo 3. Houses in the hamlet of Ikundi, at dawn. © Pierre Lemonnier (1987)

true for *Pangium edule* (known as *pangi* in French and called *aamain* in Ankave) (see pp. 64–65), takes the form of a ceremony that is akin to the sharing of pieces of pig meat in other parts of the Island, where Big Men once flourished. These figures were renowned for their oratorical talent, which they displayed at large-scale, intergroup competitive exchanges, thus acquiring prestige (A. Strathern 1971; Schneider 2017). The Ankave do not engage in these sort of exchanges and they have no figure even remotely resembling a Big Man, but their distributions of red pandanus sauce and *aamain* can sometimes have the appearance of a ceremonial gift (see photo 5: the recipient made of *a'ki'* leaves in which the tubers are placed, covered in red pandanus sauce, and brought to the guests).

The only way to prepare a large collective meal is to cook the tubers, sometimes accompanied by pig meat or marita, in a partially buried oven, also known as a "Polynesian" or "earth oven" (mumu). The task of preparing such ovens falls almost exclusively to the women. They dig a large, shallow pit and fill it with stones. On top of the rocks they place the firewood cut up by the men—that is their only contribution—and then light the fire using a burning brand so as to heat the stones until they are white hot. Once the wood has burned down, the women line the hollow with the stones, using long sticks to spread them so that the heat is distributed more or less evenly. Then they put down a layer of long, broad *a'ki'* leaves (*Comensia gigantea*) followed by several kilos of freshly peeled taros and sweet potatoes (taros next to the stones because their flesh is harder), all of which is toped off, if one wishes, by a layer of *yore'* (*Setaria palmifolia*), and then <u>marita</u>, pieces of pig meat, and leafy vegetables. The lot is then covered with more *a'ki'* leaves, and finally banana fronds, after which the food is left to steam for several hours.

Today a meal of tubers and <u>marita</u> is cooking in the earth oven. Some distance away women go about their work, while fifteen or so adult men smoke, chew betel, joke, or doze. For the most part, however, the guests wait in family groups—a couple and their youngest children—for the distribution of the red sauce. Whether in the middle of the area of beaten earth that separates the huts, under the large stand of bamboos dominating the compound, or huddled together along the wall of a hut whose overhanging roof affords protection from the sun or the rain, each little group keeps to itself. When the last of the sauce has been poured over the tubers, the youngest children take the recipients one by one and carry them to each of the families, who receive them with a simple local version of "thanks," an expression that is more like an affectionate "dear." The Ankave do not have a word for a simple thank you that can be used with everyone. Expressing gratitude and pleasure is inseparable from their tie with the person from whom they have received something. The anthropologist can suggest two interpretations of this: the first, which is unlikely, is that the notion of thanks is lacking in the Ankave language; the other, more probable, is that the notion is inseparable from an affectionate formula that goes with an already-existing tie between the people involved but that also partakes of gift-giving and social life, the meaning being therefore broader (see p. 225).

Most of the guests savor their meal of tubers topped with the delicious red sauce on the spot, and then return home when night begins to fall. Some wrap a bit of the food they have received in banana leaves to take back to family members who were unable to come. The tie used to secure the packets is long enough to form a little loop so that the treat can be suspended out of the way of greedy dogs and pigs. The shared meal is far from including the whole community, but it does considerably increase the number of those benefitting from a ceremonial distribution of food.

A few rare individuals seemed to be indifferent to the distribution unfolding slowly before their eyes and to the avid pleasure everyone else displays. It is not because they do not like red pandanus sauce that they hang back, though, but because they are obliged to abstain from it. The outside observer finds it hard to understand the reasons for this obligation, which that day applied to an old woman, whose drab ornaments showed her to be a widow; to a bare-chested man some forty years of age dressed in a tattered loincloth; and to two young men with bark capes suspended from the top of their head. As no man ever wears this item of clothing that way, the altogether singular silhouette of Timiès and Luc was an unmistakable sign that their first child was going to be born sometime in the coming months, making them fathers.

The prohibition on consuming red pandanus sauce incumbent on these four people had been imposed for different reasons. This food, appreciated by one and all, is available during the wet season, in other words from September to April, depending on the variety. The local population considers it to be a vegetal substitute for blood (Bonnemère 1996a: 248–56), and its regular consumption enables one to begin the driest season, or what passes for such in this very wet equatorial zone, with a renewed supply of blood and consequently the capacity to withstand any hardship.

The two persons wearing the drab clothing and ornaments did not take part in that particular collective meal because they were in mourning, one for her husband, the other for his sister who had died in an accident a few weeks earlier. Local people say that if a man or a woman in mourning abstains from ingesting this tasty sauce, it is because they were accustomed to consume it with their close kinsman who had just died (spouse, sibling, child, uncle, aunt, mother, father, etc.). The deceased would be displeased if they continued to enjoy these pleasures in life from which they were now excluded, and they might therefore take revenge by casting a spell on the consumers or their descendants (Lemonnier 2006a: 324–33).[3] In the case of the two young men, this food taboo was part of a set of constraints associated with their status as the future father of a first child and that were meant particularly to protect their wife from complications during the birth.

A few months earlier, Timiès' parents and parents-in-law had told him they had noticed his young wife was pregnant. A certain Ankave told me, "for them [the young parents-to-be], it's their first time, they can't figure it out for themselves." At the same time, they had informed him that he was going to have to make himself a new bark cape and wear it on top of his head for the duration of the pregnancy. They also made it clear that he was going to have to stop eating

---

3.   Whereas the women believe that men in mourning are held to the same prohibition on red pandanus sauce that they are, in fact those who wish can consume it, as they learned when they were little boys (see p. 94).

red pandanus sauce, game, or pig meat. He was also forbidden to drink water but he could quench his thirst with sap from a wild bamboo or by sucking on sugarcane. Furthermore, he was forbidden to do anything involving the making of knots, which kept him from taking part in building a house or a fence, from laying traps, or from making a bow and arrows.

As we see, a man expecting his first child is sidelined from ordinary male activities. If he does not respect these restrictions and continues to go about his usual business the birth might go badly, for the slightest intake on his part of the red pandanus vegetal blood would place his wife in danger of hemorrhaging during the birth. The activities reserved for men, especially hunting, would prevent the fetus leaving the uterus. These beliefs are taken very seriously and, although a young man may sometimes take a notion to shirk his obligations as a father-to-be, for instance, by asking a brother to help him make the bark capes or by bartering for them, he would never dare violate the prohibition on red pandanus sauce. Among the tasks he is supposed to perform is the preparation of three capes made from the beaten bark of the ficus: one for his wife, one for his sister, and the third, as we have seen, for himself. The giving of these bark capes establishes—we could almost say institutes—a trio whose actions are interdependent and have closely connected effects before, during, and after this primordial event that is the birth of one's first child.

In addition to the two members of the married couple, this group is made up of one of the husband's sisters,[4] and all three are the principal actors in the public ritual that follows the secret rite in which a ritual specialist, together with all the men who want to take part, has led the young father through the ordeals of the third and final stage of the male initiations, conducted in a forest area not far from the hamlets. Meanwhile, the young mother and the young father's sister have been led to a spot known only to the women. The public ritual, which follows these moments experienced separately, ends the first-birth ceremonies and celebrates the appearance of a new parental couple at the same time as it makes a man into a father who is, not only conscious of his new status and responsibilities to his child but also to his affines, the child's maternal kin. In the course of this process, which unfolds over a long span of time, the participation of two women to whom the young man is closely linked, his wife and his sister, is indispensable. It is at the moment when a man becomes a father for the first time

---

4.   For a long time I thought this must be an elder sister. In fact, though, the ideal sister is one who has reached puberty, may be married, but who does not yet have children.

that his sister last intervenes in his life. When he was initiated some ten years earlier, she had also accompanied him in his ordeal by respecting certain food taboos, while their mother remained secluded for the duration of the rituals. As we will see, the necessity of this sister's presence at the birth of her brother's first child is to be related to the highly valorized status of the maternal uncle, a status he will acquire when his sister has her own children.

For the Ankave, a male person is thus constructed gradually at major stages in his life thanks to the presence of kinswomen, and it is this gradual construction of the person that I will attempt to reveal by examining these key moments. We will be looking at how an Ankave becomes an adult woman or man: What are the major steps in this process? What part do rituals play? And what roles are assigned to close kin in each? A simple overview of the ethnographic material shows in effect that the participation of others is deemed to be crucial if a person is to develop properly. Throughout a person's life, a certain number of kin adopt behaviors believed to help him (or her, but on a lesser scale) grow and remain in good health, and to ensure that a future event will go smoothly. Such a system of thought and practices reveals that, without the direct intervention of others, a man or a woman cannot successfully pass from one stage of life to another. At the heart of this set of representations, we find the idea that it is possible to act on someone else by performing an action on oneself, on one's own body. The Ankave even place the ingestion of food, one of the most personal activities there is, in the category of actions that can be performed on someone else's behalf. And it is only logical that its opposite, the prohibition of a food, should also be effective: during the initiations, for instance, the novices' mothers cannot eat foods that become sticky when cooked so as to ensure that the wound caused by the piercing of the son's nasal septum will heal properly.

This situation is apparently hard for a Westerner to conceive, since even the anthropologist Meyer Fortes remarked that, "[eating] is a socially licit yet peculiarly individual activity. Everybody must eat for himself." And further on: "Eating is a direct and one way relationship between the actor and a natural product. No other person is necessarily included, as in the sexual and in other social relationships" (alluded to in Strathern 1988: 20).[5] In revealing the

---

5.   Unfortunately, I have been unable to locate the exact quote (which is not in *The gender of the gift*), but I assume M. Strathern is referring to page 16 of Meyer Fortes' article "Totem and taboo," published in 1966.

obligation certain kin categories have to abstain from eating foods endowed with specific properties in certain life contexts (a mother at her son's initiation, a husband for his pregnant wife, a sister for her brother whose wife is pregnant, etc.), the Ankave ethnographic material contradicts Meyer Fortes' position and exposes a system of thoughts in which action on and for another person is manifested also in this eminently personal act that is eating.

For the Ankave, the fact of acting—or abstaining from acting—on behalf of another person is visibly marked by the unusual fact of wearing an ordinary item of clothing on one's head: the bark cape. As we saw, when a man walks around the village with a bark cape on his head when it is not raining, it means that he is obliged to respect taboos so that his pregnant wife will be delivered safely and the baby will be in good health. For their part, when the mothers of the young initiates remain secluded in a large collective house and wear new bark capes prepared for the occasion, this means they are avoiding doing anything that might keep the wounds in their sons' septums from healing. For each imposed behavior, therefore, there is a particular physical attitude and silhouette, which advertises that several people are interacting and that the actions of one affect the other. In the case of a father-to-be, these behaviors define the existence of a specific relationship: that which grows up between the two members of a conjugal couple when they are about to become parents for the first time. When a man wears a new bark cape on his head and at the same time adopts certain attitudes and respects strictly codified taboos, the Ankave are showing that he is in a particular relational state, which has its place in the gradual unfolding of the person's transformation.

My primary aim is to reveal and to attempt to understand this process by analyzing the rituals the men, and to a lesser extent the women, must go through over their lifetime. The research on which this book is based is in line with the publications devoted to personhood and life cycle rituals in Melanesia since the early twentieth century, which have been on the increase since the 1950s. In the studies on the region occupied by the Anga groups in particular, a set of groups that includes the Ankave but also the Baruya and the Sambia, several anthropological studies have been devoted to the male initiations, which were interpreted, as we saw, as an institution for the reproduction and the legitimization of the women's subordination to the men, founded on the exclusion of the women and on the belief that they are a source of pollution, and that the maternal relationship prevents boys from growing into adult men (Godelier [1982] 1986; Herdt 1987).

One effect of the analysis of the third-stage initiations detailed in the present book is to challenge the idea that this is a purely male ritual. It confirms the findings of some of my earlier fieldwork on the collective rituals of the previous stages, in which I showed that the presence of the novices' mothers and sisters was indispensable (Bonnemère 2004b). In other words, unlike my predecessors, I defend the idea that the initiations do not concern the men alone. To be sure, among the Ankave too, entire sequences unfold at length in the forest far from the women, and the discourse emphasizes the ordeals endured by the boys. But without the involvement first of their mothers and then of their sisters, the ritual could quite simply not take place. Two spaces, one masculine and located in the forest, the other feminine and in the village, are thus linked within a same ritual process.

The number of stages in the initiation cycle varies within the Anga group: the Baruya have four, the Iqwaye have five, the Sambia, six, and the Kamea[6] only two (Bamford 2007: 96). But these are mere details. In every group, the first stages are collective and obligatory for all the boys in an age group. The other stages, which begin when the boys become old enough to marry, are centered more particularly on a single individual. From the ethnography collected by Sandra Bamford, it appears that these more individualized stages did not exist among the Kamea. What could we say about the ritual that would be the equivalent, in the northern Anga groups, of the third and final stage for the Ankave, the *suwangain* rite organized for the birth of a man's first child, which we have already briefly discussed? Among the Baruya, the Iqwaye, and the Sambia, a ritual is performed on a similar occasion, but it is never clear whether it is for the birth of the first child of the woman, the man, or the couple, whereas this is very clear for the Ankave, for whom it is the man's capacity to become a father that is celebrated. Maurice Godelier, Gilbert Herdt, and Jadran Mimica have written little about this ceremony, and especially, as I have indicated elsewhere, they wrote only about what happens—or used to happen—with the men.

For Godelier, the rite the Baruya organize on this occasion "continu[es] and complete[s] the young man's initiation" (1986: 38). There is no special term for

---

6.   The Kapau-Kamea's territory (see p. 5n5) is by far the largest of all the Anga territories. It is located to the southeast of the Ankave (see map in Bamford 2007: 17). Sandra Bamford worked in a village called Titamnga at the beginning of the 1990s and witnessed the final public phase of the second and last stage of the initiations (2007: 103–11).

this, and the young man remains a *kalave*, in other words a fourth-stage initiate, a status acquired in a collective ceremony performed once his parents have found him a wife (Godelier [1982] 1986: 35–36). On the occasion of the birth of each subsequent child, a simplified version of the same ritual is conducted. From his short description, nothing in these rites seems, at first sight at least, to differ from what goes on in the collective rites:

> Stripped of all clothing and adornment save the pulpul, he goes with his co-initiates to the ceremonial site, where he is pushed into a kind of tunnel made of leaves and branches, rather similar, though shorter, to the one through which as a young initiate he had so frequently been forced to pass, pushed and supported by his sponsor, and at the far end of which the older initiates and the (young) married men used to wait and beat him with nettles. This time, after he emerges from the tunnel, the mature men await him and rub his stomach and belly with nettles. (Godelier [1982] 1986: 38)

In the case of the Iqwaye, Mimica explains that the birth of a man's first child is the occasion to organize the fifth and final stage of the initiations (1981: 52). At this time, his status as a virile man is affirmed, which is marked by the fact that he has become a father, the ultimate state of full manhood. Unlike the two other northern groups mentioned, but like the Ankave, there are no female initiations here. In their stead, we would be tempted to say, a special ceremony for the birth of a woman's first child is organized at the same time as the fifth-stage initiations. As for the Sambia, the birth of a woman's first child, Herdt writes (1987: 167), is the occasion to organize the sixth and final stage of the male initiations, called *moondangu* (1987: 107). Here, too, fatherhood is the equivalent of full manhood. In this rite the young man learns additional purification techniques to help maintain his virility: nose-bleedings each time his wife withdraws to a menstrual hut and consumption of vegetal semen-substitutes. At this time, a particular period of his life comes to a close since he will no longer be able to have homosexual relations with the young boys. At this time, too, he learns the most secret myth of all: that of male parthenogenesis, which recounts the origin of ritualized homosexuality (1987: 167–68).

It should be noted from the outset that these three analyses of equivalent rituals never envisage that they might concern the parental couple. Even when there is also a rite for the new mother, as is the case among the Iqwaye, the two are treated as almost independent events that concern only one individual at a time: the man and then the woman. Yet even if it seems legitimate to include the first-birth ritual in the series of the other initiation stages, there is no reason to leave aside the woman who has just given birth to their child. In any event, it is clearly not the way the third and final stage of the rituals organized in the life of an Ankave man can be envisaged.

THE ANGA AND THEIR ANTHROPOLOGISTS

Several years before looking into the male initiations and the activities associated with them from the women's standpoint, I had read the studies on the rituals of all the Anga groups visited by other anthropologists. These groups total a population of over one hundred thousand persons,[7] of whom we know from oral history, linguistic studies, and research in molecular biology that their remote ancestors occupied a single territory and spoke the same language. Over the centuries, the millennia even, the original group, which lived in the vicinity of Menyamya, a government station at the center of the present-day Anga territory, split following internal strife. Today, the Anga speak twelve different languages, classified as Papuan or non-Austronesian (Wurm 1982: 140–42), which have more similarities with each other than with the languages of any of their non-Anga neighbors. Together these languages constitute a family, with its own phonological and syntactic features (Lloyd 1973). The studies carried out since the 1930s in certain Anga groups by a succession of anthropologists have helped build an image of their culture that corroborates the picture drawn by the genetic and linguistic work. We find a strong homogeneity of social organization, residence patterns, and forms of power as well as variations, sometimes merely nuances, whose heuristic importance has been shown by the most recent studies, in the context of a comparative analysis of male

---

7.   The population of Papua New Guinea has grown considerably: in the Anga territory, it has increased by 25 percent in ten years, hence the new figure with respect even to my recent publications. This number is based on the 2011 census, but unfortunately it has had to be estimated, for the inhabitants of the groups in Gulf Province, living in the mountainous interior, seem to have been counted by agents working for other provinces. This was the case for the Ankave on the occasion of a much earlier census taken while we were there.

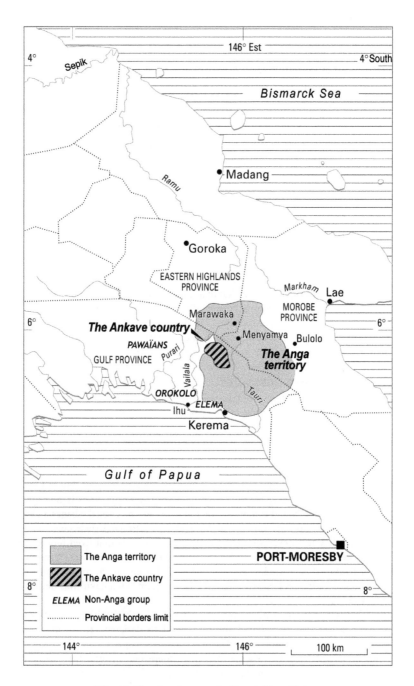

Map 2. The Anga groups in Papua New Guinea.

initiations, gender relations, and representations of reproduction, death, and shamanism.[8]

Beatrice Blackwood, then a young Oxford graduate, was the first anthropologist to visit an Anga group, designated at the time by the term "Kukukuku,"[9] which anthropologists later learned was derogatory in all the local languages and which they therefore dropped. Blackwood set out for New Guinea in 1936, to a zone under Australian administration, with the intention of describing the technical system of a people still using stone tools (Blackwood 1950). She managed to reach the territory occupied by the Nautiye, a Kapau-Kamea group living to the east of the Anga (see map 1), a few hours by foot from the Bulolo airstrip (see map 2), which had been opened by the Morobe Goldfields mining company some ten years earlier. In addition to the work cited, Blackwood

8. As an anthropologist doing comparative work with the Anga in the late 1970s, Pierre Lemonnier was the first to present systematically these social and cultural variations as he had observed them in the different groups he had visited in the territory (1981, 1997, 2005a). For newer comparative studies more centered on specific topics, the reader can consult the last two chapters in Bonnemère (1996a: 369–392) as well as two articles on Anga initiations (Bonnemère 2001b, 2004). Finally, Lemonnier's more recent work contributes essential elements for comparison in the domain of the representations and practices connected with death and mourning (2006a), and the attendant myths and rites (2010).

9. Although it has been clearly established that the term "kukukuku" comes from the Motu, one of the country's three official languages alongside English and Tok Pisin, which is spoken around the present-day capital, Port Moresby, several interpretations exist. That proposed by Hallpike in his book *The Kukukuku of the Upper Watut* (see Blackwood 1978), seems to be the best supported. He concludes that the term derives from the Motu word "kokokoko," meaning "cassowary." His argument runs as follows: Motu merchants arriving in the region of Kerema probably heard their exchange partners talking about stocky men who were ferocious if not actually cannibals, and who would run out of the forest to raid the coastal villages and wore grass loincloths and bark capes. The Motu then constructed their own image of these men they had never seen from that of the big birds that lived hidden away in the forest, could not fly, were dangerous when surprised, and were covered not in real feathers but in quills, whose color ranged from brown to blackish brown according to their age. Everyone agreed that the term "kukukuku" was derogatory and insulting.

That is why, upon hearing the Baruya and the Simbari, with whom they were working, assert that they hated the term used to designate them, missionary-linguist Richard Lloyd and doctor Carlton Gajdusek suggested substituting a word found in all the languages spoken by these groups occupying a territory 130 by 140 kilometers to the east of the Vailala River (map 2). The word was *anga'*, which means "house." It was promptly adopted and written as "anga."

published an article on their use of plants (1940) and another on their myths (1939). Her unpublished field notes were collected by C. R. Hallpike into a volume, which appeared in 1978, so that, thanks to his happy initiative, we have at our disposal ethnographic material not only on an Anga group but above all on a people living in the southeastern part of the zone, a region that was not studied again until the early 1990s (Bamford 1997).

Hans Fischer was the first anthropologist to return to the Anga territory—thirty years after Blackwood's visit—this time to the Yagwoia, Iqwaye speakers living north of the Menyamya Valley. Although he never went back, he did publish a monograph (1968) in German on these people. Godelier, in turn, was the first French anthropologist to live with the Anga, this time among the Baruya of the Wonenara Valley, where he took up residence in 1967. Herdt, for his part, was the first American anthropologist to stay with another Anga group living in the northern part of the territory, the Sambia, in 1974. Under the direction of Kenneth Read, he prepared his doctoral dissertation on this society, which was similar to the Baruya in a number of respects. Both Herdt and Godelier published books, a year apart, centered on male initiations (Herdt 1981; Godelier [1982] 1986). Although their approaches to these rituals were different—Herdt had also trained in developmental psychology—the two eminent anthropologists both interpreted the initiations as institutions designed to reproduce male domination. In 1977, Jadran Mimica, at the time a young doctoral student in Canberra, undertook to study the Iqwaye, the Ankave's closest neighbors in the Suowi Valley (see p. 26n1).

THE ANGA IN *THE GENDER OF THE GIFT*

Critical analysis of the anthropological studies on the Anga occupies a large part of Marilyn Strathern's major work, *The gender of the gift*. She takes particular interest in Herdt's interpretation of the symbolism of the flutes secretly shown to the novices to teach them, as it were, the practices of ritualized fellatio that will follow. Herdt believes that these flutes must be regarded as substitutes for the mother's breast, which the novices must now renounce forever. Before proposing an alternative interpretation of these basic musical instruments, M. Strathern situates Herdt among the anthropologists whose work she describes as having a "prefeminist cast" (1988: 58). The sexual-antagonism model used by Read as early as 1952 and repeated into the 1980s is criticized here, not so much in the manner of the feminists who were content simply to say that these studies are strongly marked by the anthropologist's sex but because they place the question of sexual identity at the heart of their problematic (M. Strathern 1988: 58). Yet, as M. Strathern argues, even if Melanesians make an imagistic use of gender, we cannot affirm a priori that sexual identity is central to their preoccupations, for concern with identity as an attribute of the individual person is a Western European phenomenon (1988: 59). Nevertheless, she goes on to credit Herdt with including in his analysis something of the relational view of gender and society that she herself defends, but considers that the persistence of the "sex-role model" leads him to see the ritual as being centered on the individual, whom Herdt regards as a sort of "responsive self" (M. Strathern 1988: 60). The sexual-antagonism model that has framed the analyses of male rituals in this part of the world, promoting an approach to gender in terms of individual identity, has led anthropologists to suggest that the male rituals "make" men—in other words, they give men "a sense of maleness." For M. Strathern, however, this idea is without foundation, whether anthropological or feminist (1988: 58–59).

Personally, I would say that if we study what goes on in the forest away from the women and if we listen only to what the men say, we will believe we are using the expression "making men" correctly to qualify the male initiations. But as soon as we expand our scope to include what all participants in the ritual do and say, the expression begins to look inadequate.

The analysis of the Ankave rituals presented here in a way finds both its echo and its justification in M. Strathern's views, for the ethnographic material I gathered in 1994 while working with the Ankave women during the initiations corroborates the idea that these ceremonies, organized for the boys to be sure, concern more than them alone or more than the men's community alone. If only because of the necessary presence and participation of the boys' mothers and sisters, each in their own way, this ritual can no longer legitimately be seen as acting on only the person of the novice. Its analysis must therefore include the relationship that this presence reveals.

In other words, I argue that the initiations do not concern the men alone (Bonnemère 2004b). Once again, many parts of the ritual are secret and restricted to one of the sexes, but, as we will see throughout this book, these rituals cannot be reduced to such moments. When I gave a paper on Ankave women's participation in the male rituals in a symposium organized by Gilbert Herdt and I in 1998, the idea was well received, almost with a sentiment that it was self-evident. That prompted me to wonder why, if the women's participation in male rituals was so conceivable, had I never read in the ethnographies on these large-scale, collective events that other participants were intervening at the same time but in a different space?[10] The time had come to challenge the paradigm dominating the anthropology of gender as well as that of male initiations since the 1950s, not to mention Kenneth Read's major pioneering work on the Gahuka-Gama (1952), who live near what is today the town of Goroka but at the time dwelled in the isolated mountains of the eastern central Highlands. However, all Oceanists are deeply indebted to this anthropologist, who is still today, over fifty years after his first writings, an author whose pioneering authority and vision as expressed in his work on gender and personhood in Melanesia are undeniable. But if the idea that male domination is the only possible way to explain the existence and continuation of the initiations was to be proved wanting, this could only be achieved through the most fundamental ethnographic research, based on fieldwork with women, whose invisibility and inaction had been assumed.

It so happens that the Ankave of the Suowi Valley were the first people to furnish this valuable information. It was in the autumn of 1994,[11] when Pierre Lemonnier and I were working there, that the ritual expert decided it was high time for twenty-six of the boys to have their noses pierced. Preparations for the initiations could then begin. At the same time, the door that was to allow me to write the present work opened a crack.

A brief explanation is needed, for the reader unfamiliar with the geography of Papua New Guinea might well wonder about the legitimacy of comparing observations of rituals made in the 1950s (Kenneth Read) with others carried out in the 1990s. In reality, the two situations are comparable because, although the Ankave saw white men for the first time in 1938 (so only a few years after the Gahuku-Gama), today they have just seen a few planes land on their little slope of an airstrip that opened in 2011, while the Gahuku-Gama live near the

---

10. In point of fact, a few authors had noted that women were not totally absent from male initiations (Sørum 1982; Gewertz and Errington 1991) but did not propose a revision of the existing analyses. Bamford (2007) offered a new interpretation of the Kamea male ritual based on the involvement of the boys' mothers to which I will turn in chapter 5.

11. The Ankave do not show their initiations to just anyone (including other Papuans), and they waited several years, until our fourth trip, before doing this.

"highway," the only long road in the country, which runs down the center from east to west.

Having studied Western Highlands societies that do not have initiations, M. Strathern did not think of the participation of real women when she criticized the writings on gender in Melanesia. She placed her emphasis on the mixture of gendered metaphors, whether these were included in objects or in persons. For this author, "collectivization" is always effected through single-sex association, which does not preclude cross-sex dependencies often being brought into play through emphatic assertion or, on the contrary, denial. The excluded sex is thus "present," and this presence is constructed as deliberate absence (1988: 120). The ethnographic material I collected shows that, for the Ankave, neither sex is excluded from the ritual process, and the presence of the "other sex" is not on the order of a presence purportedly manifested by absence. It is a flesh-and-blood presence.

As I showed elsewhere with the help of several colleagues (Bonnemère 2004b), we need to consider the various possible forms this female presence can take in male rituals. The presence is not merely virtual, metaphorical, symbolic, or whatever, or an existence via its opposite, absence, as several anthropologists have maintained.[12] The women's presence is altogether real, observable, and it is the different modalities of female presence in male rituals that we must try to understand, while at the same time keeping in mind M. Strathern's message that it is not necessarily because they are female that they symbolize femaleness in a given context, since neither objects nor persons can a priori be defined as such. If we retain her principal hypothesis, then men and women are not differentiated by their attributes but by their actions, which are themselves gendered. As for the objects, those that circulate in transactions, for example, these are male or female in virtue of their origin and their usage, and not because of any inherent qualities they might possess.

This way of thinking, we should remember, developed gradually and gained ground in reaction to a critical statement made by Annette Weiner in her landmark book published in 1976, *Women of value, men of renown: New perspectives in Trobriand exchange.* Accused by the latter of male bias and not

---

12. This was a subject of debate at the session I organized in Hawaii at the 1999 meeting of the Association for Social Anthropology in Oceania (ASAO), since certain participants argued that absence was indeed a form of presence (Bonnemère 2004b). See also Josephides, Rapport, and Strathern (2015: 205).

paying attention to the women's exchanges of netbags, M. Strathern defended herself, as we have seen, using what she termed a "strategy of negation" (1987a: 12), which aimed to deconstruct the concepts currently in use in Western anthropology and so to reveal their ethnocentric character. This approach, which underscored the gap between our analytical concepts and the systems of representations we were studying, found its audience in the so-called postmodern trend that was emerging in the social sciences at the time, and particularly in the United Kingdom and the United States. Taking advantage of the invitation to give the 1980 Malinowski Lecture in London, M. Strathern responded to A. Weiner's criticism by showing that the Melpa women's netbags could not be described as female objects. To be sure, they were made by the women, but they circulated little and only between women, without entering into the exchanges that engage the reproduction of the society, as is the case in the Trobriand Islands mortuary ceremonies A. Weiner had analyzed. M. Strathern went on to argue for cultural relativism, using two ethnographic situations in Papua New Guinea to show that it is impossible to view the category "woman" as a universal given (see p. 9), contrary to A. Weiner's conclusion to her Trobriand Islands study: if women there had a timeless power to regenerate the society and the cosmos, it was, she argued, in virtue of their belonging to the female sex and the power they have to give life ([1976] 1983: 234). For M. Strathern such a claim was patently unacceptable, for representations of femaleness vary widely with the culture. The outcome of this deconstructionist reflection, which she conducted not only on the category of "woman" but also on the dichotomies "nature/culture" (1980), "subject/object" (1984a) and "private/public" (1984b), was its concretization in the publication of *The gender of the gift: Problems with women and problems with society in Melanesia* (1988).

Although I do not adhere to the postmodernist current in anthropology, M. Strathern's strong insights are still highly conducive to progress in the way we think about Melanesia, particularly her criticism of the notion of men's appropriation of women's reproductive powers. As we have seen, this notion assumes we agree to see gender as a personal attribute or property, a conception she vehemently opposes. But before presenting M. Strathern's theory in detail, I would like to discuss the elements of Ankave ethnography that authorize a singular perspective. Three successive chapters will, therefore, be devoted to describing the birth of a man's first child, together with the before—the pregnancy (chapter 2)—and the after—the rite itself (chapter 4).

"Your wife is pregnant. Cover your head!"

Today is a day that broke the monotony of the preceding days. That is what I thought on that night of July 26, 2002. For the first time in the fifteen years I have known the Ankave of the Suowi Valley, I have just attended the entire sequence of events surrounding the birth of a man's first child. I know Thomas well; he is the youngest son of a good friend of Ayakupna'wa, and his father is one of the principal ritual experts for the collective stages of the male initiations. This responsibility does not give his father any particular prestige or power, merely that of being listened to on this occasion. He is a member of the Idzadze clan, the most populous clan, the one that makes the smallest clans fear that some of its land-poor members might covet tracts. Idzi beri, Thomas' wife, is from Ikundi, the neighboring village located at some 30 minutes walk to the east, where the Kwowi River flows into the Suowi (see map 1). She too belongs to the Idzadze clan, whose demographic growth—today it makes up half of the valley's population—has obliged the Ankave to relax their marriage rules. Even though clan exogamy is still the official rule, they have had to resign themselves to accepting that the Idzadze can marry among themselves, providing, however, the ban on marriage within the same lineage—that is the subdivision of a clan that includes all descendants of a man whose name is known—is respected.[1]

---

1. In 2003, probably in the wake of questions raised by the visit of an oil company, the inhabitants of the Suowi Valley spoke of lineages (<u>lains</u> in Tok Pisin) within the Idzadze clan.

This is the case here, since Idzi beri is Thomas' classificatory patrilateral parallel cousin,[2] who would be a second cousin in our terms.

It was neither in Ikundi nor in Ayakupna'wa that she gave birth to their little girl on the morning of July 17, but in Pena'akwi, two hours on foot from there, near the camp a relative had set up on the bank of the big river. Many people were living in the vicinity because the pangi fruits (*Pangium edule*) were ripe and ready to be made into a thick sauce, the only way they are edible (Bonnemère 1996b). It was what they call the dry season.

Photo 4. A young father, carrying the *me'we* trunk at the end of which the ornaments for his wife have been hung, comes down from the forest after having undergone the third-stage *suwangain* ritual. The two men accompany him because they underwent the same ceremony shortly before. To their feather headdresses they have added a strip of the *ogidje* cloth which the initiate prepared during his wife's pregnancy. When they emerge from the forest, they will head toward the hamlet of Ayakupna'wa where the public phase of the *suwangain* ritual will soon take place. © Pierre Lemonnier (June 1997)

At midday, Thomas and two men whose first children had been born recently, and who accompanied him for this reason, came down from the forest in all

---

2. In other words, she is placed in the category of the daughters of Thomas' father's brother.

their finery: they were each wearing a red headband of beaten bark, *ogidje*, (see photo 4) and the *suwangain* ornament characteristic of this stage around their neck. This ornament is made of a rattan ring to which are attached two curved tusks from a male pig. It is worn only on this day[3] and is passed down from father to son. A few hours later, when the tubers of the ceremonial meal had been eaten, the pace of the conviviality calms down and the villagers sit around in small groups. And yet the tension rises from time to time, because this is also one of the few times when everyone is there to hear people vent their grievances and feelings. Village gatherings are often the occasion not only to exchange news, but also to deal with potential conflicts and clear the air before they fester.

Today the respective families of the young couple are arguing about a gift of lime that was supposedly late. While I record the exchanges, which I will later be able to translate at my leisure in the little room that serves as my office, I watch the gathering closely and have a hard time recognizing Silas, the eldest son of Nathaniel, also known as Natnan, a mischievous man who died five years earlier. A new bark cape has just been placed on the crown of his head, for his young wife, Oredzi Nevai, the daughter of the current ritual expert for the *suwangain* rite, is pregnant with their first child. His expression conveys a mixture of pride and renunciation, which I imagine to be more or less the two sentiments the society expects of a young future father of a first child. Pride in being able to contribute to the perpetuation of this group that certain discourses and ritual practices show to be aware of its vulnerability (Bonnemère 2010: 126) and whose babies so often die; and renunciation of the tasty foods and the customary activities that have just been enumerated to him.

Here is what happened. One day, Silas' mother, a now remarried widow, came to tell her son that his young wife was pregnant. Immediately, like any future father of a first child, he knew he would quickly have to make three capes like those worn on the crown of the head, which can be made from any kind of ficus. Sometimes one of the husband's brothers prepares the capes, but in either case they are meant for the husband, his wife, and one of his sisters, ideally a real rather than a classificatory sister who, here again if possible, is older but still without children. All the Ankave agree that it is the pregnant woman who uses a strip of bark from the *yo'o erwa'a* ficus (*Ficus hesperidiiformis* King) to make the string that draws the cape together at one end to form the hood to be placed on the head. But they differ when it comes to knowing who is responsible for

---

3. All the men taking part in the ritual can wear theirs.

hemming one end and inserting the string to gather the hood. Some say it is the husband who does this himself, sometimes with the help of his brother's wife, others say the wife's parents are supposed to do this and that they even receive a special compensation, called *djilu'wa*. I will come back to this point (see p. 153). It is at the close of the big meal (<u>mumu</u>), organized in the following days or weeks by the couple's close relatives, that the capes will be placed on the head of the members of this triad formed by the future father of a first child, his sister, and his pregnant wife. In one case I witnessed in June 1998, it was the maternal aunt of the pregnant woman who took charge of draping the cape on the three protagonists, but other people can also do this.

One day, when her son had prepared the three capes, which we will call "pregnancy capes," Silas' mother went to harvest tubers from her own garden and from that of the young couple, then, carrying her heavy load, came back to her daughter-in-law's village. The girl's parents, too, had gone to their garden to dig sweet potatoes and taros. It was late July and there were no ripe red pandanus fruits on the husband's land, but had there been, he would have been responsible for picking some to make the sauce used to accompany the tubers. Soon the women of the two families would peel the tubers while the wife's husband and brothers would take care of the firewood for the earth oven.

A SPECIAL MEAL

This meal is the occasion to levy a number of prohibitions on the future father. These are first of all food taboos: he will be absolutely forbidden to consume red pandanus sauce, which he will take for the last time (if in season) for months to come at this meal; then the flesh of a marsupial whose fur turns a reddish brown during the season when this tree is in fruit (probably *Dendrolagus matschiei*), and, in fact, game in general. Nor can he drink water but must be content to slake his thirst with the sap of a wild bamboo and the juice of the sugarcane, clearly less thirst-quenching than the cool water of the streams that course down the mountains. Although these measures seem particularly draconian to Westerners, given the insistent messages we receive to drink a liter and a half of water a day, this prohibition does not seem to particularly inconvenience the young men of the Suowi Valley. Insofar as when they talk about good health and life, the Ankave emphasize blood and its principle source of replenishment, red pandanus sauce, if the future father finds himself in a particular state of weakness and vulnerability. In fact, I was told that his own parents, worried he would not be able to eat this vital food for months on end, told him it was possible, if the occasion were to present itself, to secretly eat the *inge' agidji'we* and *inge'pitongwen'*, birds that women and children of both sexes are forbidden to consume because, it is said, of their long tail and their predominantly red coloring, but no doubt also because these birds eat the juice of the *ika'a rwa'ne* fruits.[4] He must eat them barely cooked, because, for their flesh to be beneficial, it must be eaten bloody.

Everything suggests—and I will return to this in chapter 5—that just as red pandanus sauce is a vegetal substitute for human blood, in the animal kingdom the blood of birds fulfills this function of substituting for this vital substance par excellence.[5] The flesh of the other animals that the Ankave eat—pork, marsupials, cassowary, and eels—is always eaten well done, and no trace of blood seeps out. Furthermore, no one ever says that these meats should be eaten to replenish the blood supply. Nevertheless, there are two reasons why it is impossible to establish an equivalence between red pandanus sauce and the blood of birds: in other words, the first is not, in the plant kingdom, what the second would be in the animal kingdom. First of all, the blood of birds is compatible with the blood of male persons only (see pp. 165, 168), which, unlike red pandanus sauce, does not make it a universal substitute for human blood; and second, men turn to this source only when red pandanus juice is not available, either because it is forbidden, as in the case of the pregnancy of a wife, or because it is not the fruiting season for the red pandanus. Pending our return to this connection between birds and men, which the Ankave culture has developed to a particularly high

---

4. The *ika'a rwa'ne* (*Schefflera sphenophylla*) tree, commonly called umbrella tree, bears fruit that contains a very sweet juice consumed by certain birds. When talking about the prohibition on women and children consuming it, several men told me, somewhat embarrassed, that sometimes they drank the juice but it was something one does not talk about and that the women ignored. In an earlier study (1996a: 241), I suggested that the juice of these fruits was among the foods the Ankave men sometimes consumed to help them replenish their supply of semen. The practice of eating a food in order to replace this bodily substance is even more widespread among the northern Anga, who see the quantity of semen as being limited (see, for example, Herdt 1984: 176). But since I learned that this tree grew up there where the blood of a primordial being had been spilled (see p. 166), it would be their blood they were seeking to replenish by drinking the juice of this fruit.

5. In *Le Sabbat des lucioles*, Lemonnier mentions that the shamans use the blood of a domestic pig when a hemorrhage has been caused by the action of a malevolent *ombo'* cannibal spirit (2006a: 112).

degree, we will come back to the advice given to the future father of a first child on this day when his and his wife's families have come together for a big meal.

In addition to the food taboos that are announced, some of the most frequent everyday actions will soon be impossible for him to perform: for the duration of his wife's pregnancy he will be forbidden to make knots and will therefore be unable to pass the time until the birth of his child by making a bow or arrows, repairing his garden fence, or building a new house. The future father of a first child is placed in a situation of near inactivity, which fits with the fact that he is forbidden to consume red pandanus sauce, which is said to be the primary source of vitality and good health. He adopts a silhouette that is humble, neuter, devoid of ornaments: as the Ankave say, "he must not have fine skin," an expression that means that he must not be in especially good health (Lemonnier 2006a: 89–90), or draw attention and be agreeable to look at.

At the same time as wearing the bark cape on the crown of his head signals the state in which a man awaiting his first child finds himself, it also expresses on its own the accompanying set of constraints and obligations. This state corresponds to a unique phase in the man's existence, during which he is marginalized from ordinary social life, sidelined from activities, behaviors and vestimentary codes characteristic of the others of his gender. To be sure, other circumstances, such as mourning a wife or a sister, distance a man from those things that constitute others' ordinary life by subjecting him to obligations and prohibitions that affect his body (not shaving or cutting his hair, or even washing), the way he dresses (wearing a special loincloth called pulpul, removing his bright-yellow orchid-stem ornaments) and what he can eat (no areca nuts or red pandanus juice for several weeks); but none of these is of such an intensity whether measured in terms of duration or number of constraints.[6] In this sense, for a man, the gestation of his first child is a time in his life that not only will never be repeated but also that is only superficially similar to other times. Marginalized with respect to the other men and as though differentiated from them, everything he does has a direct influence on the body of his pregnant wife, who might suffer the consequences, as shown by the story of what would happen were he so unwise as to transgress a taboo: hemorrhage, the baby stuck in the uterus, et cetera.

---

6. For example, the prohibition on red pandanus sauce for people in mourning is sometimes broken by widowers, who consume it but always unbeknown to the women (see pp. 30, 94).

The big meal prepared by the women of the two households is not only the occasion to announce to the young man that he will have to curtail many of his normal activities and adopt restrictive behaviors. The parents of the couple also inform him, but this time indirectly, that he will have to make a certain number of bark capes during the pregnancy, as well as prepare "lime"[7] and purchase vegetal salt in view of the gifts he will have to make at the end of the ritual organized after the birth of his first child, which brings to a close the final stage of the male initiations. In some contexts, such as hunting or rituals, certain everyday words cannot be pronounced. At these times, the Ankave have special ways of speaking whose meaning all have learned in the course of their lives. This is the case in the present situation: the parents of the young couple cannot employ the usual expression to tell their children that they will have to make lime. If they actually pronounce the word *lime* (*sonkwo*), they replace the verb usually associated with it by another, with the very neutral *yarene*, which would be the equivalent of the English *to do*. At the same time, they must teach them the other precautions they must take in speaking when making this white-ish powder indispensable to everyone's well-being and to social life in general. They themselves cannot use the expression *sonkwo yarene*, and the words *water* and *frog* are also banned.[8] They will say that they have *komare yarene* and everyone will understand that they have made the lime which they will need to distribute once the secret rite has been performed.

---

7. The term *lime* may not be altogether appropriate in this ethnographic context since, to obtain it, the Ankave burn bark and not seashells or coral (Lindstrom 1987: 15; Revolon 2014: 147). Nevertheless, I resign myself to using it for two reasons: first because the product that goes by this name is used in exactly the same way as that made by the coastal populations; and, second, because those Ankave who speak Tok Pisin use the term <u>kambang</u>, which is the translation of the English *lime*. I therefore ask the reader to understand this word to indicate the astringent white powder that, associated in small quantities with an areca nut and a leaf or a catkin from the *Piper betle* tree, makes a "chaw" that produces a stimulating runny red paste when thoroughly masticated.

8. The Ankave do not say anything particular about why these two words are forbidden, but we know that frogs are associated with women (see p. 160): when a man dreams of frogs or sees one, it means a woman is thinking of him; furthermore, women catch frogs to be used as bait for eel traps. The myth says that the first eel came from a piece of an overly long penis of a man who was imposing himself on a woman. She cut off his penis and the longest piece headed down to the river, where it turned into an eel (Bonnemère 1996a: 318–22; Lemonnier 1996).

As we will see later, the process of transforming bark into this highly astringent white powder is time consuming, as is making the capes, since the young father-to-be must go into the forest with his wife and strip the bark from several different trees, soften it, and stretch out the surface by pounding it for hours with a specially polished, grooved stone or a large wood club (Lemonnier 1984b: 143). Among the pieces of bark cloth that will have to be made during the gestation of a man's first child, the most important, from the ritual standpoint, is a wide piece of cloth that will be dyed with a red pigment, which the young man, or his father (as I observed in 1998), obtains by preparing the bark of the *ika'a wawirongwen* (*Ficus variegata* Bl.). The making of the cape respects very specific rules that are social—since the pregnant woman's family can never perform this task—but also technical. Unlike the other barks that are stripped from standing trees, that of the *wawirongwen* is cooked together with the piece of trunk from the tree that has been felled in advance, which, the Ankave say, gives it the time to soften and, consequently, reduces the risk of tearing when it is stripped; this also makes it take on a white color that takes the dye well. On June 10, 1998, Wite Toradze was carrying out this operation for his son, Ngudze wi'a, whose first child had just been born and who had been unable to do this himself. The cloth that Wite Toradze had beaten that morning was still damp. To dye it, he had hollowed out a red pandanus fruit and then cut the outer, edible part into strips, which he placed in a bamboo tube to cook. Then he poured the softened seeds onto a broad *a'ki* (*Comensia* sp.) leaf and soaked the sides and folds of the cloth with the dye, kneading it carefully with the juicy red seeds, which ultimately came loose. This produced a bright orange *ogidje* cloth; all that was left to do was fold it carefully and wrap it in a fresh *a'ki* leaf so that it made a small bundle, which Wite Toradze tied up with solidly knotted rattan string and left to dry in a cordyline. The rules say that it should dry in the forest, but the day was already well advanced and the sun was too low. He preferred to place the cloth in a more open area. As we will see, this *ogidje* cloth would play an important role in the secret male phase of the ritual (see p. 83).

The other capes, the ordinary ones that the future father of a first child will also have to make, are meant for his wife, his sister, and himself. Each will wear theirs once the baby has been born and they have taken off the cape that had been placed on their head during the collective meal after the announcement of the pregnancy. The future father, particularly, had been conscientiously wearing it throughout the gestation of the child everyone was waiting for. For the young father, this substitution of capes will take place during the secret phase of the *suwangain* rite, which is performed in the forest—in other words, a few hours before the public phase. The young father's sister receives her cape from him. The new mother can put on her own cape herself, but only after she has bathed in the river, accompanied by her own sister (see p. 80).

For the time being, each person is eating a small helping of the meal cooked in the earth oven, which is the occasion to levy the prohibitions. The father of the pregnant woman—the baby's maternal grandfather—warns his son-in-law that he will also have to beat an *ijiare'* cape for the end of the ceremonies, once the secret rite has been performed, when he will have to make himself handsome (in other words "manly") and don the ornaments of his new status. Sometimes his father-in-law even offers to make this item of male clothing, which is tied at the neck and the waist with a string to hide the buttocks (see photo 4). Although it is beaten at the same time as the others, the *ijiare'* cape is not kept in the same place, at the house of the father-to-be, but hidden in the forest by the ritual expert, who will bring it out on the day of the secret ceremony.

During the gestation of a man's first child, three persons—himself, his sister, and his wife—are thus united by the fact of having received a new cape at the same time, having to wear it the same way (on their head) and for the same duration. They form a triad in which one might suppose that the actions of each have repercussions on the others. Yet this is not the case. I will discuss this at length in a later chapter, but here allow me to say that the relations members of this triad entertain with each other are not reciprocal: the sister acts on her brother, the brother on his wife, and the wife on the child she carries. It could no doubt be debated whether the child should be considered as a full member of the group, but I will resolve the question here by saying that the Ankave triad contains only active members: in other words, those persons who are defined as the "subject" of an action on someone else and who are not merely the "object" of others' actions.

If this group did not contain a man, the triadic situation would hardly stand out, since women habitually cover their head when they are carrying a netbag full of food or when it rains. But today, everyone has noticed that Silas is wearing a recently made cape on his head. Less ostentatious, because performed in a more private context, are the alimentary behaviors required of the two women. Everyone nevertheless knows that a pregnant woman should consume red pandanus juice as often as possible because the fetus owes its growth to the blood provided by the mother. She must therefore be careful to replenish her stock of the precious fluid. The juice the men extract from this odd-looking fruit is the best candidate for this role. Since the fruiting season of the fifteen cultivars of this tree is spread over eight months, it is impossible for a pregnant woman to fail to get enough for the whole duration of her pregnancy.

PREPARING THE VEGETAL BLOOD

The long, deep-red fruits that grow and ripen slowly in the shade of hard serrated leaves are cored, and the outer layer, composed of thousands of hard semi-detached seeds is cut into strips. The strips are stuffed into bamboo tubes laid on the flames or placed in an earth oven, a <u>mumu</u>. When the seeds have softened, they are easy to detach completely; they are gathered onto a leaf of the *a'ki'* tree and pressed by adult men, who strain the juice through tightly clasped hands. This is done by the men because the women clean babies' bottoms or gut marsupials, and so their hands are always potentially unclean. It is therefore impossible for them to touch this blood substitute that will mix with the life-giving substance circulating in the bodies of those who consume it. And so it is the men who squeeze the red seeds several times while trickling water over them: the product they obtain from the first pressing is called *ta'ne'*, a paronym of the term used to designate blood, *tange'*.[9] This is a thick liquid paste (photo 5), the best kind for replacing blood that has been lost after having been wounded, during menstruation, and during pregnancy, for the baby uses the supply of blood present in the mother's body, the blood that fills the uterus, which they say comes from the same source as the blood in the rest of the body. The second pressing yields a lighter sauce, *main'*, which is of lesser "biochemical" interest. Sometimes a third pressing is done, which this time produces a juice that, although still reddish in color, is so liquid that it is called water, *inenge'*. It possesses few qualities of interest for a pregnant woman.

---

9. Paronyms are phonetically similar words that, by a phenomenon of folk etymology known as "paronymic attraction," tend to be used in an equivalent way (Dubois 1974: 57). The phenomenon is usually associated with situations of taboo (Benveniste 1974: 255; Haudricourt, pers. comm.): here, pronouncing the word "blood" while squeezing the red pandanus seeds is not possible, but using its paronym is.

The father-to-be and his sister together respect an absolute prohibition on this *simangain*, the Ankave's vegetal blood, as it can legitimately be called.[10] The future mother and her sister-in-law both observe the taboo on consuming the *yore'*, a slow-growing setaria terminating in a hairy spike. It could be said that the future father's sister has a double role because she respects the prohibitions shared by her brother and by her sister-in-law. She acts as a sister for her brother and as though she was a second mother for the child to come. Yet, she is also the father's sister who, in the Ankave world has no role *of any kind* with regard to her nephews or nieces. It is the mother's sister who is a quasi-mother, as I learned one day from an altercation between a man and his sister-in-law.

A couple was arguing about their eldest daughter, who had extended her stay with her maternal aunt longer than planned. The father was worried about this woman's harmful powers—powers that are attributed to a child's maternal kin (see p. 141)—and he reproached his wife for not having forced their daughter to come home to the village, located a half an hour's walk away. The mother's sister, who was present, broke in and violently challenged her brother-in-law, saying he had no right to demand whatsoever from his daughter since she was like her own daughter, having come from a womb that was in all ways like her own. A maternal aunt is therefore truly a second mother. But in the context of a first pregnancy, it is the future paternal aunt who accompanies the pregnant mother in respecting the ban on setaria, a grass whose characteristics might harm the fetus.

A pregnant woman must also avoid all marsupials with sharp claws because the baby might clutch the walls of the uterus, or those that live in deep holes because the baby might have a hard time leaving the uterus. Those with spotted fur are not regarded with favor either because the newborn's skin might be covered in spots. In short, to best prepare a first birth, the Ankave impose personal and shared prohibitions on three persons. The husband's sister is in an in-between position; she respects both the husband's main taboo—on red pandanus—and shares the ban on setaria with the future mother. As we will see throughout the book, the position of sister-in-law varies over the different initiation stages undergone by a man, and in the end she yields to the parental couple.

---

10. In support of the expression "vegetal blood," we could add to those paronyms that apply to both blood and the product of the first pressing of red pandanus seeds the word *ke'ka'a*, which designates both a blood clot and the thin membrane covering the numerous small seeds of the fruit (Bonnemère 1994: 25–26).

Photo 5. Men press the cooked seeds of the red pandanus to extract the juice, regarded as a vegetal blood substitute. Always consumed poured over tubers, the local staple, it will be consumed collectively, as indicated by the presence of leaf-bowls that will soon be carried to everyone. © Pascale Bonnemère (November 2000)

FOOD TABOOS

In analyzing the food taboo systems in the societies they study, anthropologists usually refer to the intrinsic properties of the prohibited foods. The Ankave, too, lead us down the same path when they explain that Silas' wife cannot eat the flesh of the spotted marsupial for fear of transmitting this feature to the baby. The underlying logic is that of similitude or "sympathy" (Mauss [1950] 1968: 60–63; Belmont 1978: 286), and it is also involved in the case of the prohibitions on eating mice and other rodents that live underground since it is thought that the baby would run the risk of remaining inside its mother's body.

Furthermore, when the Ankave explain the prohibition on consuming red pandanus levied on all future fathers, they say it is because the juice is red like blood and that the wives would run the risk of hemorrhaging to death during the birth. Here, too, we apparently have a reasoning process that establishes a similitude between characteristics of the forbidden food (here, the fact of being liquid and red) and the consequences of a possible transgression (an abundant outflow of blood). Yet the second part of what the Ankave say leads us not to dwell on the relation between a food and person alone, for the harm is done not to the person who violates the taboo but to someone else. It is therefore more the relational situation established by the prohibition that needs to be studied than the characteristics locally ascribed to the forbidden food (Bamford 1998: 161). I venture to posit here that the fact that the violation of a prohibition affects someone other than the person who has transgressed is the main point we should look at. Or at any rate it is the feature that distinguishes the Ankave system of food taboos from those commonly analyzed by anthropologists (see chapter 6).

The Ankave consider that this vegetal blood consumed by the future father affects the inside of the future mother's body and produces a sort of surplus blood supply that does not mingle with the blood that nourishes the fetus. On the contrary, the juice consumed by the mother does not create any surplus in her; it goes entirely to making the fetus grow and is never superfluous, even consumed in excess. The characteristic of red pandanus juice is to make blood in the—male or female—body, but when it is consumed in the context of a pregnancy, things get more complicated owing to the different position of the pregnant woman and that of the father-to-be with regard to reproduction. When the future father consumes red pandanus juice, he creates a blood surplus in his pregnant wife, whereas she is nourishing the fetus with her own blood. The future mother is bound to her child by a nurturing relationship, whereas the prohibition places the future father in what we might term a relation of protection with regard to his pregnant wife.[11]

Aside from these food taboos, Silas and his wife have just learned indirectly that they must not only make a certain number of bark capes but also prepare lime and purchase vegetal salt from their Iqwaye neighbors, who make it from a variety of ingredients (*Impatiens*, tree fern, *Coix*) as Pierre Lemonnier showed (1984a: 104–5). But prior to this acquisition, other pieces of bark cloth must be made, for it is not possible to purchase salt with *kinas*, the national currency; it must be procured by barter. This salt must be obtained within a system of specializations characteristic of the set of local Anga groups: the Ankave provide the Iqwaye[12] with bark cloth, which the Iqwaye cannot make because their

11. As we will see in chapter 6, such conduct evokes a set of behaviors required of a certain number of persons connected with a pregnant woman, among whom her husband (Menget 1979: 247), and for which anthropology uses the umbrella term "couvade."

12. For more on this population with which the Ankave of the Suowi Valley have always entertained close and sometimes conflicting relations often based on barter and matrimonial alliances (see p. 26), see in particular Mimica's doctoral dissertation (1981) and his book published in 1988.

territory is situated at too high an altitude for the trees used to supply the right bark; in exchange the Ankave receive the salt, which they do not know how to produce (on the principle of exchange rates, see Lemonnier 1981: 57).

LIME: A MALE PRODUCT?

Lime, too, takes several days to prepare. The couple goes to a place in the forest where the right trees grow, generally *oru'wa* (*Syzygium* sp.), from which they will strip the bark.[13] They build a shelter so they can stay there for the time necessary. The first task, a male task, consists in clearing a place on the ground of all leaves and roots so that these cannot mingle with the ashes that will be obtained by burning the bark strips. After the space has been cleared, a few strips of bark are set alight, but only after having cleaned off the lichen and other dirt and dust by using a machete blade. As they burn, the man adds other pieces of bark to form a large cone (43 x 60 cm) and stirs the embers with a branch of *ika'a kwipungwen* (a member of the Laurel family) whose bark is entirely white; as he does this, he recites a magic formula that mentions the name of a wild megapod: "*ikwire ayira rware'a ira'a ere tengwerata'ne*" ("*rware'a* bird, I place you in this hot nest").[14] After an hour, pieces of bark can still be seen, but the pile has largely collapsed. The man takes care that no twig or dust comes in on the wind. When the pile is completely reduced to ashes, he gathers them up in banana or *a'ki'* leaves, which he folds to form a long package that he allows to cool completely. The following day, he and his wife pour the cold ashes into short lengths of bamboo, which they tap on the ground to make room for more. Then they add a little water to settle the ashes.

The next morning the man chops down some little trees to build a small, sloping scaffolding. Meanwhile, his wife goes to a nearby grove and cuts a large number of dry bamboos, *sere pia* or *sere robere*, which are very hard and burn only at high temperatures. The ashes from such bamboo will cool very slowly, the Ankave say. Lengths of split dry bamboos are then laid in layers on

---

13. Other species are also candidates: *ika'a relebele* (*Ficus pungens*), *ika'a siwire* (*Toona surenii*), or *ika'a ayonge* (*Cupaniopsis* sp.).

14. Note that magic formulas do not exactly follow the grammatical rules of the Ankave language. In several cases, even the vocabulary is different or the spelling is modified.

the bed of wood, each layer placed perpendicular to the previous one, until the structure has attained a height of some 1.8 meters. The layers are held in place by stakes planted in the ground along the sides of the scaffolding. Nearby, the woman lights a little fire in which her husband chars a piece of bamboo, which he then lights from another fire and places at the top of the structure. Then comes a magical gesture, which consists in blackening a very long piece of dry bamboo in the fire of the structure before planting it close by in the ground, while muttering the following phrase: *"gubare nepedje piipi kama'a a'a tem-ete ngwerata'ne"* ("these shell[15] and feather ornaments, I placed them on your head. You cannot leave"). When the fire has reached the middle layers, the man takes the length of burning bamboo and circles the structure twice. The first time around, he mutters the following formula in the Iqwaye language, as is sometimes the case in the ritual context:[16] *"wajeje youlabajeje miangwa'o oralereje"* ("this red bird [*pi'tongwen* in the Ankave language] feather, I give you the strength of this red"). And on the second time around, he adds, this time in the Ankave language: *"Pare Okaye mere mere sungwegne brombrom"* ("Look! Here come the enemies shouting battle cries, brom brom"). He then plants another piece of bamboo in the ground, which will be consumed as the successive layers of the structure burn. It is important to raise the temperature of the fire very high. From time to time the man checks the solidity of the structure, which the combustion has made unstable and, if he feels it necessary, plants new bamboo stakes to hold the layers in place. When the flames reach the middle of the structure, he thrusts in a stick while pronouncing a new phrase concerning the enemy: *"Parokaye mere awi tetea'ne"* ("Now I have you surrounded!").

As the various layers of bamboo continue to burn, the future father selects some thick bamboos growing nearby to be used to contain the little blocks of ash—solid cylindrical pieces—which he will soon collect from the middle of the collapsed structure. Three hours after the structure was built, the embers are no longer red. The man gently stirs the ashes with a long, very thin bamboo and extracts the chunks of varying size. He takes them in his hand (or with bamboo tongs if they are still hot) and piles them in a corner of the wooden bed that

---

15. The four types of shell ornaments mentioned here (*gubare, nepedje, piipi,* and *kama'a*) are worn as pendants, necklaces, or across the forehead. For further details, see the glossary.

16. People say of the Iqwaye language that it is not as "heavy" as that of the Ankave.

has not yet had time to burn. In a sort of little scoop he has made from a piece
of bamboo, he crushes one or two pieces of ash so as to be able to pour it into
the big bamboos that he gathered while the fire was burning. His wife proceeds
in the same manner with two superposed leaves of *a'ki'*. The filled bamboos are
stoppered with crushed fern fronds. Finally, the man deposits these on a fire
that has been lit near the structure, keeping a close eye on them for ten or so
minutes: he turns them regularly, wipes them carefully with ferns, and then
rubs them at length with the cold ashes of bamboos used for the structure.
This rubbing is conceived as a process of dressing, and the ashes are like the
lime's "bark cape." As he rubs, he utters one last formula: "*wewara rwa'apungwe'
puwe'raya swidenge' taorengene*" ("venomous snake, little insect, and bee, I say I
will eat you").

These various charms and the high temperature of the fire work together to
ensure that the final product has a pure white color. The Ankave comment on
the virtues of the lime they make from the bark of certain trees and compare it
to the limes that coastal populations obtain from seashells, "The lime we make
is much better because the sap of the tree goes into the lime and makes it taste
good. The product obtained by burning seashells is not as good."

This is hardly the place to go into the symbolism of lime; nevertheless, in
view of the precautions taken during its preparation (ban on words associated
with things female), the charms employed (referring to war with enemies and
uttered in the Iqwaye language, which is also used in initiation chants), and the
care taken to produce the whitest product, I would be tempted to associate it
with that male substance par excellence, which is semen. By offering lime at the
close of the rituals, the young father would be affirming, as it were, his masculinity and his procreative capacity. But that is only a hypothesis.[17]

The lime and the vegetal salt obtained by barter during the pregnancy will
be used in the ritual that takes place a few days after the birth, but the difficulty of the task sometimes makes for delays or for refusal to carry out the full
ritual. Aside from these time-consuming activities, during this entire period
the father-to-be lives as though he were shut off from village activities, since he
cannot help his brothers or brothers-in-law clear a new garden or build a fence.
Nor can he participate in staking the sugarcane, which must be done when it
grows and ripens. He can sit with the others at a collective meal of red pandanus

17. Which makes one think of Jadran Mimica's proposition that Iqwaye salt, a product
     whose production is also complex, was associated with semen (1991: 82).

juice if he wants, but he must not press the seeds, no doubt because he might be tempted to lick his fingers covered in juice, which is bland but so vital to life. For the space of several months, Silas will be reduced to almost no more than a silhouette, a shape stripped of those distinctive marks of maleness: the bare head, and the bow and arrows, and he will be forced to abstain from the activities associated with maleness.

He has been temporarily placed in brackets, as it were, segregated from active life and social activities; this is a state not shared by his wife, who continues right up until the delivery to go to her gardens and carry back heavy loads. Only a few pains sometimes force her to rest and call on the few experienced women in the valley who know how to assuage the contractions with massages, application of water, and their breath. This is the case of old Ibua akwoningi, the only midwife alive at the time, a woman of strong character who saved several women when the placenta refused to come, by introducing her expert hands into their vagina and as far as the uterus. Older by several years, Subu beri, who died in 2003, knew, on the other hand, what to do before the birth when the baby was turned the wrong way. The breath of these women, like that of the shamans,[18] allowed them to see inside the body and make a diagnosis. Relieved until the next time, the pregnant woman returns to her normal occupations; it is often when a woman is on the way back from the gardens that the baby comes. This is all the better in a certain way, for it is not always desirable for a baby to arrive in full view of everyone.

So, if the silhouette of an Ankave future father signifies a state of empathy—of osmosis—with his pregnant wife, as in the couvade described in South America, it could not be said, as has been asserted for this part of the world, that he acts as she does, that he mimes childbirth when his wife withdraws to give birth to their child, that he shares her pains (Menget 1979: 247). In fact, as Claude Lévi-Strauss had already suggested, "it would be a mistake to suppose that a man is taking the place of the woman in labour. . . . It is particularly his person which is identified with that of the child" (1966: 195). I do not know what the case is for the Ankave, but if there is a man who suffers when a woman gives birth, it is her brother rather than her husband. Michael told me that he would receive the *simo'e* gift when his nephew was initiated and when his niece

---

18. In the case of shamans, this breath is their whistling that encourages their auxiliary spirits, the *pidzemena'a* (Lemonnier 2006a: 116).

reached puberty, or earlier if she was asked for when still a young girl[19] because he had suffered when his sister gave birth to them: "I too brought them into the world" (Bonnemère 2015b). To be sure, the future parental couple formed by Silas and Oredzi Nevaye are now a unified entity from which a human being will be born, but this entity is neither autonomous nor self-sufficient enough to be the only one to welcome the child. The woman who gives birth remains tied to her brother, who will soon become an essential figure for the children she will bear: the maternal uncle. It is only from that point that the cross-sibling bond,[20] which tied only the sister to her brother, now finds a form of reciprocity by being extended by the brother in the direction of his sister's children. It could therefore be said that the influence or action a sister exercises on her brother during the different ritually marked stages in his life is expressed in the other direction, only in what I would term an indirect form, since this action is deferred and carried over to the following generation, that of this woman's children. But in what quality does he act then? Is he still his sister's brother when he becomes a maternal uncle? Does the avuncular relation subsume or absorb the cross-sibling relation? To gain a better understanding of the avuncular relation, which Lévi-Strauss showed to be a relation involving not two but four terms, since it supposes a brother, a sister, a brother-in-law, and a nephew (1963a: 41), we need to advance in the presentation of the ethnography.

19. The gifts owed to the maternal kin over the lifetime of an individual will be discussed at length in chapter 7, and particularly the *simo'e* gift because it raises a few tricky questions of interpretation (see pp. 142–46).

20. Anthropology customarily uses the term "parallel relation" for a relation between persons of the same sex and "cross relation" for a relation between persons of the opposite sex.

CHAPTER 3

Accompanying a birth

Thomas' wife felt her first pains at daybreak, whereas she had planned to accompany her mother to the garden her parents had cleared three years earlier, at Pena'akwi, a spot on the Suowi River an hour and a half walk downstream from Ayakupna'wa, one of the main hamlets in the valley. The garden was still producing taros locally known as "Kongkong" or "Singapou" (*Xanthosoma* sp.) for, although they originally came from America, they arrived in New Guinea before or during the Second World War, depending on the region, via Asian bearers. Having come into the valley over fifty years ago, these big tubers quickly became the main staple of the Ankave and the pigs they raise, adapting easily as they do to all soils. They nevertheless have one drawback compared with sweet potatoes: they are toxic when eaten raw. Ankave women are therefore obliged to cook even those they feed their pigs, whereas the neighboring populations, whose territories at a higher altitude allow them to grow more sweet potatoes (and indigenous taros, *Colocasia* sp.), simply feed their animals the smallest tubers not eaten by humans anyway, without having first to roast them in the coals. The labor connected with raising pigs is therefore greater in societies where Kongkong taro is the staple food. Unlike the sweet potato, which the specialists believe arrived in New Guinea sometime in the seventeenth century and which, if we are to believe the oral history of the Enga and the Huli, two populations located to the west in the Enga and Southern Highland provinces, became the main staple in the Highlands in the course of the eighteenth century,[1] the cultivation of "Chinese taro" has a much shorter history in the country, and this situation makes it impossible to evaluate the real impact of its introduction yet. Furthermore, the populations that took it massively into their diet and that of their pigs are much less numerous than those groups that eat mainly sweet potatoes.

Coming back to Idzi beri, there is no question of her accompanying her mother to pick any food whatsoever, as she is in the throes of her labor pains. And yet, if she has already been in Pena'awki for several weeks, it is because her family is one of those who came to this spot halfway down the mountainside to exploit the fruits of the *Pangium edule* trees planted several generations ago by their ancestors, which they tend regularly. It is July, and the fruits, locally known as *aamain*, are ripe enough for it to be time to rid them of the toxic substance they contain, a cyanogenic glycoside, so as to consume them as a sauce poured over taros and sweet potatoes. It is a time-consuming process.

First, the fruits must be gathered and placed on a raised platform so that the yellow flesh around their seeds will soften; then, the seeds must be poured into bamboo tubes, which are heated in the fire. When the seeds have been roasted, their shell is cracked with a stone or a hard wood stick, and the kernels are extracted. While the women are occupied with this task, the men clean out an old maceration pool and check all around to see that it will hold water; then in the bottom of the pool they make the wooden basket lined with long leaves of the *a'ki'* into which the kernels will soon be poured. When the basket is full, the leaves are folded over and the lot is solidly attached with vines. The pool is fed with water channeled from a nearby stream through thin bamboos split lengthwise, and, after having pronounced a charm and laid a small packet of clay on top of the arrangement, the owner of the *Pangium edule* and the pool steps out and watches it fill. The basket must be completely covered with water. The anaerobic maceration of the *aamain* kernels lasts three or four weeks, during which time it suffices to regularly—once or twice a week—check that the pool has not lost its water. At the end of this process, the kernels have liquefied

---

1.   The research on oral histories I refer to here was conducted by Wiessner and Tumu among the Enga and by Ballard among the Huli. The references for their works and many others can be found in the bibliography of the very valuable overview volume edited by Ballard et al., entitled *The sweet potato in Oceania: A reappraisal* (2005). This is a survey of our present state of knowledge and of the ecological, economic, and social consequences of the introduction of the sweet potato, which forms a sequel to Doug Yen's work thirty years earlier (1974).

and the resulting beige-colored paste is consumed during large-scale, collective meals. The women of the inviting household cook sweet potatoes and taros in an earth oven. Then they divide the tubers into equal shares and place them in leaf-recipients that have been lined up on the ground. Next, the men pour the sauce stored in the bamboo tubes over the helpings of tubers, and each family receives one or two portions, according to the number of its members. Once or twice a week, from May to August, the inhabitants of the Suowi Valley thus gather at one or another's house to take, with a certain degree of ceremony, a collective meal of these tubers.[2]

That day in Pena'awki, the families whose ancestors had originally planted the *aamain* trees and who continued to tend them by pulling the weeds at their base and cutting off the dead branches, were gathered to prepare this sauce appreciated by one and all. Before descending to these lower reaches of the Suowi Valley three weeks earlier, Idzi beri had already been having pains, which prompted those around her to consult Ibua akwoningi, already an old woman at the time; she was a shaman and particularly known for her competence in dealing with the final stages of pregnancy and with difficult births.

Ibua akwoningi is no longer with us today; we were told that she died in 2009. This woman, known for her sturdy character, had lived through all the events connected with the Australian colonial presence in her valley. She was a little girl when, one January day in 1938, Samuel W. Carey, a young geologist working for the Oil Search Limited Company, arrived in Ayakupna'wa accompanied by a no-less-young (22 years old) patrol officer, Alan T. Timperley, who had been tasked by the Australian government with the threefold mission of keeping the little team of prospectors safe, exploring the region from the headwaters of the Vailala, and making contact with the inhabitants he was likely to meet. They had left Kerema forty-two days earlier with four assistants, "policemen," as the Ankave called them, and thirteen bearers recruited at the administrative post opened in 1906 to patrol the region (Lemonnier 1999a: 109n20); they were joined by seventeen other bearers from villages they passed through on their way up the Vailala River (see maps 1 and 2).

---

2. For more about the technique for preparing this fruit, which is fairly rarely consumed in New Guinea, and about the social context in which it is distributed, it could be useful to consult an article entirely devoted to the subject (Bonnemère 1996b). In this society, the transformation of this toxic fruit into an edible sauce involves a process of maceration deemed superfluous in Southeast Asia, where it is more often eaten (it is usually judged to be enough to simply roast the seeds).

Ibua akwoningi remembers perfectly the arrival of these black men, whose skin, to be sure, resembled that of the only human beings she had seen since her birth but whose hairstyle and looks were different. Nevertheless, she had always been reluctant to talk to me about this extraordinary event, for, shortly after we arrived in 1987, I had learned from another old woman—who denied it the next day—that the white men had been violent, and the Ankave's response was just as violent but less "effective." The *Kukukuku*, the term used at the time to designate the Anga,[3] had the reputation of being warriors who lived dispersed in the forest rather than in villages and who regularly launched "bloodthirsty" raids in the lowlands. The members of the expedition were therefore particularly on their guard, and their apprehension added to the fatigue that was beginning to weigh heavily both on their physical form and their morale. Many bearers had already deserted, and others left the expedition after their sinister passage—for both parties—in the Suowi Valley. Some *Kukukuku* observed the white geologist from a distance as, accompanied by his little team of prospectors, he spent the better part of his time winding slowly along the river. Others sized up the second white man who, usually at the rear of a long column of bearers, took a path further up on the ridge. This extreme attention to their slightest movements was interpreted as an aggression by these men, exhausted by so many days of canoe travel followed by an arduous trek.[4]

Years after these remote times that the oldest Ankave do not like to evoke, Ibua awkoningi was already an elderly woman whose tongue was feared by all. She was the daughter of an Idzadze clansman and a woman from a neighboring group to the north of their territory, the Iweto (see p. 26n1). As a shaman, she was qualified to make a diagnosis and, in most cases, to treat sicknesses ascribed to the action of evil spirits, whether they lived in human bodies or came from other forest-dwelling beings (Lemonnier 2006a). She had also acquired a special knowledge of which no male shaman in the valley could boast, which consisted in intervening in problematic births or placenta deliveries. Consulted by the families of future mothers who were worried about the course events were taking, she would hurry to the parturient, after she first equipped herself with the usual, ultrasimple shaman's gear: a bamboo tube filled with water and a few stalks of *andiwaye*, a dark-rose colored impatiens that commonly grows in the

---

3. See p. 38n9.
4. A summary of this incredible journey, which lasted three months, can be found in Bonnemère and Lemonnier (2009: 304).

many damp and shady spots in the surrounding forest. Given the scattered distribution of the hamlets and her advanced age, it often happened as of late that she lived too far away to arrive in time to relieve a woman about to give birth. Generally, the placenta had been successfully delivered, but on several occasions she was obliged to detach it and thus save two lives.

Here is what the old "midwife," as it would be almost legitimate to call her, told me during the early months of my ethnographic adventure with the Ankave, well before I had the chance to see her at work.

> I heal by blowing. I lay my hands on the belly and the baby moves down. The woman feels better then. If she suffers, I rub her with *andiwaye* flowers and the pain eases. I use the water from the bamboo to wash her skin and I also pour it on the flowers before rubbing them on the woman's belly. And I blow. I get behind the woman who is about to give birth and I press on the top of her belly with a steady pressure, and I blow at the same time. That way I turn the baby around, with my hands. And the baby can descend and get into the right position. (Ayakupna'wa, June 29, 1987)

Ibua akwoningi had learned these gestures from her maternal aunt because her own mother, who had also been a shaman and "midwife," had died before her daughter was old enough for her to pass on this knowledge. Yet there is nothing automatic about this transfer of knowledge between a parent and their children. Beforehand, they must have noticed in the children's behavior, a perspicacity, and a certain gaze that indicates they can be taught to see what is going on inside bodies.[5] In 1987, two of Ibua akwoningi's three children were shamans; and since her twenty-six-year-old daughter had never been pregnant, she had not yet transmitted her midwifing skills to her. Ten years later, Sari wiei was considered to be infertile,[6] but her mother had taught her to help women who

---

5. For a description and detailed analysis of the shaman's skills and actions, see Pierre Lemonnier, *Le Sabbat des lucioles* (2006a: 108–12).

6. In a work on parenthood, the question of sterility inevitably comes up. The Ankave do not stigmatize barren women—it is considered to be impossible for a man to be sterile, despite in some cases evidence to the contrary—but a man who does not have children with his wife will look for a second wife in order to become a father. In the Suowi Valley, there was only one childless man; this probably was painful for him but nothing distinguished him from a man with children, if not the fact of not having gone through the final stage of initiations. In this society adoption is not an option.

were having difficulties in childbirth. In other words, it is indeed a matter of skill stemming from a certain form of shamanistic knowledge that is determining and not the experience of motherhood. Having had children is neither sufficient nor necessary, but that still does not mean a man can intervene in such a situation. I have heard that it has happened in the past that a male shaman has taken such an initiative, but always in exceptional circumstances, because there was no woman nearby and his wife's life was in danger.

The shaman's ability to see through the skin using their breath allows them to both make a diagnosis and to heal. When Ibua akwoningi said the baby had descended and was finally in the right position before coming out, it was because she had *seen* that it was turned the wrong way, and that was the cause of the future mother's abnormally long labor. As the old woman had stressed to me several times, here the eyes are the principal organs at work; when shamans talk about their skills, they say they see things that ordinary people, including those who know about healing magics, do not. Having seen through the skin as though using an X-ray, they are able to intervene on the painful spots, those where the anomalies are concentrated: a clogged artery due to a spirit's malicious action (Lemonnier 2006a: 108) or a baby turned the wrong way.

Idzi beri had not needed to call on the shamans' knowledge during her pregnancy, and until that July 17, 2002, she had never felt the baby weigh so heavily on her lower abdomen. It had apparently turned and was ready to leave the womb, and the birth was imminent. At dawn that day, only the women were awake; they had already stirred the embers in their fireplaces to rekindle the previous day's fire because it was chilly out. Erauye onexei had gone to her daughter, and told her to breathe gently, then, when the contraction had slowly released its grip, had helped her stand up and led her some distance from the zones where the temporary leafy shelters had been erected.

Ideally, a birth should take place away from inhabited places, in a space often only a few tens or hundreds of meters distant, in the middle of the wild grasses or on the edge of the forest. Formerly, women even went into the forest to bring their children into the world and only returned to the village three or four days later, after having completely cleansed themselves of the excreta whose polluting effect on their own bodies the men so feared. Today, because the men are no longer warriors responsible for defending the group from enemy attacks, the rules concerning the birthing spot have been relaxed.

Another time, on August 17, 1990, Idzadze onexei had left the house only when her pains became unbearable. Night had fallen several hours earlier and

Gideon, her husband, was playing cards inside with several men. She gave birth to her child nearby, with the help of her mother and Tumnuku beri, the wife of her brother-in-law (her husband's brother), who lived close by. The next day, at dawn, Gideon built her a shelter and covered it with *a'ki'pungwen* leaves; it is in such a shelter that every Ankave woman stays with her baby until she can go down to the river and bathe. With a first birth, this bath takes place only once the men have caught the marsupials, at dawn on the day the ritual is organized. This time, Idzadze onexei's shelter adjoined the house where her husband was sleeping with their other children.

In the fall of 1994, while the male initiations were in full swing in Ikundi, one of the novices' mothers, who was secluded in the collective women's shelter as was required of all novices' mothers (see pp. 97, 99), was obliged to leave suddenly to give birth to her second son. She did not go far either; she simply hid behind some bushes close to a path not often used during rituals when everyone is very busy. The symbolic charge of the situation struck me, for my earlier analyses of the collective male initiations tended to show that the men performed a—classic—rebirth of the boys:[7] now Idzi beri's youngest son had just been born at the very moment when her eldest was undergoing something like a second birth in the forest, in the hands of the men. Unfortunately, neither lived very long, but to my knowledge those commenting on their deaths did not imagine that a possible explanation could be found in this unusual situation.

Childbirth is thus an event that is less and less supposed to take place away from village life; nevertheless, today the husband still does not take part, and nothing to do with newborn babies can be discussed between men or in their presence. More generally, no man ever touches a baby before it has grown chubby or got its first tooth. Someone remembering Maurice Godelier's book, *The making of great men*, devoted to the Baruya, whose territory lies five days walk from the Ankave's valleys and who, like them, belong to what are known as the Anga groups (see pp. 36–39), would automatically think this is because a baby is polluted, having come out of a woman's body, and is therefore a source of danger for men (Godelier 1986: 61). The fact of being the baby's father in no way alters his vulnerability as a man. This is not the way Ankave men and women think, however; they agree in saying that, if a man, including the baby's

---

7.   On this topic, see Arnold van Gennep's pioneering article ([1909] 1981). For the Anga, see Godelier ([1982] 1986: 51) and Bonnemère (1998 and 2001b).

own father, were to touch it, it is the child who might fall ill. A father, or any other man for that matter, may look at a baby, at least once the marsupials caught by the men have been presented to the new mother, but he cannot take it in his arms. The rule underpinning the necessity to avoid any physical contact between a man and an infant, or a baby only a few months old, follows a logic based more on the incompatibility between the two states of the persons involved (a male adult and a baby newly born from a female body) than on simple pollution, as seems to be the case elsewhere in New Guinea. This is so even if some Ankave men consider newborns to be defiled by their stay in the mother's womb.

A birth is, therefore, strictly women's business. When a woman feels her time has come, she asks another woman to come with her to support and, eventually, help her. To convey her message, if need be, she will say, even to her own sister: "I have a headache (or a backache) and I can't walk." Tenawi had stayed with her elder sister, who had said this to her, whereas she was planning to leave for several days with her husband and their children to gather seeds from the high-altitude pandanus. It was the very end of the month of October 1987, and on the 21st of the month, Obeni, Onorwae's eldest daughter, had gone to Pudzipukwo, where Ibua akwoningi lived at the time. Returning together at the end of the day, and as night was coming on, they were obliged to sleep over in Ikundi. Nothing problematic was discovered following the midwife's diagnosis, but Onorwae curtailed her activities, leaving her sister and daughter to look after her gardens.

She would give birth to her fifth child on November 2nd, in the dead of night, slightly down the slope on which the hamlet of Ayakupna'wa has stood for generations. Young Obeni had awakened me and led me, hidden from sight, to the spot; in the past no child of a pregnant woman, even a very small daughter, could follow the women to the place of birth. Onorwae had given birth to a daughter, her second; it had not been an easy birth since the baby was breech, provoking severe back pains. When I got there a good half hour afterward, she had already wrapped the umbilical cord and placenta in an old bark cape and tied the three centimeters she had left on the baby with a piece of bark cloth. In the chilly night, the baby, whose name—Obeni akwaei without having been given yet—was implicitly known because of its birth order and sex (see pp. 224–25), was also wrapped in a worn bark cape. Going back up the slope to the hamlet at four thirty in the morning, Obeni and I stopped in front of the family house to tell Paul he had a daughter. At daybreak, around six a.m., I returned alone to see my friend, then came back two hours later with my young interpreter, Matrena.[8] Onorwae's last two sons, aged three and six, were with her; the youngest was even trying to get so close to her that he was told to stay back. He turned his back on her, sobbing. He knew very well that the breast he still took in his mouth from time to time, essentially for the pleasure of it, would soon and definitively be denied him. At the end of the day, Onorwae takes her baby back up to the village and to the shelter adjoining her house, where she would stay until she had bathed in the river in a day or two.

Six years later, Onorwae's own eldest daughter, Obeni, gave birth in the shelter next to her house. It had been built for her co-wife, who had had a child a few months earlier, and had not been torn down. That a birth can take place in a domestic enclosure and the same space can be used for such an event and then later used to prepare a meal does not really occasion disapproval. As long as the new mother does not come back into the main house until she has cleansed herself from the pollution of the birth and tubers have not been cooked in her presence, her husband has nothing to fear from this formerly ill-reputed proximity.

"TOK PIKSA," "TOK BOKIS": PICTURE TALK

The practice of dissimulated speech ("tok bokis" or "tok piksa," in Melanesian Pidgin), used by Onorwae to tell her sister that her time was near, is widespread among the Ankave and is used in well-identified circumstances. The forbidden words are replaced by others when the context requires it, and they are not learned outside this context. It is consequently not possible to understand this dissimulated language at first, to the extent that Rick Speece admits that sometimes during his early years as a missionary-linguist he had taken what had

---

8.   When we arrived in Ayakupna'wa in May 1987, the family of Joseph, a Lutheran pastor from a northern Anga group, the Watchakes, had been living in Ikundi for several months (Bonnemère and Lemonnier 2007: 50). His oldest daughter, Matrena, spoke Ankave and Tok Pisin, and accompanied me during the first months of our stay, until November when everyone suddenly returned without warning to their own valley. The Ankave regularly give me news of Matrena, who is now the mother of several children and teaches at a school not far from Menyamya. Without her help, it would have been much harder to gain access to the women's world and would no doubt have taken longer.

just been said literally, without the slightest idea of what was really meant. And
as you can imagine, asking for clarification on the spot would be unthinkable.

A hunter or a woman out catching rodents in the forest cannot talk about
potential game using the proper term for fear of gravely angering the animals'
protecting spirits (the *pisingain awo'*), which might no longer allow their proté-
gés to be captured. Nor does one pronounce the word "taro" (*a'we*) in the forest,
so as not to make them jealous of human food. Likewise, as I have said (p. 51), a
couple making lime cannot use the word "water" (*inenge'*), an element necessary
for cooking the bark. Samuel's daughter learned about this particular linguistic
taboo one day in October 2006. Her father had told her, "*okaje! komare sere geni-
abe*." She quickly seized one of the short bamboos full of grayish, cold, bark ashes,
since she already knew that the word *komare* was used as a replacement for "lime"
in this context. In fact, her father complicated the picture further since he was
asking her to give him the long, thin bamboo filled with water.

The interpretation of dreams, too, is based on this metaphoric language understood by everyone, since, for each forbidden term, there is another, very specific term known by all adults. A man who dreams of a frog understands that
a woman is interested in him; if he dreams he has harvested large quantities of
areca nuts, he knows that the trap he recently set has caught a cassowary or a
marsupial. During sleep, one of a person's two spirits travels, attending events
that really happen or reading other people's thoughts. For instance, it is because
her spirit visited me that I had dreamed about her the night before, Obeni told
me without hesitating when I told her my dream on waking. A few years earlier,
when relations with the members of the neighboring valley were not at their
best, Omadze Nguye dreamed he had caught some fish on a fish-poisoning
expedition. All the inhabitants of the Suowi Valley deduced that the Angae villagers wanted to poison them.[9]

In the past and until the end of the 1960s, dreams played an important role
when going to war with neighboring groups because they offered a reading of
events past or still to come. One night, the maternal uncle of Sandze Omore,
who had gone out to set a trap for cassowaries, dreamed of a broken bow. Everyone deduced that enemies had attacked his nephew. They called him, they looked
for him, and eventually, the next morning, they found his body. The enemies had
struck him down with an ax and thrown his body into the river after he had

---

9.   Mutual accusations of sorcery peak during an epidemic, that is when too many
     deaths clearly point to human malevolence at work (Lemonnier 2006a: 133–34).

shot one of their numbers through the neck with an arrow. People linked what had happened to the dream of Sandze Omore's maternal uncle. Dreams thus provide access both to the intentions of others and to often-dramatic events. It is because they provide information that can turn out to be valuable that no one ever keeps his dreams to himself and that everyone can join in their interpretation.

So Idzi beri had announced to her mother that a headache kept her from getting up. And, as she would have done upon hearing any first-time-mother-to-be make such a statement, she helped her daughter by trying to ease her pain and indicating the best position to adopt so that the baby would not be too long in coming. To assist the mother, a big stick is pounded into the ground. Then the woman squats down and when a contraction comes she breathes out strongly to help the baby be born. That day, not far from Pena'akwi, Erauye onexei was trying to relieve her daughter by sprinkling her with cool water, telling her to breathe slowly and to support herself with the stick to which she clung with both hands; sometimes, too, she would place herself beside her daughter and push down on the top of her abdomen. Fifteen years earlier, Onorwae too had used a stake and had pushed on her abdomen, but alone, by squeezing a folded bark cape between the top of her thighs raised by the squatting position and her chest, which was bent forward. This was effective since her youngest daughter, Obeni akwaei, came out "by the feet"; in other words, she was a breech baby. I even attended the first birth of a shy, young woman whose mother had placed one or two flat pieces of wood on top of her abdomen; my notes are vague on this point because Idzadze wiei was almost entirely covered by her bark cape and because, finally, I was uneasy at being there despite having her permission. This practice of pushing down on the abdomen, with its variants, indicates that the pushing is not ensured so much by breath control, the way we do—where all pregnant women are taught to pant "like a dog"—as by exerting physical pressure on the uterus.

When the hours go by and the baby still has not shown any sign of an imminent passage through the vagina, a shaman, sometimes a man, goes to tell the future father that he must undo the knots of his bowstring and dismantle the bindings of his arrow heads. Formerly, if he had an ax, he had to remove the stone blade from the handle; in other words, he had to undo the bindings. Sometimes he would go as far as to destroy one of the stakes in his garden fence. It is therefore to the future father that people look and on him that the suspicion weighs when a baby is long in coming. He is called in to reduce the

potential obstacles to the delivery because it is his activities that might be the
hindrance. While the husband does everything he can, other women approach
the woman in labor to try to reassure her, to make her forget her suffering for
a while, and help her perform the useful gestures. That day, Imine beri, one of
her classificatory paternal aunts, had traveled to be with her as soon as she had
gotten the news.

A few hours later, a baby girl gave her first cry and the tired young mother
sat down next to her on the bark cloth that had been laid under her to receive
the child. The grandmother cut the umbilical cord with a bamboo knife.[10] Then
they waited for the placenta to be expelled, a moment always fraught with worry,
given the numerous women who have died from an infection of the uterus following the incomplete delivery of the placenta. Over a twenty-year period, six
women died in childbirth; the majority already had children. This is clearly not
something new, and I was told about several deaths of the kind that had occurred in the past. All women are familiar with this danger and dread it. When
it seems to be taking too long, they manipulate their abdomen, firmly pressing
down with their hands, pushing sharply, doing everything in their power to
hasten the process. At the Goroka Institute of Medical Research, where we
were received for many years, I heard doctors say that the uterus of the women
in New Guinea often became sluggish after a large number of births; in other
words, the uterus no longer contracted strongly enough to expel the placenta
without outside intervention. This is usually not the case for first-time mothers,
and only half an hour after having given birth to her little daughter, Thomas'
wife was wrapping the placenta that had nourished the fetus in a leaf to be laid
in the hollow of a nearby branch, safe from hungry pigs and dogs.

Idzi beri's mother let her daughter rest stretched out alongside the newborn
baby and returned to the shelters along the Suowi River. Everyone was now
awake. Sitting around the fire, each person was eating a taro or a sweet potato
that the women who had risen early had placed in the hot ashes. Erauye onexei
announced the birth of her granddaughter. Another step had been taken: the
day of the *suwangain* ritual was approaching, but first the new parents had to
observe a fast. For three days, the young father, who has not yet seen his baby,
is not allowed to swallow anything at all: no food is allowed and he can take
neither water nor sugarcane juice. The young mother must observe a total fast

---

10. Had the baby been a boy, she would have used a piece of pitpit cane (*Saccharum
    edule*).

the day following the birth, but beginning on the second day she must drink sugarcane juice to bring in her milk. The Ankave believe that the colostrum, which flows spontaneously and is not regarded as a good food for the newborn baby, changes into nourishing milk only if the mother consumes sugarcane juice, which her sister will have taken care to bring her. For the Ankave, mother's milk not only makes the child grow, it also enables the child to produce blood in its body, thus continuing the process initiated by the red pandanus juice consumed in abundance by its mother during her pregnancy (see pp. 53–54).

When the baby has been born, there is no longer any question of the mother eating red pandanus sauce or chewing betel; moreover these two prohibitions are particularly specified for both parents, so great would be the danger to the woman's body, not yet safe from a hemorrhage, were they to be violated. These three days of transition between the long wait of the pregnancy and the rituals to come are devoted to rest and abstinence.

When a woman gives birth close to the village, her family and friends immediately hurry to build a temporary shelter, usually, as we have seen, adjoining the house, where she will spend three or four days after the birth. In the present case, where the birth took place at Pena'akwi, in other words several hours walk from Ayakupna'wa village, the young parents' families came only a week later. Immediately, one of her sisters—but the mother, a sister-in-law, an aunt, or more rarely the husband can also do it—built a lean-to next to the house and covered it with fragrant leaves from the *ika'a denge'* tree (*Acalypha insulana*) and then with broad leaves from the *a'ki'pungwen* (*Comensia* sp.), which are used only in this context. Lastly, the lean-to was covered with long, leafy stems of the *ara' su'e* (not identified), which is also pleasant smelling. In the past, these female shelters (called *meemi anga'*, "birth houses") were put up away from inhabited places, on the edge of the forest. In other Anga groups, like the Baruya, there are even whole areas below the villages reserved for leafy shelters where the women give birth (Godelier [1982] 1986: 10). They go there not only to bear their children but also to isolate themselves during their periods, for menstrual blood is considered to be an important source of pollution, which can endanger the men's health.

Among the Ankave, the length of time spent in the *meemi anga'* depends on the marsupial hunt. But before going into the forest to catch these animals, the young father gradually resumes a more or less normal diet. At least three days after the birth of his first child, at dawn, the father receives from the hands of the ritual expert sugarcane (*ungwen*) from three different varieties (*sindere', rarena', and imenegne'*), after the ritual expert has blown on them (Bonnemère 2002).

That is the only food given to him. The following day, the expert leads him into the forest to feed him the halves of two varieties of endemic taros *a'we* (*Colocasia* sp.)—*imema'we* and *ayonge'*, which he dug the previous day in his own garden. His wife, or a woman from one of the two young parents' clans, cooked them before daybreak. The expert has performed a magic ritual before cutting up the two tubers. In the morning, he takes half with him. It is around 8 a.m. The woman who has cooked the tubers takes the other half to the young mother, who is still in the special shelter built for her. In her case, the taros will not be eaten alone but added to a dish of setaria and leafy vegetables, *yaa* (*Rungia klossii*), both forbidden during pregnancy. One of the husband's sisters is responsible for gathering the setaria and the greens, but if that is not possible, the wife of his maternal uncle does this. The dish is called *meemi sare'*, "birth salt."

Today it is Iwasi, wife of the new mother's maternal uncle,[11] who is in charge of preparing and cooking the mixture for Idzi beri. She has cleaned the setaria, cut up taros to be added to those brought to the young mother, and gathered the *kwininge'* leaves, whose licorice smell is much appreciated. She is seated outside on the ground in front of the house, and, carefully mixing the ingredients, she fills the five bamboo tubes she went out to cut a few hours earlier. Then she lights a fire with a few pieces of wood gathered nearby and places the bamboos on the fire. While they are blackening, she goes out to cut a few long *a'ki' pungwen'* leaves, of the same variety as those used to cover the young mother's lean-to, on which the food will be placed. The bamboos are turned over regularly so that the flame will reach them uniformly. After half an hour, Iwasi opens the bamboos and pours the cooked food onto an *a'ki'* leaf. Her small five-year-old daughter would very much like a taste of this good-smelling dish but she is quickly dissuaded by her mother, who shoves her away. Shortly afterward it is the turn of her youngest daughter, a two-year-old, to approach, but because she has just stepped on one end of the *a'ki'* leaf holding the food, she finds herself sharply reprimanded. Iwasi quickly dusts off the spot where the child has stepped, for the preparation of the *meemi sare'* meant for the new mother demands a few precautions: no bit of grass or soil must be allowed to contaminate it.[12] All that remains to do is season the dish with salt mixed with

---

11. Note that here this is a classificatory maternal uncle—in this case her mother's father's brother's son (MFBS).

12. This is also the case of the ground on which the bark is burned to make lime (see p. 58).

some strongly lemon-scented *sijiwi'* leaves. Iwasi chews a leaf after having re-moved the central vein, which is too stiff, then pops a big handful of salt into her mouth. She then spits the mixture onto the dish. Women are chatting nearby, commenting on the preparation of the dish: "I used to chew *komeye'* leaves as well," said one old woman. Another turns to Tumnuku beri, but I deduce that the information is also directed at me: "You, you are the mother of Thomas, you can't eat setaria because you already had the *meemi sare'* when he was born." "Yes, that's true, I have already eaten this dish; it is the turn of the other women to consume it," she replied. Obe wiei, still a girl, asks Iwasi: "Aunty, can I eat some too?" "No, you can't." And Tumnuku beri adds: "You are the only one besides me who can't have any of this good dish." In effect, the first cousins of Obe wiei's father (his father's brother's daughters) are Erauye onexei, the mother of Idzi beri, who has just given birth, and Tumnuku beri, Thomas' mother. But it is above all because of this last relationship that she is forbidden to eat *meemi sare'*, since the members of the maternal kin group of the young man who will soon become a *suwangain* cannot share in this very special dish. After a long discus-sion, the women decide it is time to take the mixture, which is said to tone the uterus, to the new mother.

The two young parents have just shared two taros that have been magically treated by the ritual expert. Each has eaten half, in different places and one after the other; but they are the same tubers and that is why we can legitimately speak of sharing. Most of the prohibitions that had been placed on the young parents are now lifted, with the exception of those on red pandanus juice and areca nut. It is time for the men to go hunting. While waiting for them to come back with the *meemi tse'* marsupials (literally "birth marsupials"), the young mother remains secluded with her baby under the lean-to. The hunt takes place in two stages: the men related to the young father by kinship (his brothers, father, ma-ternal uncle) and by marriage (his wife's brothers, his father-in-law) all leave to-gether to hunt game, on anyone's territory; they spend two or three nights in the forest, the time it takes to find enough meat to allow each of the village women to receive a small share; this applies to almost all the women for, as we will see, some cannot touch this meat. In the second stage, the young father goes out alone to set traps and hunt on his own clan territory; the marsupials he catches at this time are primarily for his wife. After having cleaned the marsupials in the bush, or in the village for those he has caught nearby, the fur is singed off over the flames and they are cooked in a piece of bark or in an earth oven, depending on the quantity. It falls to the sisters of the two young parents to cook one of the captured animals together, preferably a *tse' arma'*, in other words a small, long-tailed, hairless marsupial rat (see p. 89). They cook it directly on the fire before cutting it up, but neither can eat any. In the present case, the marsupials were cooked at Pena'akwi, where Idzi beri had her little girl. Kiau'ni, one of the young mother's classificatory aunts,[13] brought them in a netbag concealed under her bark cape. There were five, which she left at home until she could bring them to Idzi beri, after the close of the *suwangain* ritual, planned for the next day.

13. In this case, her father's mother's sister's daughter (FMZD).

CHAPTER 4

──────────────

Transmitting know-how

On the day chosen to celebrate the birth of a man's first child, most of the village has risen at dawn. Separately, the young mother and father will soon be getting ready, assisted by close kin of the same sex, for the public phase of the ritual, which will be held when the sun reaches its zenith. And so, on July 26, 2002, toward 5 a.m., several of Idzi beri's kinswomen, accompanied by the young father's sister and two women who had recently given birth to their husband's first child, went to the shelter under which the new mother and her baby had been confined since their return from Pena'akwi. The sound of the women's footsteps and their whispering slowly roused Idzi beri. She sat up and laid her still-sleeping baby on her left thigh. A few embers continued to glow in the little fireplace at the center of the space available under the shelter. It was still dark.

Soon the women invited the young mother to step outside and come to sit next to them, a few meters from her place of seclusion. Erauye onexei, Idzi beri's mother, then stood up and struck the roof of the lean-to several hard blows with a stick, and the shelter came tumbling down. The other women watched her and burst out laughing, for the baby was a little girl. If it had been a boy, they would have sung a few notes of an initiation song.

Shortly afterward, before the sun had come up, they left the spot and set out down the narrow path to the Suowi River. No one spoke as they filed down the trail slowly so as not to trip over the roots in the path, which the pale light revealed only at the last moment. The young mother carried a new bark fiber skirt in her arms, which, in this case, her maternal uncle's wife had made for her. Sometimes it is the young mother herself who strips bark from the appropriate tree, heats it, beats it, and then tears it into strips, which she assembles parallel to each other to make the piece of clothing. The new cape she had put on over the netbag holding the baby had been made by her husband, who had had it brought to her. Twenty minutes later, the women were seated beside the big stream, fairly deep at this spot, from which no one ever takes water to drink.

Idzi beri's mother was standing to the back, and it was her eldest sister who had gathered the lemon-scented *robere* leaves (not identified) whose fresh scent eliminates the smell surrounding birth. This is not described as a "bad" odor; it is simply specific to this event and is not like any other. In fact, it is given a special name: *meemi denge'* (literally "birth smell"). Idzi beri was still wearing her old skirt and had sat down in the cold water with her legs outstretched; her sister, Iwasi, carefully scrubbed her body from head to toe with a bundle of sweet-smelling leaves. Then she repeated the process with a piece of soap purchased at Menyamya. When Idzi beri had dried, she put on her new skirt. The young mothers who accompanied her also washed, but without using *robere* leaves because they had given birth several weeks earlier and for them the odor of birth had already disappeared. The older women seized the opportunity to get themselves wet and to wash their small children, who did not at all appreciate the water temperature this early in the morning. Only the baby was not dunked in the icy water. That would come later.

Toward 7 a.m., it was full daylight; the women filed back up the slope, but as they reached the village, the young mother, her sister, and the two women accompanying them split off on a little side path that would enable them to more discreetly reach the spot where, hidden in the tall grasses, they would cut their hair, decorate their faces, and especially await the signal that would tell them they could now come out in full view and join the others on the village ceremonial ground where the public phase of the ritual was to be held. Before going down to the river, Iwasi had remembered to pick a fruit from the *airo'* tree (*Bixa indica*), which contains soft, bright-red seeds. She had taken it from the tree planted by Nathaniel several years earlier because it grew not far from the spot where her young sister was secluded. She had placed the seed in a box, together with a few personal effects (a comb, a razor blade, a bamboo blade) that she always carried in her netbag. When they were settled away from prying eyes, she took out what she needed to cut her sister's hair. After having shaved the top of her forehead, her neck, and her temples, she crushed the *airo'* seeds, took some of the colored paste on a stick, and carefully drew several vertical lines on her sister's forehead where it had been shaved. The two young mothers who accompanied them with their infants in their netbags, shaved and decorated each other in the same way. All that was left to do now was to wait patiently until they were called from their hiding place. A strange sound rose from the forest above the village; it was the humming of the bullroarers, which the women, it is said, take to be spirit voices.

While this little group of women was escorting the young mother to the river, several other members of the couple's kindred—for example, the wife of the young father's brother or some aunts—had begun to peel the many taros and sweet potatoes they had harvested in their gardens the previous day. Their husbands had gone to chop down a few trees for their trunks, which they would bring back and cut up so as to be able to heat the stones placed in the shallow circle of the earth oven. At six in the morning, Tumnuku beri (Thomas' mother), together with her two young daughters, went up to the place where the public phase of the ceremony would be held to ensure this task. At the end of the afternoon, a large meal would in effect bring the day's festivities to a close. It would take many hours to cook the food in the earth oven and therefore everyone had to get an early start.

The men, too, were up early.[1] Well before sunrise, the two men who were at that time the last in the valley to have graduated to the rank of *suwangain* went to Thomas' house to conduct him to a remote spot in the forest. They took the young father there, where they themselves had been led by their respective sponsors a few weeks or months earlier, to gather a certain number of plants that he or his wife would need a few hours hence. The two other men told him first of all that he needed two different varieties of areca nuts: he must therefore gather a cluster from a wild areca palm (in this case, a *nengiye aobungwen*) and another from a tree that had been planted (any variety of *nengiye*), and also pick a few leaves of *Piper betle* (<u>daka</u>). The young father hung the two clusters of areca nuts on his <u>pulpul</u> instead of placing them in his netbag, as he would normally have done. They next told him to gather some wild ginger, *ara' sorebe* (*Riedelia*, a member of the ginger family), and a leaf of *ara' era'a* (*Asplenium* sp.) grass. Then they went to the source of a river deep in the forest to collect some yellow clay *rwa'a omore'*, with which he mixed the *sorebe* ginger and the *era'a*

---

1. My description of the secret male phase of the ritual is essentially based on Pierre Lemonnier's observations and video recordings.

leaf after having cut them into tiny pieces. The whole mixture was wrapped in an *ara' kiringi* leaf (also a *Riedelia*) picked nearby. Last of all, he had to chop down an *ika'a me'we* tree (*Cryptocarya* sp., a member of the Laurel family) and cut it just above the fork in the trunk.[2] As he had already watched the public ceremonies organized for other young fathers, he knew that this long piece of wood would be used to carry the ornaments he would give to his wife when he came back down from the forest following the secret *suwangain* rite (see photo 4). One of the men with him stripped the bark from the trunk and cleaned the surface of the wood, but it was the young father who carried it on his shoulder. It was not until midmorning that the various ingredients needed to continue the ritual had been gathered, for the area of forest they had to comb to find them all was vast. The young father's sponsors then led him close to the spot where the secret male phase of the *suwangain* rite would take place; it is this phase that authorizes Anga specialists to regard this event as a stage of the male initiations.

Yet for the Ankave, this is only one moment among others in the ritual that includes, as we have just seen, a secret female phase and a public phase, which I will soon describe. Near each hamlet in the Suowi Valley is a place in the forest that the Ankave have found suitable for preparing the *suwangain* ritual space. This is defined by the indispensable presence of one or several *ika'a saore'* trees (*Elaeocarpus sphaericus*). The tree is one of the few species that, in this tropical world populated by evergreens, have leaves that turn red and fall; that is the reason the Ankave give for its use in the ritual. For the last several years, the *suwangain* rites have been organized in a tiny clearing upstream from Ayakupna'wa, no doubt because this hamlet stands at the center of the valley and it extends over a large cleared area—which since January 2011 has become the only landing strip in the valley, but which the Ankave had called "future landing strip" ever since they had undertaken to level the ground more than twenty years earlier.[3] There, a large number of people can gather easily.

Several hundreds of meters from the ritual space, Thomas and the two men with him stopped, unable to continue until they received the signal. Several men were already in the space, busy sweeping away every leaf and branch littering

---

2.   The trunk can also be split at one end and the ornaments inserted into the cleft.

3.   Construction of the landing strip is another aspect of our life as anthropologists, which would be too long to recount here (Bonnemère and Lemonnier 2012; Lemonnier 2016).

the ground and scraping the bark of the *saore'* trees to rid them of every speck of dust. The atmosphere was already charged. The expert had prepared a ritual platform at the foot of a tall *saore'*. Such an altar is composed of several wooden stakes pounded into the ground, over which is stretched a red bark cloth dyed with the *ogidje* Thomas had prepared during his wife's pregnancy.[4] On this stand, the ritual expert had laid out the shell headbands, those made of white cockatoo and parrot feathers, and the orchid-stem chest ornaments for the three men, the *suwangain* ornament made with pigs' teeth for the young father, the shell and bead necklaces for the young mother and the new pulpuls. The ornaments had not been laid out at random on the *ogidje* cloth but approximately according to where they are worn on the body. In other words, the headbands were placed at the top of the cloth, close to the trunk of the *saore'*, the chest ornaments just below it, the belt below that, and at the bottom of the cloth, the pulpuls. The arrangement gave this altar a vaguely anthropomorphic appearance. Next, all around the altar, the expert planted the reddish-purple cordylines (*wareba oremere'*) he had gathered from his own garden that morning. Finally, he positioned himself under the altar, lit a fire with a splinter of wood that burns without smoke, and waited for the principal figures to arrive, all the while shaking the *ogidje* cloth gently,[5] which made it seem as though the altar was taking quick shallow breaths, like the mythic hero, Natemowo (Lemonnier 2005b: 246, 2010: 215).

The story of Natemowo can be compared to the myth of the nameless man, as we call him, which tells that, when the first men came out of the ground at Obirwa, the birthplace of most of the Anga groups, only one was unable to say his name, for which the others killed him. His blood flowed out onto the ground. The part that hardened, the clot, became the red cordyline, *oremere'*; where the blood seeped into the ground there grew up a red pandanus of the *perengen* variety, the first of the season to fruit (see p. 138). The fifteen varieties of marita come into fruit one after the other, from the month of August to the month of April. One, which ripens in March, bears yellow fruit and is therefore not associated with blood as the others are. Nevertheless, the latter still differ in their capacity to renew the blood according to the intensity of their color. In the

---

4.   In rare cases, it may also happen that some other man does it for him (see p. 52).

5.   When not actually under the altar, the expert can move it from a distance using a vine he has attached to the cloth.

myths, it is the *simangain perengen* variety—the first to fruit—that is mentioned as representative of all red pandanus. Likewise, when available, it is the variety preferred for ritual use.

The man's spirit next appeared in a dream to the ritual expert, who at the time only pierced the young boys' nose, to tell him that henceforth he would have to add another ritual operation: rubbing them with red pandanus seeds. Because "this fruit came from my body; it did not come from nowhere; you will rub it on the boys cheeks and shoulders to make them grow by making the juice of the red pandanus enter their bodies" (see p. 137). These were the primordial man's last moments, when he could still take shallow breaths, materialized here in the form of an anthropomorphic altar.

Once the sacred altar had been set up, all the men present, with their chests bared and an ax or a club in hand, stomped on the ground to tell the three young men that they could now come. They immediately set out on a headlong race to the ritual space that had been created nearly from thin air. The young man must arrive there with lowered eyes. Then he would receive the order to look. There, grimacing men, with their ax or club raised and ready to strike or their bow drawn, were jumping up and down aggressively as the warriors of old used to do to impress the enemy. The confidence of the three men was shaken.[6] They would soon be beaten and then lectured. One man began: "Look! Look at that! Are those bank notes? And these shells, do you know what they are? Now that you have seen them you must not run away from the enemy!" Another added: "When we are at war, you must take the ornaments you see here on the platform. You must take them with you before going into battle!" Then: "We made new ornaments for you! You cannot go in the garden of another man to steal game or a pig. You must not go away with the wife of another man, and this *suwangain* pig-tooth ornament is no laughing matter. You must not take the wife of another man! You must not go and steal from the garden of another man!"

Then the ritual expert ordered first Thomas and then the two others to join him under the altar. They squatted there and their elbow and wrist joints were heated, almost to the burning point. Other men came up and held their own hands over the fire. When everyone had heated themselves, the expert extinguished the fire and told the three protagonists to stand up and move slightly to one side before he, too, came out of hiding.

---

6.   And even more than that if I am to judge by Lemonnier's memories of facing a man
      with a raised ax during one of the first *suwangain* rituals he attended.

He then took a red cordyline (*wareba oareso'we*) and a piece of ginger and, holding them in one hand, struck Thomas successively on the shoulders, the chest, and the cheeks, and then repeated the operation on the two sponsors. Then it was time to lift the ban on areca nuts that had been enforced since the child's birth was announced. As when any ban is lifted, but perhaps even more so here because of the lesson that goes with it, this takes the form of a ritual. The expert asked the young father and his two sponsors, who also had obeyed the prohibition since the baby's birth, to chew an areca nut of the wild variety *aobungwen* (or *imoere'*) but without using lime, and then to take a leaf of one of the *saore'* trees before spitting the milky juice on the trunk of the tree at the foot of which the anthropomorphic altar had been built. Numbers of purple and red cordylines had been planted on this precise spot. The ritual expert then gave a lecture meant primarily for the young father, but which was no doubt useful for the two sponsors to hear once again. He spoke loudly: "When you have another child and you have to lift the ban on chewing betel that was imposed at his birth, you will have to come here alone to chew an areca nut without lime and spit the white juice on one of the *saore'* trees growing in this place. Today we showed you how to do it. In the future you will have to perform this gesture on your own." The young father was then made to chew and then spit out the piece of wild ginger, *sorebe'*, he had gathered at dawn.

Then it was time for the three young fathers to put on their finest body ornaments, made of shells and colored feathers. In addition, Thomas had to don his new pulpul, his new *ijiare'* bark cape—the one that falls down over the buttocks—and place around his neck the rattan *suwangain* collar with its attached pig teeth, the sign of the new life cycle stage to which he had just graduated. The ornaments remaining on the *ogidje* cloth were for the young mother. They were hung on the forked—or split, depending on the case—end of the *me'we* log, while the cloth was cut into strips and immediately distributed to all the men present who tied an orange band around their forehead (see photo 4). Then they could chew another areca nut, this time in the ordinary way—in other words, adding a bit of lime and a leaf or catkin of *Piper betle*.

By then it was almost noon. The sun had reached its zenith and blazed down on the men's colored decorations. It was now time to descend to the public gathering ground—the so-called "landing strip"—where the women who had prepared the meal were sitting by the oven, hermetically covered with banana leaves, whiling away the time smoking and chatting. When someone came to tell them the men were about to arrive from the forest south of this clearing, one of the women jumped up and went to where the young mother, the two women accompanying her, and her sister-in-law were waiting. The latter left their hiding place, slightly downhill to the east of the strip and began to advance, their backs bent parallel to the ground and their bodies almost entirely covered—except for their legs— by their bark capes (see photo 6); then they stopped just before entering the open space, since their arrival and that of the men had to be perfectly synchronized. When they heard the singing and saw the line of men descending from the forest with the new father and his sponsors in the lead, they resumed their progression, their backs still bent. The effect was powerful: the men held themselves particularly erect, proud, scintillating in their feathers, while the three women adopted a bodily attitude that a Western eye could easily see as submissive. The image this posture spontaneously brought to my mind—after several years of acquaintance with the Ankave cosmology—was that of the cassowary, an animal closely associated in their mythology with women (see chapter 8). In effect, all that could be seen were legs surmounted by a brown horizontal mass made up of their backs and heads covered in long bark capes, somewhat like this big bird, whose long thin legs support a massive body covered in black feathers—which are brown on the young birds. But let us set aside this interpretation for the moment because the Ankave put forward another: for them, this posture is reminiscent of that adopted by women suffering from the pangs of childbirth.

One thing is certain: the staging of this simultaneous arrival of the men and the women on the village gathering ground captures the imagination of everyone there. It has a graphic dimension, as it were, since the women's path is perfectly perpendicular to that of the men and, when seen head on, the final view is that of a line of men drawn up to full height towering over three women walking all bent over. That day, the young father's kinswomen cried noisily, as they do each time the initiates return to the village after a stay in the forest. "Today, they told me, he has become an adult man and now the decline has begun";[7] one generation replaces another.

The three young women sat down in a semicircle and two of them clasped the base of the *me'we* trunk that Thomas had brought back from the forest. While they held it upright, he removed the shell and bead necklaces hanging from one end and gave them to his wife, who immediately slipped them over her head.

---

7. When the mothers of the young first-stage initiates, whose initiation takes place as a group, cry when their sons come back from the forest, it is because they no longer recognize them, they say, so great is their physical transformation (see pp. 101–02).

Photo 6. The young father carrying the *me'we* trunk and his two sponsors must arrive at the same time as his wife, his sister, and the wives of the sponsors at the place where the public phase of the *suwangain* ritual will take place. A woman greets the men as they come down from the forest, rubbing them with the yellow clay used when the first- and second-stage initiates came out of seclusion, which is the same as that used by mothers to rub on the body of their new baby. © Pascale Bonnemère (June 1998)

She now looked nothing like a cassowary; she could almost compete in beauty with the men. He and the ritual expert then distributed a few areca nuts from the two varieties that had been gathered in the forest (the wild *aobungwen* and the cultivated variety), together with lime and *daka* leaves (*Piper betle*), to the women so that they too might lift the ban on chewing betel a little later.

One of the three young *suwangain*—this can more rarely be the ritual expert—then carefully split the wood into kindling sticks some twenty centimeters long, which he then planted in the ground in front of the three seated women. The sticks are supposed to form a circle of ten or so centimeters in diameter, the center of which is then filled up with more—even smaller—sticks before setting fire to the base. It is sometimes hard to light this little bonfire, but when it is the new father who blows on it, they say, it immediately bursts into flame. Nevertheless, that day the fire would not catch, despite Thomas' best efforts. Those present immediately set about looking for explanations, and Joel put forward the idea that the argument that had flared up earlier between the mother of the parturient and the husband's family had something to do with it. Erauye onexei had publicly complained to Thomas' mother about not receiving either braided orchid-stem ornaments (*iru'gwa'*) or a new skirt, as is the custom.

Everyone had witnessed the altercation, including this anthropologist:

TUMNUKU BERI. You weren't there when we told you there weren't enough ornaments?

ERAUYE ONEXEI. He's not that young; he couldn't go get the orchid stems needed to make the ornaments?

T. B. His brother didn't help him, so it was hard for him to go for them alone. If your son had been alone, I would have said to myself that it was going to be hard for him to go gather the orchid stems.

E. O. Big sister! Since you say that about the orchid-stem ornaments, quick, give me the lime and the bark capes.

T. B. Your daughter had the baby earlier than expected, and so we weren't ready.

E. O. You acted like she wasn't pregnant and you took your time.

T. B. Even Thomas has an old pulpul. And I, his mother, am not in good shape.

Other people, all members of the young mother's maternal clan, then had their say: first her maternal uncle, very angry that his niece was not going to be able to look pretty; a more distant female relative, too, who had demanded the capes owed to her and pointed out that the maternals are the first ones the husband's family should think of when having to make the various gifts that accompany the birth of a first child. Kiau'ni then jumped in, on behalf of the husband's family: "We told you it would be impossible for us to make the bark capes and prepare the lime because of having to organize the end-of-mourning ceremony for the son of Erauye ognorwa, Thomas' cousin." Leven, the new mother's classificatory maternal uncle retorted: "Since that's the way it is, this young woman will not wear a new bark skirt but will simply wrap herself in a bit of cloth. Yet I prepared the *ogidje* cloth and the women are going to use it to make loincloths for their children." Then only half joking, the women had threatened to strip off Thomas' pulpul and ornaments if they did not receive lime and capes: "He's going to find himself naked!" a threat that had prompted general mirth. To which Thomas had replied: "Let them go ahead! Take off my feather ornaments; I'll go bare-headed and that's all there is to it!"

According to Joel, an altercation like this, which casts disgrace and shame on the young father's family, was enough to keep the fire from catching, and everyone accepted the idea. The young mother's maternal aunt expanded: "You didn't give the bamboo filled with lime, so this fire, it won't light correctly." It took a good deal of patience before the pieces of *me'we* wood began to blacken. The argument had also died out, finally, without serious repercussions on relations between the two families.

Over the fire, the husband's sister, joined by the sister of his wife, placed a *tse' arma'* marsupial captured during the hunt following the birth, in order to burn off the fur and gather the ashes in a banana leaf. They then mixed these ashes with the yellow *omore'* clay that the young father had just given his wife. If the *tse' arma'* is the preferred choice among the birth marsupials, *meemi tse'*, it is because it grows fast, a quality they would like the baby to possess as well. But if no one had caught a *tse' arma'*, another marsupial would have done.

The mixture is immediately rubbed onto the baby's body, either by its maternal grandmother or by the two sisters of the couple who prepared it. After having rubbed the baby from head to toe with the clay, the old woman passed the child quickly over the fire and then gently massaged its joints and pulled its arms before handing it back to its mother (see photo 7). Other mothers then brought their young children to her so she could do the same with them; their treatment was shorter, no doubt because less was at stake and they had already been rubbed by their mother when they were born, or, if they were their father's first child, by their grandmother, their aunt, or an experienced woman, as in the present case.

Then came the moment for the young mother, the sister of the young father, and the two women who had accompanied the young woman to lift the ban on areca nuts that they had been respecting since the baby's birth. The procedure is similar to that followed by the men in the forest, except that instead of spitting the whitish juice produced by chewing a nut of an *imoere'* wild areca with a leaf of *Piper betle* (*daka* leaf) on a *saore'* tree, they spit it over the *me'we* fire. Once the ban has been lifted, they can once again, like their husbands, chew betel with lime and spit the red juice. The fire was then allowed to die out and the ashes were recovered by the child's mother, who would later deposit them at the foot of a big clump of *a'ki'* leaves (*Comensia gigantea*).

Then it was time to eat. As the afternoon was drawing to a close, the women who had been cooking since dawn unfolded each of the banana-leaf packets, revealing the sweet potatoes and taros that had cooked for several hours in the

Photo 7. The maternal grandmother of this firstborn passes it over the fire lit with wood from the *me'we* trunk that the young father has brought down from the forest.
© Pierre Lemonnier (June 1997)

earth oven. Others fashioned the serving dishes, in fact a sort of small trough made from two *a'ki' abare'* leaves, the broader end of which is folded back on itself so as to produce a deep hollow able to contain a large portion of food, as is done for all collective meals. Each family receives one of these generously filled receptacles, which they can carry away from the oven and eat as a group. But today, the men and the women cannot eat together; and so people will not eat these tasty tubers as a family but with persons of the same sex. Slowly cooked in an earth oven, the sweet potatoes and taros melt in the mouth in a way they do not do when cooked in the ashes. When the light began to fail, everyone went home. It was at that moment that the *meemi tse'* marsupials were brought to the young mother, here by Kiau'ni, who had kept them at her house after they were brought back from Pena'akwi. A young man cut them up and the young father's sister parceled them out.

Only women can eat these "birth marsupials," and their distribution always begins with the couple's closest female relatives: the sisters and the mother of the young mother, her maternal aunts (mother's sisters and maternal uncles' wives), and if there are any pieces left over, all the women present share them with their small female children. The young father's grown sisters and his mother are not allowed to eat any, for "it would be like eating the child." Moreover, and probably more significant, people added that they had already enjoyed this meat when the new father was born some twenty years earlier. The new mother, on the other hand, receives only the marsupials caught by her husband on his own clan territory. It is not until this exclusively female food has been eaten that the young parents can once again stay in the same house, from which the woman has been absent since she brought her child into the world.

Today was a day of lessons for Idzi beri and Thomas:[8] a sister, men and women of the same generation, a mother, and a ritual expert accompanied them and performed in their stead, one might almost say, the gestures they will have to reproduce when their other children are born. Together with them, the community has welcomed their firstborn child, but henceforth they alone will perform these gestures at the birth of their other children. A new parental couple has come into existence.

---

8. Let us note that this was also the case of the "sponsors" of both sexes, who now better understand what they had experienced some time before.

CHAPTER 5

A long ritual journey[1]

The ceremony accompanying the birth of a man's first child is an important life event since it is the occasion for him to go through the third and final episode in a long ritual process that began years earlier when he was still a young boy. The first two phases of this ceremonial cycle had mobilized the male community, and beyond that, a group of women connected with the novices, in the forefront of which were the mothers and older sisters. Many other women had contributed their labor to feed the principal participants (the young novices' mothers and the novices themselves) during the weeks of seclusion and intense ritual activity, and provide the finery they would don at each new stage of their physical—since the collective rites are meant to "grow" the boys—and social development, which go hand in hand with instilling in them their society's moral code of conduct.

In the present chapter, I will lay out the full journey that, at the close of the three initiation stages, will have taken a boy from the status of childhood to full manhood, of which fatherhood and access to the position of maternal uncle are the crowning achievements. This requires dwelling, as we did for the first-birth ritual, on the two collective phases of this cycle. These rituals—which are obligatory for all boys and are organized for a group (twenty-three boys in 1994)

---

1. Parts of the analysis presented in this chapter have already been published (Bonnemère 2008).

of nine to thirteen-year-olds—form a whole, distinct from the third and final ritual which, as we know, focuses on one man whose first child has just been born. Whereas the third phase involves only the ritual specialists, the young fathers acting as the novices' sponsors, and those men who want to accompany them to the sacred forest site, the first two ceremonies are collective and the entire community takes part. These two ceremonies are usually separated by several months or even a year, but they can sometimes be organized one immediately after the other, as in 1994, when Pierre Lemonnier and I were there. Each of the first phases is distinguished by a name, which is that of the primary ritual act undergone by the boys: "nose-piercing" (*itsema'a*) for the first, and "rubbing with red pandanus seeds" (*semayi'ne*) for the second. Several years before the collective rituals, a secret rite had been organized for the five- to six-year-old boys. At that time, the men had taken them to a spot where red cordylines had been planted. There the boys had discovered that first-stage initiates and men in mourning may consume red pandanus juice and they understood that they too would be able do this, out of the women's sight, between the two phases of the collective rituals and when they were in mourning.

During the several weeks of their forest seclusion, the first- and second-stage novices undergo various body treatments:[2] not only do they have their noses pierced, but they are also struck with switches, their arms and legs are pulled, and their skin is rubbed with the leaves or fruits of certain plants and with earths. They are required to fast on several occasions and, at other specific times, they are made to swallow mixtures intended to heat or cool their body, which is also subjected to extreme temperatures—for instance, by placing them close to a huge fire and sprinkling them with icy water. The novices have to perform physical feats, like crossing a stream on a slippery log or running as fast as possible after having swallowed vegetal salt, which at high doses is a violent poison since it's basic component is potassium chloride. They are also made to pass through narrow corridors of branches while being beaten from outside with cassowary quills; they must show no emotion when thrown into the air against a tall tree, in other words not try to catch hold and land upright on the trunk used to launch them. They are also subjected to mental ordeals such as repeated sleep deprivation, threats of death were they to tell the women about the rituals, an obligation to wait until the very last minute to leave their hut

---

2.   I will not dwell on the events that take place in the forest, as their analysis is not
    necessary to the argument developed here.

when deliberately set on fire, deceptions—false enemy attacks, encounters with living dead—and the revelation of secrets. All this transpires in a highly charged atmosphere (Bonnemère 2001a). Throughout the rituals, the future initiates share wood- and water-collecting chores, collective hunts, and great promiscuity insofar as meals are taken together and nights spent in a tiny hut. They are also obliged to adopt restrictive behaviors and attitudes: they must squat or sit in line, stretch out their legs, go everywhere in single file and only when they are told to do so. At other moments they are enjoined to close their mouth and squeeze their lips together, to bow their head, and to remain silent for long periods of time. They can eat only when given permission to do so. They are also taught lessons in various forms. Directly, when the necessity of sharing and mutual aid is explained to them, or when the moral rules and behaviors that will be expected of them as adults are set out for them—not to cry, to control their anger, be self-contained, help each other, overcome fear—or the obligations and prohibitions that will flow from certain occasions later in life—not to covet another man's wife, not to go near someone else's traps, etc.. And indirectly, when they watch skits miming events situated in a primordial past or ritualized fights between men of different generations (Bonnemère 2001a).

Ankave male initiations thus entail a series of ordeals in a variety of forms, the explicit purpose of which is to toughen up the boys and prepare them for life as adult men; until recently (the late 1960s), this consisted in fighting to defend the members of the tribe from enemy attacks. But these are also times for learning the proper rules of conduct and a place where certain mythic foundations of their culture are expressed in a metaphorical and fragmentary manner. Such conclusions can be drawn simply from observing what the men do in the forest during the rituals. But among the Ankave—as perhaps elsewhere in New Guinea, but this is no longer possible to ascertain—the men are not the only ones who have a ritualized activity during initiations. We will now turn to the other important participants in these collective phases of the initiation cycle, who have more often than not been forgotten in the analyses of such rituals (Bonnemère 2004b).

THE UNFOLDING OF COLLECTIVE RITUALS

We are now going to immerse ourselves in the rituals organized by the inhabitants of the Suowi Valley in the fall of 1994. In late October of that year, the rainy season already having set in, everyone had gathered in the village of

Ikundi and was preparing to spend several weeks living to the rhythm of the male initiations. The building of the two big collective shelters for the novices' parents, that faced each other from some fifteen meters apart, was in full swing. From dawn to dusk, men busily carried posts and branches, while the women brought the broad *a'ki'* leaves to thatch the roofs. Soon the fathers of the boys in the same age group would spend the night in one of these shelters, while their mothers would be secluded day and night in the second one (see photo 8).[3] A few hundreds of meters from there, in the forest above the village, other men were building a rudimentary lean-to shelter that would house the twenty-five novices for the duration of the rituals. Everyone was in high spirits, for here these ceremonies are still considered indispensable for the boys' maturation, and no one would dream of not performing them.

On October 27, when the sun had reached its zenith, old Idze Erauye invited the novices' mothers to come out of their hut and follow him to the top of the village, to the head of the path that leads into the forest. The women stopped near an empty house, then flattened themselves on the ground and covered their bodies with their bark capes (see photo 9). A short time later, the novices' sisters arrived and immediately sat down, lowering their gazes. Kiau'ni explained to me that they had come here to listen to the sounds the men made when piercing their boy's septum. And in effect, we soon perceived vague words, movements, and the words of the spirits, which we anthropologists know to be the sound of the bullroarers. For several dozens of minutes, the women remained there listening, in silence, unable to see anything, trying to determine the origin of the different sounds the men produced, before going back to the village. The mothers were the first to return, and all sat down under the porch of their temporary hut, while the sisters, who had followed close behind, were allowed to resume their occupations. A few hours later the cracking of whips could be heard, and I learned that the novices and their fathers were being beaten. The echo of all of the noises coming from the edge of the forest reached the collective female shelter in a very muffled form. Although the women were unable to see or to hear everything, they could nevertheless follow at a distance the ordeals their sons and brothers were undergoing. My women friends told me that if I spoke to any man that night I would fall gravely ill. Pierre, in turn, had been told to sleep in the front part of our temporary house, the one we had set up for the duration of the rituals, while I would sleep at the back with Camille, our five-year-old daughter.

---

3.   Unlike the mothers, the novices' fathers can move about freely.

Photo 8. For the duration of the collective rituals, the novices' mothers are secluded together in a big shelter on the outskirts of the village and obliged to adopt certain behaviors and obey prohibitions that are identical to those imposed on their sons secluded in their forest shelter. © Pascale Bonnemère (November 1994)

THE WOMEN'S INVOLVEMENT

Anyone observing such a scene might conclude that the women merely listened passively to the echoes of the male rituals. Yet this is far from being the case, for the efficacy of these ceremonies depends on the women respecting a number of behaviors. For the many weeks of these rituals, the activities of the boys' mothers—and to a lesser extent that of their older sisters—are highly controlled so as not to pose a threat to the novices' health and survival, and to ensure their unencumbered passage to adulthood. Even the men believe that this major step in a man's life can simply not happen without the presence of these two categories of women.

We must therefore examine the forms taken by this involvement in the Ankave male rituals. The women concerned are, on the one hand, the novices' elder sisters and, on the other hand, their mothers, whom we have already seen being auditory witnesses to the scene of the nose-piercing, but in a manner that is distinct from and more marked than their daughters'. The difference in posture, the mothers lying flat under their bark capes, the sisters sitting with downcast eyes, continues

Photo 9. A ritual expert has led the novices' mothers to a place not far from the site where the nose-piercing ritual will soon be held. They must flatten themselves on the ground and cover their bodies with their bark capes, for only the sounds of the ordeal must reach them. In no case can they see what is about to happen.
© Pascale Bonnemère (October 27, 1994)

in various forms for the duration of the ritual. While the mothers must remain immobile or only move bent over and remain in their collective shelter, the sisters stand around outside and can go to the gardens to harvest food for everyone. By contrast, the only movement allowed of the boys' mothers takes place once a day, in single file, at a specific time of the day to perform a very specific gesture. And when the ritual experts act on these women, to lift a taboo, for example, they can do this only after having had them sit down side-by-side in a line.

For anyone who has seen what happens in the forest with the boys, the analogy of the staging, here in the village and there under the trees, is stupefy-ing: a collective of barely individualized beings receives the same treatment or performs the same gestures. And when a detailed comparison is made of what happens at the same time in the two spaces, the parallel is, despite each having its own constraints, altogether significant. Nothing as systematic connects the group of novices with the group of their older sisters.

The parallel between the novices' ritual actions and those of their mothers can be seen as much in the nature of these actions as in the moment they in-tervene. Both groups receive bark capes, made for the occasion by members of their kindred, which are then gathered up and handed out by the ritual experts. In the mothers' case, the cape is worn under their old, everyday cape; in the case of the novices, it is a new item of clothing that they place on their bare head. After the noses have been pierced, the mothers and sons go every morning at dawn to the stream nearest their respective spaces of seclusion and soak their new cape in the water before putting it back on without wringing it out, then they return to their shelters. What the women say about this gesture refers to the novices' infancy, a time in their lives where they were afraid of the rain and were disobedient. As for wearing the cape, the women do not elaborate; they simply say that, when they put it on, they are in sympathy with their son and do not move so that the wound in the septum will heal correctly, since the slightest gesture could hinder or prolong this process.[4] The healing takes place in several stages spread over four or five weeks, during which the nose plug is changed three times and certain bans are lifted.

The mothers, the older sisters, and the novices are also united in respecting a number of attitudes, some of which have to do with food. At the beginning

---

4.   As Lemonnier points out (2010: 213n3), the liminality with death that precedes the boys' symbolic rebirth during their initiation is very real: any infection of the wound can be, and sometimes is, fatal for the novice.

of the rituals, these three categories of persons receive, each in their own space, a mixture based on vegetal salt whose ingredients vary slightly but which have a similar aim: to raise the temperature of the body. More precisely, we are told, it is supposed to heat the liver of the novices, whose symbolic death is beginning, and simultaneously to remove all trace of the boy's birth from the mother's womb. Then only the mothers and the initiands receive sugarcane so as to produce a cooling of their body. Then comes the time to levy several food taboos. Red pandanus juice, areca nuts, water, leafy vegetables that become sticky when cooked, and several varieties of tuber are forbidden to the mothers, older sisters, and initiands from the moment the boys' septum has been pierced. These restrictions are gradually lifted as the nose plug is changed, except for the bans on consuming red pandanus sauce and chewing betel, which are kept in place until the meal marking the close of the ceremonies. The lifting of these two major prohibitions—because they last a long time—is characterized by a high degree of ritualization whose modalities once again bring out the differences in the treatment of the mothers and the sisters.

In all cases, the procedure for lifting a taboo begins with cooling the body; this is done by pouring water over the head from a bamboo tube. But the mothers are given the two areca nuts used to lift the ban by the ritual experts while the sisters receive them from their newly initiated brothers. The sisters are the last to be freed of the taboos, at the very end of the ceremonies when the men and boys return to the village. In addition, unlike the mothers, they were not rubbed with clay when the novice's nose plug was changed for the last time. Taken together, these variants emphasize the special involvement of the mothers in the collective phases of their son's initiation.

During the period of strict seclusion corresponding to the time it takes the boy's septum to heal, not only do the mothers abstain from several foods, but, like their sons once again, they must not scratch their skin or scrape away the black layer from the tubers the other women have cooked for them in the ashes. In the same manner, as soon as they hear the call of a bird of ill omen or the buzz of an insect—especially a fly—mothers and sons must immediately stop chewing the food they have in their mouth and, often, spit it out. Because flying insects and these birds are associated with decay and death, their manifestations must be canceled when the main participants in the ritual are ingesting a food in order to prevent these vectors of death stealing into their body if they were to swallow. The call of certain birds is supposed to evoke the name of the female genitalia, which here again requires that at least the boys immediately spit out the food they have in their mouth. Finally, the husks of the sugarcane that the mothers and their sons eat at well-defined moments of the ritual are gathered up by the experts from the two spaces, respectively the village and the forest, and deposited in spots known only to them. The mothers' actions and those of the novices are thus perfectly similar, but are performed in distinctly separate spaces, for these two categories of ritual actors must absolutely not meet.

Once the boys' noses have healed, all the women set about making the items of clothing and body ornaments the initiates will wear when they return to the village. This preparation takes about two weeks, during which time the boys hunt together in the forest and continue to undergo various ordeals designed to toughen them up. On the day chosen for them to emerge from seclusion, food is cooked in a big earth oven. Two experienced women, members of two different clans, have previously brought back *kiringi'* leaves and yellow-orange clay (*rwa'a omore'*) from the headwaters of a river. The leaves are used to wrap up a sweet potato and a *Colocasia* taro for each of the initiates, and then the parcels are placed in the center of the oven. While these cook, the boys file down from the forest, richly adorned and accompanied by their respective sponsors, initiates from the preceding group who have accompanied the boys throughout their ordeals; the rest of the men follow. When they come to the outskirts of the village, the same two experienced women are waiting for them, and rub their heads and chests with the clay they have brought back. Accompanied by a formula, this gesture is identical to the one the new mother performs on the body of her newborn baby, yet another proof that, in accordance with Arnold van Gennep's ([1909] 1960) analyses over a century ago, initiation is modeled on birth.

Immediately after having been rubbed by these two women, the initiates and the rest of the men parade at length all through the village. Then, after having filed before their mothers, to whom they have given areca nuts and some small game, the boys go to a secluded corner of the village where they sit together while the tubers continue to cook and the other men gather near the fathers' shelter. When the tubers are ready, the women gather around the earth oven and each takes one of the bundles wrapped in a *kiringi'* leaf and places it on her new bark cape given to her at the beginning of the ritual, and then, one by one, each mother calls out the name of her son. Each boy files by, picks up the bark cape on which the bundle, composed of a sweet potato and a *Colocasia* taro, has been placed, and takes it back to the corner where they were gathered. When they have eaten this food, they bring the cape and the *kiringi'* leaf back to their mothers, who are clearly saddened by the radical change in their sons. The men even say that they have changed so much their own mothers don't recognize them! All the leaves are collected, and the two experienced women deposit them in the spot where they gathered them. Then life resumes its normal course, and the initiates' parents return to their home where the initiates will not join them until the following day.[5]

In the previous chapters we saw that, years later, when these boys have grown to adulthood and are preparing to receive their first child, their sisters will once again accompany them, again respecting a ban on red pandanus juice and areca nuts, donning, like them, a new bark cape and joining their sisters-in-law for the public phase of the ritual. Alternatively, the role of the mothers is over once the collective phases of the initiations are over.

Photo 10. The long line of initiates and their sponsors arrive in the village following the collective rituals of the first two stages. They are greeted by two women, who rub them with the same clay that is smeared on the *suwangain* initiates' shoulders and on the body of newborn babies. © Pascale Bonnemère (November 1994)

---

5.   Formerly, the young initiates' return to the family home took place much later. In the meantime, they would sleep in a special house in the village, and the women would bring them food every day.

Photo 11. Back in the village, the first- and second-stage initiates give their mothers areca nuts and the few small animals they caught while they were in the forest. In return, their mothers will soon give cooked tubers to them. This exchange indicates that, at the close of the ritual, the nature of their relationship has changed: it has lost the symbiotic character it had in childhood. © Pierre Lemonnier (November 1994)

What is the nature of the relations revealed by this system of prohibitions and attitudes to which the members of the novice-mother-sister triad are subjected? What the Ankave themselves say sheds light on the specificity of the role of the boys' mothers. During the 1994 initiations, one of the ritual experts told the mothers: "You are one body with your sons." One of the women commented on the fact that they had to respect the food taboos, saying: "We carried him in our belly, this son who is now being initiated, so when he is hungry are you going to eat?" And to explain why the novices' sisters were not obliged to remain immobile during the weeks their brothers' noses were healing, one woman pointed out that they had not given birth to the boys, but "were helping their brothers."[6]

---

6.   Here, cf. what Sandra Bamford reports on the silence of Kamea women about these
     matters: When the ethnographer asks them via a male interpreter "how [they]
     perceive their own role in initiation and how does their presence enhance the efficacy
     of the rites . . . they smile mysteriously at him and respond with what must strike
     them as an obvious adage: he is a man—that it is not his place to know what happens
     with women at this time" (2004: 51). We may suppose that if Bamford had talked
     alone with the mothers of the initiates, she might have received a different answer.

It would therefore be because the mothers carried the boys in their womb and then gave birth to them that they are secluded during the rituals. What Onorwae explained to me in the mothers' house goes in the same sense: "When they pierce our son's nose, we mothers think of the taboos we respected when he was in our womb." These continual references to pregnancy and the nearly complete[7] parallel between the gestures performed, the precautions taken, and the prohibitions followed by the mothers and their sons allow us to describe the bond between them as "symbiotic."[8] The vocabulary, too, points to a similar reading of the mother-son relationship, since the Ankave language has a term, *renamia'*, which designates the unit formed by a female and her young or a mother and her nursing baby.

It is the child's or the young's dependence on its mother for its survival that founds this representation of an entity whose constituents cannot be envisaged independently of each other, a mother and her children forming a totality (Barraud 2001: 63). Similarly, Kathleen Barlow writes of the Murik, who live in a mangrove colony at the mouth of the Sepik River, "a mother-child dyad, especially for firstborn children, is a fairly exclusive relationship" (2004: 527). We could therefore ask whether, for the Ankave, the mother-son

---

7.   While the ban on red pandanus is officially respected by everyone, the boys in fact breach it once the wound in their septum has dried (see p. 107n15). In the utmost secrecy—and as far as I know, the women are not aware of this—they ensure their own growth, which, as I have shown elsewhere, is modeled on gestation (Bonnemère 2001b: 24). Pregnant women must consume great quantities of red pandanus sauce to make the fetus grow and provide it with blood. Very young boys, together with the men, also consume it for several years before being initiated (see p. 94). (For another example of symbolic gestation in male initiations, this time in Senegal, see Troy [2008: 59].)

8.   The conception of the mother-child relation as symbiotic is far from being restricted to the Ankave, as is shown by several anthropological studies conducted in the Americas or Australia. Among the Shoshone Indians of North America, for example, women who had just given birth observed a 30-day period of seclusion in a shelter regarded as an extension of the womb. Whatever the young mother thought, did or ate could have a direct effect on the baby's development (Gould and Glowacka 2004: 185–86). In Amazonia, mother and child were treated as a unit during the six weeks following the birth, during which time they were secluded. As Beth Conklin and Lynn Morgan wrote: "in early life a Wari' infant's blood is considered to be merged with its mother's blood, and they essentially share a single social identity" (1996: 672). Among the Aranda of Australia, "a woman and her son are designated by the term *chuaninga*, which means 'couple,' 'pair,' 'one body,'" Marika Moisseeff reports, quoting Spencer and Gillen from 1927 (1995: 105).

bond is seen as a relationship or whether it would not be better described by the term "undifferentiation."[9] Whether or not that is the case in no way changes the fact that a modification to the nature of this bond must come about in the course of the initiation. And the ethnography shows that the two components of the relation must be present for it to be transformed. Given such a system of representations, the physical presence of the boys' mothers is indispensable.

"Kamea women figure intimately in the proceedings of the men's cult" (Bamford 2004: 35),[10] but Sandra Bamford denies the embodied character of the relationship between a Kamea woman and her child. Although she analyzes the taboo conditions on smelly game that connects a mother and her son at some point and disconnects them at another (see chapter 6) as "presenting an image of a singular body wherein the eating habits of one party directly affect the health of the other" (Bamford 1998: 162), "the nature of the connection is not based on the notion of 'shared substance.' Instead, the bond between a woman and her child is based on that act which brought the relationship into being in the first place—the very act of 'containment' itself" (Bamford 2007: 95–96). Her interpretation of the Kamea initiation cycle runs counter to the existing ones that emphasize the reproduction of "a hierarchy of gendered states," proposing instead that "it is only through initiation that a woman's son is finally 'de-contained'" (2004: 41).[11] As Bamford sees it, the Kamea conception is thus not based on shared substance and symbiosis but on "containment," which, together with its opposite, "decontainment," are the keywords of her whole analysis. This process of decontainment is staged during the final dancing phases of the initiation sequence when women collectively surround the men

---

9. In all events, this is an internal relationship, as are all the relations transformed by the ritual: "an entity is 'internally' related to another if this relationship is part of its definition" (Holbraad 2008: 231).

10. Bamford also writes that "a boy is not initiated into the men's cult so much as he is detached from an encompassing female form. Women are not incidental to the process; they furnish the ground and the motivating force against which it takes place" (2007: 99).

11. Indeed, as Bamford puts it, "until he is initiated, a boy is, in a sense, still 'contained'" (2004: 41). As far as we can tell from the food taboos that fall on both the boys and their mothers, and although the term used and the underlying conception is different from that of the Ankave, the unit formed since pregnancy between a mother and the child she carries is viewed in both groups as lasting well beyond the birth and even the weaning.

and boys and when the men suddenly extract the boys from the ring, "detaching them from the containing influence of the mothers" (Bamford 2004: 54). Indeed, as we'll see shortly, even the tabooing of smelly game for both mothers and sons, as it is organized throughout their lives, is interpreted in this way. Like Ankave mothers, Kamea mothers are confined in a collective dwelling, raised like the men's cult house during the opening phase of the initiation sequence (2007: 99–100). Bamford reports one man's comments: "The only thing mothers can do is sit in the house. If they leave it, the noses of their sons will break" (2007: 100). For Bamford, "the image we are presented with is that of a container who is tightly contained" (2007: 100).[12] However, from her ethnography, we learn that "one of the most important tasks assigned to Kamea women during their seclusion[13] is to guard the bullroarers (*mautwa*), the preeminent symbol of male cult life throughout Melanesia" (2004: 45). Here, for once, Beatrice Blackwood's material is quite different from what Bamford collected among the same language-speaking people some sixty years later, since she wrote that "it is supposed to result in death for a woman to see a bull-roarer" (1978: 124). This statement is also present in a long myth that relates how the first men come out of a tree, how women's vaginas were pierced, how water came out, and, in one version, how bullroarers first appear. Blackwood writes that at this point of the narration, "the women who were sitting within earshot were sent away" (Blackwood 1978: 159). Here is how the part of the story concerned with bullroarers goes:

> The women do not know about the bullroarer. The man heard it and got this thing (showing one), it cries, the woman went close to it, the man sent her away. The man heard it cry, he went and got one and swung it, so that it cried. The women must not see it, if they do they will die. They hide the bullroarer in the bush, and it sounds in the bush. (Blackwood 1978: 159)

---

12. As is clear from the description of the Ankave mothers and their son's behaviors in two different spaces during initiation and the relevance of their similarity to understand what is going on (see above), among the Kamea the analogy between what they both do only concerns the taboo on smelly game and on "greasy" food (Bamford 2007: 100).
13. Bamford writes that the mothers' cult house is located in the bush, although she does not elaborate (2004: 44) while, as we remember, Ankave mothers are secluded in a large collective house built at the edge of the hamlet (see photo 8).

Although Bamford writes that "certainly, no woman ever admitted to me that she had handled the bullroarers" (2004: 205n20) and that "according to men, women are not fully cognizant of what they are holding on to" (2004: 44), she adds that "this may be a 'publicly acknowledged' secret—known by all but admitted by none" (2004: 205n20) and that "the bullroarers are wrapped in leaves and pieces of bark cloth before being presented to women so that only the tip of one end is exposed" (2004: 44). The mothers of the boys are given the bullroarers by men, along with instructions to watch over them carefully, just before they go into seclusion; the men will take them back during the first stage of the rituals and show them to the boys for the first time. We will never know whether the accounts of the two ethnographers are different because they worked in different Kapau-Kamea villages or because the practices related to bullroarers changed between 1937 and 1990.

Let's now come back to the Ankave, for whom the bullroarers do not concern women at all and who do not tell any myth in which bullroarers are even mentioned in passing. For the relation between a mother and her son to be transformed, the symbiotic or undifferentiated character of their bond must be reasserted by imposing the same attitudes and prohibitions on both terms of the relation, until the novice has come through the symbolic death represented by the piercing of his septum, which sets off the first stage of the initiations. For the mothers secluded back in the village, lifting the ban on chewing betel and the principal restrictions on their movements signals the moment when this transformation takes place. And the game the son gives his mother when he comes out of seclusion, following a precise ritual code already described, is the tangible sign (see M. Strathern 2013: 202) that the nature of the relationship between the two has changed (cf. Gillison 2016: 20–21).[14] The formerly symbiotic bond has become a relation in which exchange is now possible.[15]

Traces of the symbiotic bond nevertheless subsist, as shown by the ban preventing a mother eating the first eels or the first cassowary caught by her son (see chapter 11). The women explain this ban once again with reference to

---

14. In Bamford's terms, this would be the moment when a gendered state is created for the man (2007: 94).

15. It must be added here that, between the staging of the undifferentiated state at the start of the ritual and this mutual exchange of food that closes the first stage, the transformation of the nature of the mother-son bond is effected through a differentiation of the first-stage initiates' behaviors from those of their mother from the moment the wound in the boys' septum has dried.

pregnancy: "My son was in my belly. So, if I put the game he has killed in my belly, he will not be able to catch any more." The relationship between a mother and her children is thus forever marked by the children's stay in the womb and by the symbiosis or undifferentiated state it implies.[16] It can also be seen in the fact that a girl's mother is forbidden to consume the marriage gifts paid in kind by the family of her future son-in-law before her daughter has reached puberty (see p. 212). So closely are these foods associated, in this context, with the girl's body that were the mother to eat any of this game or some of the domestic pig, it would be, people say, an act of cannibalism.[17]

While this transformation of the mother-son relationship is taking place, the collective initiations also say something about the bond between a brother and his older sister. During these rituals she obeys the prohibitions she shares with her brother and their mother, but when he comes back from the forest following the first-stage ordeals, he gives his sister a bird he has hunted and some areca nuts, which in this case do not indicate a change in their relationship—unlike the small game a son gives his mother, who gives him food in return. The areca nuts lift the ban for the two of them, but the gift of the bird places a taboo on game that they will have to respect until the beginning of the second-stage ceremonies. At this time he will give her game once again, but this time they will eat it together, for the last time in their lives. Later, as the maternal uncle of his sister's children, he will eat the game his brother-in-law must give him to ensure the children's good health (see pp. 140–41). Unlike the mother-son bond, the brother-sister relation is here established through a ritual and not a transformation for, as we have seen, it is with her brother's initiation that a girl begins to take an active part, by respecting specific behaviors and prohibitions, in the important events that will mark his life, in particular when his wife

---

16. Analyzing the Aranda male rituals from the extant literature, Moisseeff similarly associates the lifting of the bans with recognition of the circumcised son's newfound autonomy from his mother (1995: 125), while also pointing out that "the mother-son bond is never completely severed" (1995: 134–35), despite the rituals of physical individualization endured by the son and in which his mother intervenes.

17. The picture is totally distinct from the Kamea situation, where "unlike boys who labor under an onerous array of dietary restrictions, Kamea girls are free to eat virtually anything they please. Indeed, some women will enjoy a taboo-free existence until the day they die; the determining factor is the sex of any offspring they may carry. Should a woman give birth to a child of the same sex as herself, her life will continue pretty much as before" (Bamford 1998: 161). See also chapter 6.

is expecting and then gives birth to his first child.[18] We can already suppose that her presence is connected with the status of maternal uncle, which ideally every man should attain. Indeed, this is the only status that makes a man capable of acting for someone else—and in particular of having his nephews reborn during initiations—whereas all women, as I have said, have this capacity spontaneously.

This description of the gestures and conducts of all the participants in the initiation cycle opens avenues of analysis rarely glimpsed before. As soon as the anthropologist shifts her attention from the forest space, where only the men officiate, to another space, that of the village outskirts where the mothers' shelters have been built, the initiation rituals appear in a new light. And we discover that the boys' access to adulthood requires the transformation of the relations they had with a certain number of persons, in the forefront of whom are their mothers and sisters.

And yet, as I wrote in the opening pages of this book, in the descriptions anthropologists left of the Anga initiations in the 1980s, the women were totally absent.[19] Based on the fact that they were excluded from the forest space, that the boys were—literally—torn away from their mothers, that secrets were revealed to the novices, that nothing must transpire of the homosexual relations between the boys and their unmarried sponsors, and that the initiates did not go back home but would sleep in the men's houses for years to come, Gilbert Herdt and Maurice Godelier interpreted these rituals as initiations whose organization and content were directed against the women. According to Godelier, the women were held responsible for the need for men to grow and fortify these boys who had up to that point been cared for by women. The male initiations were therefore described as institutions for the legitimization and the reproduction of male domination of women (Godelier [1982] 1986: 62). In other words, the focus was exclusively on what the men did and on the forest space where their activities took place, without taking into consideration what the novices'

18. It should be remembered here that this is most often the couple's first child, but that, in the case where a young widow with a child from her first husband remarries with a man who has no children, the ceremony must once again be organized to celebrate the arrival of this man's first child.

19. With the already mentioned exception of Blackwood's and Bamford's descriptions, respectively in the 1930s and the 1990s, of the public phase of the second and last stage, called the marita ceremony among the large southern Anga group known as Kapau-Kamea (see p. 4).

mothers and sisters, and more broadly all the women of the village, were doing in the meantime.[20]

Several factors, having as much to do with the characteristics of fieldwork in New Guinea as with anthropology as it was done at the time, might explain the women's invisibility in the anthropological studies of the rituals of the region. The first anthropologists to work in the Highlands—in the 1950s—of what is today the independent State of Papua New Guinea, were men,[21] and given the strict division between male and female spheres of activity, their informants were also primarily, if not exclusively, men. Their only access to the women's world was through men, while at the same time the male discourse was characterized by the systematic disparagement of female practices and an emphasis on the danger inherent in associating too closely with women.

In these conditions, it is easier to understand that these pioneers did not hear about the possible role of women in the rituals organized by the men and designed to grow the boys. And it followed that the male anthropologists would go into the forest with the other men without much concern for what the women might be doing in the meantime, or without thinking to ask them later what they had actually done. It took nothing more for an important ethnographic reality to vanish and for the "women's analytical 'invisibility'" (Moore 1988: 3) to be perpetuated in the anthropological writings on the rituals of this part of Melanesia.

Having worked with the Ankave as a couple, we are in a position today to put together our information and observations on both the men and the women, and to attempt to provide an interpretation of the male initiation rituals that combines the analysis of the men's activities in the forest with that of the behaviors required of certain categories of women. Insofar as the women intervene mainly by obeying bans on foods and certain behaviors on behalf of their sons or brothers, we must now try to understand how this system of prohibitions is organized and discover what it tells us about local conceptions of male personhood and the transformation a man undergoes over his lifetime.

---

20. For a systematic inclusion of the role of women in several male rituals in New Guinea, including several Anga groups, see Bonnemère (2004b).

21. With the exception already mentioned, in the case of the Anga, of Beatrice Blackwood, the first anthropologist to have gone to the region (in 1936). That being said, since she was interested above all in the material culture of the Nauti, a Kapau-Kamea tribe in the eastern and southern Anga territory, she limited herself to a careful description of women's participation in male rituals but did not engage in its analysis, contrary to what Bamford did sixty years later (see Conclusion).

CHAPTER 6

Abstaining for oneself, abstaining for others

As I have mentioned several times, a series of dietary and behavioral restrictions and prohibitions are imposed at times during the rituals that punctuate Ankave life.[1] Most of these have features that distinguish them both from other local prohibitions and from the modalities organizing similar systems in other societies: their specificity has not so much to do with the banned foods or behaviors, as one might expect, as with the persons concerned by the prohibition. Indeed, the person who obeys the prohibition is not the one who benefits from it (see also Bamford 1998: 162); in other words, the prohibitions imposed at very specific moments in the life cycle always establish a relation between two individuals that is mediated by a food or a behavior.

Two situations are possible: either one person respects the prohibition for another person, or two persons respect the same prohibition at the same time. Inasmuch as the person for whom the prohibition is respected is not the one who respects it, the first case differs from the most frequently occurring configuration in the taboo systems found the world over, which require one to respect a prohibition for oneself, violation of which would have a negative effect only on oneself as well. It should be noted that this situation is attested whatever reasons

---

1. For Émile Durkheim, prohibitions are part of what he calls "negative cult." But far from inhibiting activity, they exert "on the individual's religious and moral nature a positive action of the utmost importance" ([1912] 1995: 441).

people advance to justify the ban and whether it is permanent (a Jewish person will never eat pork) or temporary (in the event of mourning or pregnancy, for example). The prohibitions we are discussing with respect to the Ankave life cycle are never respected for oneself; they are meant to benefit someone else: one's son, younger brother, pregnant wife.[2] This is an important distinction because it obliges us to examine not only the justifications offered for levying a restriction on a particular food or behavior but also, and probably above all, the relation between the two persons involved.

In the case of two persons respecting the same prohibition at the same time, the problematic varies little; this particular configuration simply leads us to wonder if each person is respecting the same prohibition for him- or herself or for the other person. What the Ankave have to say will help us answer this question, but we can already note that the simultaneous actions underscore the existence of a relation between the two persons respecting the same prohibition. Because if each person observes the ban for him- or herself, why do it together? Meyer Fortes suggested an answer some fifty years ago when he wrote that, "sharing or abstaining from the same food, means uniting in common commitment" (1966: 16). The analysis proposed by Bamford to account for "one taboo complex [which] stands apart from the rest . . . by its capacity to knit boys and women into a single cultural image (1998: 161) echoes Fortes' statement. The taboo on "smelly" game, falls on a mother and her son, and has a temporal dimension. Small boys cannot eat rats and other species, like marsupials, that emit a strong odor when cooked. But, "from the time that her son has his nose pierced during the first phase of initiation, all of the food items [smelly game] that were taboo to him now become taboo to his mother as well" (1998: 162). The taboo will be lifted for the boy once the initiation is completed, while his mother will never again eat smelly game, "until a dying day," Bamford continues. What is truly specific here is that, if the boy's mother were dead, he could eat this game,[3] and he would also be "not barred from the secret male proceedings" (Bamford 1998: 165) and "free to take on many of the prerogatives normally reserved for older men, including the right to handle the bullroarers" (Bamford

---

2. Note that the situations concerned here by such a taboo system are thus more numerous than among the Kamea, where only mothers and sons are involved (Bamford 1998). But, in both cases, our "concern lies less with analyzing the semantic content of these prohibitions than it does with explicating the specific form which they take" (1998: 161). I, of course, could not agree more.

3. See details in Bamford 1998: 161.

2007: 172). Among the Ankave, all the boys are initiated and were the mother of one to die, another kinwoman would take her place and do exactly what his mother would have done. Maybe this difference has to do with change, since in the past all Kamea boys were initiated "regardless of whether their mother lived or not" (Bamford 2007: 172n14). Today, only twenty to thirty per cent of them choose to go through male rituals, which are, moreover, held in a truncated form,[4] whereas this is not (yet) the case in the Suowi Valley.

Prohibitions for others are levied only at very specific points in a person's life, and all have to do with the "making" of a human being: when a man is expecting his first child, at the birth of this child, and to a lesser extent, at the time of subsequent pregnancies and births, but also during the male initiations, where the boys go through something like a second birth. We see that these special moments need to be supported by prohibitions respected by several persons at the same time: a mother and her son undergoing initiation, a woman and her brother who will soon be a first-time father; or by one person for another: a man for his pregnant wife, for instance. Relational configurations thus emerge, and we must, on the one hand, unearth the logic behind them and, on the other hand, seize the transformations these relations undergo over a person's lifetime if we are to understand how people in a given place conceive of the development of the person and access to the status of parent.

But before undertaking to decipher this very special system of prohibitions,[5] let us first consider those that a person respects for him- or herself. These are uniquely food taboos imposed in respect of criteria having to do with age and sex. For example, certain foods are not proposed to children because of characteristics they possess: the flesh of the white cockatoo, whose feathers, of the same color as the hair of the elderly, would cause premature aging in children who consumed it; likewise, the fruits of the two squashes, *rwonangwen* and *ya'me*, take too long to ripen for them to be eaten without compromising the child's growth. Nor are children allowed to eat echidnas, whose backs are spiny, certain insects whose bites cause itching, or their eggs, or the eggs of the cassowary, for

4.   As Sandra Bamford writes, "a truncated form is emerging wherein boys are taught all the secrets of the men's cult and are shown the bullroarers (*mautwa*) but refrain from having their nose pierced" (2007: 97).

5.   I never read about similar taboo conditions in any ethnography, and even among the Angans this is not a common practice since only the Kamea share some of the characteristics—but not all—encountered here (see, for example, p. 108n17; p. 210n12).

fear of causing boils to appear on the body. When the female cassowary sees her empty nest, it is said that she beats her beak on the ground, which produces sores in the armpits and the groin of children who had chanced to eat her eggs. No question either of eating the meat of the little gliding possum known as the glider, or *tse'pipia'wo*, since a membrane might grow along the side of the child's chest and out to their arms. Aside from these prohibitions, which apply to children of both sexes without distinction, girls are forbidden to eat praying mantises because their hands and arms would contract like the front legs of this large insect, later preventing them from working in the garden, or the sugarcanes *ungwen rarena'* and *imenegne'*, which are the varieties given to boys during their initiation (Bonnemère 2002: 182). By respecting these few restrictions, children are protected from the undesirable effects the consumption of foods with properties inappropriate to their age might have on their immature body and their tender skin.

When children reach adulthood, they respect food taboos for the benefit of someone else. These prohibitions apply only as long as they are of an age to reproduce: and if the elderly can eat whatever they want, it is not so much due to their age itself as to the fact that they are no longer potential parents.

That is why a pregnant woman and her husband must abstain from certain foods believed harmful to the child in the womb. According to local ideas about reproduction, a child is the product of its mother's blood and its father's semen. Once conception has occurred, the blood—which usually drains away during menstruation—remains blocked in the uterus and makes the fetus grow. This blood is the child's only food and makes the child's own blood.[6] Of all the foods a pregnant woman eats, red pandanus juice occupies a unique position because it turns into blood. As a vegetal substitute for this life-giving substance, it is highly valued during pregnancy since the need for blood increases. The future mother therefore consumes great quantities of the red sauce, thus increasing her own blood supply, part of which will serve to nourish the baby she carries and ensure it develops properly.

The extreme permeability of the fetus to its mother's intake[7] has negative effects too, as shown by the numerous restrictions imposed on her to preserve

---

6.   For a detailed presentation of these ideas on reproduction, see Bonnemère (1996a: 223–29).

7.   In an article entitled "Making kin out of others in Amazonia," Aparecida Vilaça says she "feel[s] very uncomfortable with the notion of permeable boundaries, since it supposes the existence of something like a solid or fixed body" (2002: 362n14). See below as well.

her child from harm. The Ankave say clearly that the animals whose flesh is forbidden have physical or behavioral characteristics they would not like to see transmitted to their coming child: marsupials with spotted fur, for fear the child's skin will be similarly covered in spots; those that live in holes in trees or the ground, frogs or eels that hide under rocks, certain insects that live inside bamboos, for fear that the baby will remain trapped in the womb, thus making for a slow, difficult birth. Eating certain plants might also hamper the birth process: certain climbing squashes are to be avoided so that the umbilical cord will not wind around the baby like the stems of the squashes around tree trunks. When it comes to the setaria *yore'* (*Setaria palmifolia*), a hairy grass, no pregnant woman would eat it, for if she did her baby's skin might become covered in sores.[8] Aparecida Vilaça reconsiders the question of the couvade in the light of "perspectivism," a concept developed by Eduardo Viveiros de Castro (1998). As she presents it, "Amerindian peoples conceive the world to be inhabited by different types of subjects, all possessing souls, who apprehend the world from distinct points of view related to their bodies (2002: 351). In Western Amazonia where the Wari' lives, "the body runs the risk of being made like the body of other types of people (or simply animals)" (2002: 359). "By observing taboos, the parents . . .finish making the child's body similar to their own" (2002: 357). That is why "couvade restrictions . . . avoid 'corporeal' associations with beings of other species" (2002: 360). Although perspectivism has not been attested for New Guinea (but see Brunois 2007), Ankave comments on their taboo observances during pregnancy point to a similar fear that may indicate conceptions of interspecies relationships and mutability close to South Amerindian ones.

Aside from these restrictions applying to all pregnant women, certain foods are forbidden to female members of a given clan.[9] This type of prohibition applies not only when they are actually carrying a child but also throughout their

8.   While all these behaviors and justifications may seem quite exotic to you and me, an article entitled "Are pregnant women fetal containers?" easily has its place here. In effect, women in the West are subject, de facto, to recommendations from the medical profession, which, if not followed (for example, in the case of hard drugs) can lead to legal action (Purdy 1990: 274). In this case, as among the Ankave, pregnant women are seen as being one with the fetus they carry, and their dietary behaviors (alcohol consumption, for instance) affect it directly.

9.   This information does not figure in my earlier book, *Le Pandanus rouge* (1996a) because I received it only in 1998.

reproductive years. For this reason, from puberty to menopause, women of the Idzadze clan do not eat duck, for their future children might be born with webbed fingers. Ngude and Omore women abstain from eating the *newimbere'*, the Raggiana Bird of Paradise (*Paradisaea raggiana*), because this bird loses part of its red feathers at the end of the red pandanus fruiting season (in April). A baby born to a woman from one of these clans who happened to eat this forbidden flesh during her pregnancy, or even before becoming pregnant, would be bald as an adult. Sometimes it is enough for a pregnant woman out walking in the forest to pass near a spot where a forbidden bird has made its nest for the animal to become disgruntled and act negatively on the fetus.[10] The Ankave do not offer an explanation for these clan prohibitions and, aside from the ban itself, there is no specific relation between the members of the clan and the forbidden animal. In particular, we are not looking at the social phenomenon anthropologists have christened "totemism," where "each group of humans claims to share with a group of nonhumans a collection of physical and psychic dispositions that distinguishes them, as an ontological class, from others" (Descola 2013: 167).[11] For even aside from the fact that the prohibitions do not apply to all clan members but only to the women, and among these, women expecting a child, no relation of identification can be established between the animal whose flesh is forbidden and the humans who obey the prohibition. In other words, we cannot espouse Fortes' idea that totemic taboos set aside the person who obeys them, together with their co-agnates, from persons of other lineages and clans in a total scheme of group relations with which they and the others are identified (1966: 17). Let us note, too, that, in their modalities of action, these prohibitions designed for the pregnant women of a specific clan are no different from those imposed on all women: in both cases they are meant to protect the children they are carrying or will carry in the future.

Can we call the prohibitions that pregnant women respect prohibitions "for others"? They are expressed as such, since it is the child she carries and not she herself who would be affected by their transgression. Just as children need to be protected from foods that are not appropriate for beings whose growth

---

10. As anthropologist Michael Lambek wrote about a Malgache population on Mayotte, these beliefs reveal the existence of "a theory of contagion in which the foetus is felt to be extremely susceptible to the experiences encountered by its parents" (1992: 264n12).

11. For Claude Lévi-Strauss, "the term totemism covers relations, posed ideologically, between two series, one *natural*, the other *cultural*" (1963b: 16).

is incomplete, fetuses cannot tolerate certain foods their mother might ingest harmlessly if she were not pregnant or of childbearing age. From this standpoint, the child in the womb is regarded as a separate being from its mother. At the same time, pregnancy creates a situation in which the woman is closely bound up with the baby she carries, such that anything she eats immediately finds its way into the fetal body. As we have seen, it is precisely this symbiotic bond typical of pregnancy that, many years later, the initiations seek to break and transform into another type of relation.

Although the father-to-be is not in such a relation with the coming child, he too must obey several food taboos. However, the person he is protecting is not the baby but the woman who will soon bring it into the world. I have already said that the main food banned for the husband of a pregnant woman is red pandanus juice: were he to consume any, his wife might hemorrhage during the birth. Reproduction is the only situation that creates this triadic entity in which the behaviors of a future father affect the future mother and sometimes, through her, his child. Clearly nonreciprocal, the impact on others is indirect but is experienced as being altogether real; it reveals the way the situation of "making" a new human is conceived, with a fetus acted on—in other words, the beneficiary—a woman placed in a position of agent with respect to her child and beneficiary with respect to her husband, and a man whose acts affect his pregnant wife and who is never, in this specific context, in the position of beneficiary. The actual properties of the forbidden food matter little for understanding such a configuration;[12] it is enough to know *for whom* the prohibition is obeyed. The Ankave system of food taboos therefore cannot be dealt with simply by analyzing the intrinsic attributes and qualities of the banned foods (see also Bamford 1998). The actors involved in the process—both those on whom the prohibition is imposed and those who benefit from it—are equally important for understanding what is at stake in such a system. Pregnancy thus establishes a triadic relational configuration such that the dietary behaviors of the future father impact on the body of his wife and the taboos she must respect have an immediate effect on the body of the child she is carrying.

---

12. Ultimately, we could almost restrict our interest to the ban on red pandanus sauce, which has special properties, to be sure, since it is deemed a vegetal substitute for blood.

But diet is not the only area of social life where the relation of a man to his pregnant wife is played out through the respect of prohibitions; we have also seen that he is forbidden to perform any task involving the making of knots, for fear of inhibiting the birth. He therefore cannot make arrows, build a house, or repair his garden fence. And when the birth threatens to be difficult and the baby is long in coming, a close relative will ask the father-to-be to dismantle his arrowheads so as to free the child from the uterus in which it is trapped.

COUVADE AND ITS INTERPRETATIONS

Couvade practices are well known to anthropologists; widespread in South America, such practices have been grouped under this single term.[13] *Couvade* designates a situation where a father-to-be and sometimes other close kinsmen respect a set of dietary and occupational restrictions or prohibitions during the pregnancy, at the time of the birth and sometimes several days after, and in some cases even simulate the act of childbirth.

As early as 1910, James Frazer had identified two different types of couvade: "One of these customs consists of a strict diet and regimen observed by a father for the benefit of his newborn child, because the father is believed to be united to the child by such an intimate bond of physical sympathy that all his acts affect and may hurt or kill the tender infant. The other custom consists of a simulation of childbirth by a man, generally perhaps by the husband, practised for the benefit of the real mother, in order to relieve her of her pains by transferring them to the pretended mother" (quoted in Menget 1989: 91).[14]

It was first thought that a man ritually placed himself in a situation parallel to that of his pregnant wife and that, like those restrictions on the future mother, the restrictions imposed on his own activities were meant to protect the coming child. In fact, the two forms of couvade also differ according to the identity of the person for whom the prohibitions are imposed: the first consists

---

13. I am talking only about the couvade ritual and not about any psychosomatic manifestations shown by some men whose wife is pregnant, which have often been referred to by the same term (Kupferer 1965; Newman 1966).

14. He had suggested calling the first kind "postnatal or dietary couvade," which would come under the heading of magic by contagion, and the second, "prenatal or pseudomaternal couvade," which would fall under the rubric of imitative magic (Menget 1989: 91). See also Munroe, Munroe, and Whiting (1973: 35).

essentially in food taboos aimed at protecting the baby, while the second is designed to accompany the mother in labor (Newman 1966: 155n3).

The history of the interpretation of the couvade is exemplary of the evolution of thinking in anthropology. These prohibitions were first assimilated to a form of sympathetic magic based on the belief that the characteristics of an animal or a plant consumed by the future parents could be transmitted to the child. Obeying food taboos was thus regarded as a measure designed to protect the child. An attempt was also made to include the couvade in the then-prevailing evolutionist thinking by considering the father's involvement in the birth as an indication of the passage from matriarchy to the patriarchal form of government believed to characterize more evolved societies.[15]

Over the following decades, most interpretations tended in the same direction and regarded the couvade as a rite of fatherhood. Bronislaw Malinowski posited that, in the Trobriand Islands where descent is reckoned matrilinearily, couvade practices aimed to legitimize the father's role in making children (1927: 192). Along the same lines, for Alfred Métraux these practices were "an expression of the close bond between the father and the infant's clinging soul" (1963: 374). And Mary Douglas expressed a similar idea when she found, in societies practicing the most extreme form of couvade—in which the man takes to his bed when his wife is in labor and, often, simulates her pains—the existence of a fragile matrimonial tie and a desire on the part of the husband to assert his rights over his wife and her children (Douglas [1966] 1981: 24).[16] In this case, it would be a matter of the husband establishing, as it were, a bond with his child of the same sort that his wife automatically has with it, in which she combines a visible biological function and a recognized social role.

Another set of interpretations invokes factors of a psychological order. For instance, based on a sample of twenty-two societies located in various parts of the world, Robert and Ruth Munroe, in collaboration with John Whiting (1973), affirmed the existence of a correlation between couvade practices and the absence—or the weak presence—of the father during the child's early years. This interpretation holds that paternal distance is directly linked to residential arrangements in which young children sleep with their mothers. According to these authors, such spatial arrangements create identification in male

---

15. For an overview of the anthropology of the couvade, see Fitz Poole (1982: 54–57) and more recently Albert Doja (2005).

16. I cite the first reprinting of the book (1981).

25

individuals with the opposite-sex members of the family, of which the couvade, by having the father play the role of the pregnant woman or of the woman in labor (or both), is one of the manifestations in adulthood. Studies influenced by psychoanalysis saw this practice as a behavioral consequence of the various conflicting images of the opposite sex formed during childhood, such as penis envy, unconscious hostility to the opposite sex, or the desire to appropriate women's procreative capacities (Doja 2005: 925–26). Here too we find ourselves confronted with interpretations that place the father in a relation of identification with his wife at the time of birth.[17]

Yet in *The savage mind*, Claude Lévi-Strauss challenged the idea that, in the couvade, the man takes the place of his wife in labor and advanced instead that the father was playing the part of the child (1966: 195). What he seems to be affirming here is rather the existence of an identity of substance between the two parents and the newborn child; this is precisely what Janet Chernela's analysis of the couvade, as practiced by the Garifuna of Honduras, illustrates: the father is not simulating his wife's convalescence and therefore is not acting "like a woman," he is staging his own bond with his offspring (1991: 62).

For Patrick Menget, who specializes in such questions, if the couvade cannot be regarded as a device for legitimizing the child or the couple, it is for the simple reason that the marriage tie or the social recognition of a union exists, in most human societies, before the child is born (1989: 92). In other words, "the father's legitimacy is established by the marriage and not by the physiological theory of conception or by the practices that follow the birth" (Menget 1979: 259). In his 1974 "Malinowski Lecture," Peter Rivière also sets aside certain earlier interpretations and instead suggests that the father's actions during the couvade do not concern the child's physical being but its spiritual existence (1974: 431). The creation of this spirit in each human being is nevertheless, in his interpretation, modeled on human physiology: "All or part of the processes of pregnancy, parturition and nurture serve as a model for the spiritual creation" (Rivière 1974: 433). In other words, for Rivière, the couvade has to do with the creation of a whole person, made up of a body and a spirit; it is one of the many institutions dealing with the universal issue of man's duality (Rivière 1974: 434). It is as though the mother gave birth to the body of her child while the father looked after its spiritual birth.

---

17. Concerning this hypothesis, see the discussion published in *American Anthropologist* (Broude 1988, 1989; Munroe and Munroe 1989).

Since the pregnant woman also respects numerous taboos, it is hard, in the case of the Ankave, to qualify the couvade as a rite of fatherhood, as a large number of anthropologists have suggested doing; instead it becomes, to adopt an expression used by Laura Rival in talking about the Huaroani of Amazonia, "a rite of co-parenthood" (1998: 631), which attempts to neutralize, as it were, the difference between fatherhood and motherhood. Although most specialists of this part of the world, where the practice is widespread, have noted that the prohibitions are levied on both parents, they deal only with the father's participation, as though the ritual restrictions imposed on the mother were normal and did not demand special analysis (Rival 1998: 630). For the Ankave, the prohibitions imposed on the pregnant woman should no longer be considered separately from those incumbent on the father-to-be, for it is together that they form a meaningful system, in which the father abstains from eating foods that might turn into blood and cause his wife to hemorrhage or from performing tasks that might cause the baby to be retained in the womb, while, by excluding certain foods from her diet, the future mother is taking care not to harm the child she carries.

Both cases are a matter of respecting prohibitions "for others," a concept generally applied by the Ankave, which dictates that the state of a person's health depends as much and even more in certain circumstances on the actions of others than on the person's own actions (see also D. Taylor 1950: 343). In all events, the joint participation of the two future parents in their child's birth led me, in an earlier chapter, to interpret the first-birth ritual, of which the couvade is part, not only as the third stage of the male initiations, but also and especially as the moment when the existence of a new parental couple is manifested.

In the wake of a number of other authors (Broude 1988: 908–9; Chalifoux 1998: 119; Menget 1979: 263), I would add that the couvade should not be regarded in isolation but as part of a set of practices connected with key moments in the life cycle. Among the Ankave, prohibitions on foods and behaviors are imposed on several occasions in a person's life, and from this standpoint the couvade is not a separate institution. It can no more be isolated than the initiations or the funeral rituals can, all of which entail similar behaviors. The social practices that accompany these stages in an individual's life must therefore be analyzed together, for each one reveals a conception of the person and their development in which the participation of others, through positive actions as much as prohibitions, is indispensable.

As we saw in the earlier chapters of this book, the arrival of a first child in Ankave society is, more than for the other children, the occasion for imposing ritualized behaviors, not only on the future parents but also on a certain number of persons connected to them. The husband's sister has an important place here: like her brother, she must abstain from red pandanus juice for the duration of her sister-in-law's pregnancy, and like her, she must not eat the hairy setaria grass (*yore'*). In addition, for the three days following the birth, she will join the couple in respecting the ban on chewing betel. This behavior marks the end of a man's accompaniment by his sister, which began at the time of his initiation some ten years earlier.

ANTHROPOLOGY OF PROHIBITIONS

If we restrict ourselves to the analysis of food taboos usually proposed in anthropology, it is hard to account for a system of representations and practices in which a person who respects the prohibition is not the one liable to suffer the consequences of its violation. In fact, all have attempted to describe and interpret systems in which the prohibitions are both permanent and meant for the person respecting them. Among the Ankave, these taboos are levied at well-defined moments in a person's life and for someone other than that person. This situation therefore leads me to look first of all at the persons concerned by a prohibition, whether as an agent or a beneficiary, and only afterward at the food's properties. The majority of the anthropological analyses we have focus solely on these properties and seek to understand why a given food cannot be eaten by a given category of persons. Nevertheless, the situation of prohibition sometimes entails more elements, as in certain Australian groups, where "the restrictions surrounding the distribution of food depend on the particular food, the technique of gathering and preparation as well as the relationship of the persons involved" (McKnight 1973: 194).[18]

This is also the case of the food taboo systems found among the Hua, a people living in Papua New Guinea's Eastern Highlands, to which Anna Meigs

---

18. It also happens that a prohibition respected for oneself in fact hides a triadic situation: in Amazonia, for example, a person abstains from a food in order not to interfere with the relation established with a given class of nonhumans. This relation is thus part of the taboo situation (Anne-Christine Taylor, pers. comm.).

has devoted an entire volume. She distinguishes two modalities of prohibition: "absolute" prohibitions, which establish a relation between a food and a category of persons ("X must not consume *a*"), and "relative" prohibitions, which pose a relation between a category of persons and a food but the food depends as well on its human origin (so "X must not consume *a* that comes from Y"). As the author stresses, what matters here is the social relation between the consumer and the person who gathered or grew the food, or who raised the pig, and that nearly independently of the nature of this food itself (1984: 17). The risk involved in eating such a food stems from the human life-substance, called *nu*, which permeates the plant as it is produced. Food grown by a woman past menopause is therefore much less dangerous than food produced by a newly married woman from a different village than that of her husband (Meigs 1984: 20–21). Yet despite the fact that this system of food taboos has a relational dimension, which we have seen to be very present in the Ankave situation, it differs from the latter in that it takes into account the identity of the person who produced the prohibited food.[19] Alternatively, when an Ankave woman cultivates her gardens, she does not infuse the taros and sweet potatoes with her own life-substance, and if certain foods are prohibited, it is because of their intrinsic properties and not because of any that might have been conferred on them while being grown.

These types of analyses seek to explain why these complex and widespread practices known as food taboos are varied. They differ according to whether the elements underpinning them are regarded as sociological, psychological, or are bound up with the relations the populations entertain with their environment (let us call them *ecological*). Émile Durkheim, regarded as the founder of the French school of sociology, and in his wake the British school of social anthropology, understood prohibitions, whatever their nature, as social facts and as such amenable to a sociological analysis of the classification systems that organize and articulate the components of the living world: animals, plants,

---

19. The local system of food taboos, where the identity of the food-producer is a parameter to be included, recalls the situations in which the fact of eating tubers that grew on the same clan lands creates an identity of substances that can make strangers into kin (Bonnemère and Lemonnier 1992: 135). In both cases, a cultivated food is more than a simple food insofar as it contains something of the person who worked the land or of the clan that owns it. Or, as Almut Schneider writes for the Gawigl living in Western Highlands Province, food "carries something of the relation between the land and the gardeners, those in the present like those in the past" (2017: 69).

and human beings. We will later take a closer look at the work of Douglas, the main proponent of this approach. Nevertheless, some anthropologists have considered that, in the particular case of prohibitions, a sociological analysis is not enough, and that the origin of the taboos must also be sought among reasons of a psychological order, such as aversion or disgust formed in childhood, but without resorting to the idea of psychological universals, which clearly cannot account for specific cultural configurations (for example, see De Vos 1975: 78). Others still have seen cultural dietary regimes as adaptive systems aimed at managing the local environment for the best (for example, see Ross et al. 1978).

I am not going to list all the studies on food taboos—which would exceed the scope of my competence—but I will propose, on the basis of a few examples, a sort of overview of these three approaches, none of which, as we will see, is truly capable of accounting for the ethnographic material I gathered among the Ankave. In all the above studies, the properties of the forbidden foods are considered to be the key to their explanation, whereas, as I have already said, in this society, the determining parameter is as much the identity of the persons concerned by the prohibition as the properties of the food itself. This specificity is directly linked to its configuration, which brings three terms into play: a food and two persons, one the agent and the other the beneficiary of the prohibition.[20] In contrast, the prohibition systems analyzed elsewhere in the anthropological literature have only two terms: a food and a person, in whom the positions of agent and beneficiary of the prohibition are merged.

When it comes to anthropology of food taboos, inevitably the name of Mary Douglas springs to mind. Starting from the prohibitions set out in the Biblical books of Leviticus and Deuteronomy, this famous British anthropologist proposed a symbolic and sociological reading of prohibitions in general, which deeply influenced later ethnographic studies touching on the notions of taboo, impurity, and pollution. Although her book *Purity and danger*, published in 1966, has been abundantly discussed and criticized, it remains a major contribution. In it the author calls on the idea of "classificatory anomaly" to account for the case in which an element assumed to belong to one class—here, mainly the pig but also the pangolin for the Lele of the Congo—possesses a feature

---

20. With a variant in which two persons respect the same prohibition at the same time. In this case we must ask ourselves whether we have here two agents and two beneficiaries, or two agents and a single beneficiary (see beginning of the present chapter).

incompatible with the prototype of its class. Taken to be "anomalous" in however slight a way, the animal in question was forbidden to eat. This was also the case of fish without fins or scales that "are swept away by the current, unable to resist the force of the stream" that were not eaten by Jews in the early Christian era, not because of this failing advanced by the speakers but, Douglas suggests, because of their strange aspect that set them apart from other fish ([1966] 1981: 59). Anomaly creates disorder because it challenges the clear-cut lines between the classes of elements generated, by definition, by all classification systems. And since disorder is nefarious, "our pollution behaviour is the reaction which condemns any object or idea likely to confuse or contradict cherished classifications" (Douglas [1966] 1981: 36). The notions of contamination and pollution make it possible to protect and preserve the social system, as it were; they are a technique for dealing with these anomalies represented by elements that are not in their proper place in the classifications characteristic of each society.

This analysis is in line with the positions advanced by Durkheim and Marcel Mauss in their famous study *Primitive classification* ([1903] 1969), in that Douglas considers social facts to be at the origin and the heart of all symbolic systems. At the close of a long inquiry into the origin of classification systems based on a detailed presentation of ethnographic examples—essentially from Australia and North America—Durkheim and Mauss assert that "the first logical categories were social categories; the first classes of things were classes of men, into which these things were integrated" ([1903] 1969: 48–49). As Douglas spelled out in an article published in 1972, her wish had always been to "take seriously Durkheim's idea that the properties of classification systems derive from and are indeed properties of the social systems in which they are used" (Douglas 1972: 34). For instance, Douglas regards the body as a symbol of the society: "The body is a complex structure. The functions of its different parts and their relation afford a source of symbols for other complex structures" (Douglas [1966] 1981: 115). And so, just as ideas about pollution and contamination surround the secretions and fluids that flow from the body, and therefore cross its boundaries, food taboos apply to the anomalous elements in the classification system. And these representations have repercussions on the society insofar as, she writes, they express the risk of danger on the margins. The author takes the example of the Israelites: "In their beliefs all the bodily issues were polluting, blood, pus, excreta, semen, etc. The threatened boundaries of their body politic would be well mirrored in their care for the integrity, unity and purity of the physical body" (Douglas [1966] 1981: 124). Her work is thus much more than an analysis of food taboos; it presents a strong hypothesis concerning the way societies deal with elements whose characteristics do not lend themselves easily to inclusion in a given classification system. As Edwin Ardener reminded us in his review of *Purity and danger*, several solutions exist to cope with such a situation: the elements can be brought under control while ignoring their ambiguity by avoiding them (thus strengthening the definitions they do not conform to), or by labeling them as "dangerous" (1967: 139). The solution adopted by a very large number of societies, according to Douglas, is to set restrictions on the consumption of the flesh of animals located at the margins of the categories in which they are classified, as can be seen in her wide-ranging comparison at the end of her book. We have here a major reflection on classificatory logic and the consequences of its weaknesses. Nevertheless, it is incomplete from the standpoint of food taboos, properly speaking, insofar as it considers only the *properties* of the banned foods and fails to address the *status of the persons* bound by the prohibitions. The ethnographic examples chosen to illustrate the thesis suit such a vision since the prohibitions they reveal were permanent and affected the population as a whole. The examples therefore highlight neither particular moments in the lifecycle nor specific relational situations, as among the Ankave.

Another anthropologist, Claudine Fabre-Vassas, has also contributed to the interpretation of prohibition systems in a meticulous analysis of the representations and practices surrounding pigs in Christian Europe from the Middle Ages to the present. Attempting to understand what she calls an "ethnological paradox," which says that "contrary to the universal rule that associates the other, the outsider, with what he eats, Jews are assimilated to the flesh they prohibit for themselves" (1994: 108), the author investigates the way pigs are raised, thought of, evoked, killed, and eaten in Europe, particularly in the French Pyrenees region. She begins her reasoning by a Christian myth with numerous variants: it tells that Jews do not eat pork because, since Christ turned the children of a Jewish woman into piglets, for Jews to eat this animal it would be the same as eating themselves. This Christian interpretation of the Jewish ban on pork is based on nothing less than the prohibition of cannibalism, since the piglets are none other than the changed Jewish children. And with that, the author notes, "Jews are assimilated to the animal" (1994: 14). For Christians, on the other hand, every part of the pig is good to eat; it is in a sense because the Jews do not eat pork that Christians feast on it. This is a way for Christians to set themselves apart from Jews and, at the same time, to stigmatize them while incorporating them following a sacrificial logic (Fabre-Vassas 1994: 360–64).

The Ankave justify the respect of a taboo in a similar manner, in this case the ban on consuming the game given in the context of marriages, by idea that its violation would be tantamount to an act of cannibalism (see p. 108). Assimilation of the flesh of an animal to human flesh is thus far from being an isolated representation, as Alfred Gell showed in his reflection on the disgust shown by his Umeda friends in Papua New Guinea when he had automatically sucked the blood running from a cut in his finger. For Gell, "Umeda ideas of taboo had little or nothing to do with real or supposed anomalies within their system of animal or plant classification, and everything to do with avoiding eating one's own self" (Gell 1979: 135). It would be more often the horror of cannibalism—real or metaphorical—than the nonconformity of the prohibited animal with the members of the class to which it is supposed to belong that underpins the existence of certain food taboos.

The reader will have understood that these two authors' analyses, insofar as they fail to call on the properties of the banned foods or on any classificatory order, do not support Douglas' hypothesis. For Fabre-Vassas, the Jewish ban on pork has to do with the association of this animal with the children of a woman from their religious community. For Christians, consuming this food is a means of affirming an identity by setting oneself apart from the dietary practices of another group. The idea that diet might be used as an identity marker and/ or as a means of setting oneself apart from other populations one regards as inferior (for example) is found in numerous studies, whether by anthropologists like Ellen Basso, specialist of the Kalapalo Indians of Central Brazil (Ross et al. 1978: 17), or Kaj Århem, who has studied the East African Maasai (cited in Simoons 1994: 91),[21] or by historians looking to explain the Jewish taboo on pork (Simoons 1994: 93). The mental operation consisting in identifying a group with what it eats is apparently widely shared, and dietary practices are therefore a powerful means of defining oneself and others. In numerous cultures and parts of the world (and for many anthropologists), adopting food taboos that others do not respect is a way of saying one is different from them. There are obviously many other ways as well, and we might well wonder why eating is better suited than any other social practice to contribute to defining a group. But that is not within the scope of my subject.

Although the reasons given by the authors I have just cited are different, their interpretations all refer to cultural representations found in the societies

21. See also Garine (2001: 487) and Mintz and Du Bois (2002: 109).

that follow these prohibitions. This is not the case of other interpretations that reject such approaches as "mentalist," "structuralist," or "symbolist," in which the culture is seen as a system or a code of ideas that assigns values to the physical components of the system (Ross et al. 1978: 1). These interpretations favor what they call a "materialist" analysis, in which food prohibitions are manifestations of the population's adaptation to its environment.[22] One of the most widespread ideas is that the adoption of prohibitions is a response to a situation in which game is in decline; prohibitions would make it possible, as it were, to avoid its depletion or extinction. However, if it is altogether possible that ceasing to consume certain animals has contributed to their perpetuation, it is doubtful that the populations consciously banned certain animals for this purpose. For every anthropologist knows that, contrary to what Westerners often imagine, the inhabitants of tropical rainforests are far from always acting with the preservation of their environment foremost in mind.

From an ecological school of thought in the 1950s–1970s, this trend, purportedly more scientific than interpretative anthropology, owing to its concern with the underlying causes of social behaviors, went on to become a psychologically based form of determinism. As an example of the relative continuity between these two research avenues, let us look at the studies conducted in a geographical zone close to that discussed in this book and on which there is something of a tradition of research in human ecology: the Mountain Ok, living in western Papua New Guinea near the border with the Indonesian province of Western Papua. A study by George Morren, published in 1986 but based on a 1975 doctoral dissertation, sought to understand the relations the Miyanmin entertain with their natural environment. To this end, the author adopted the presuppositions of ecology and biology to explain human behaviors, in this case the idea that societies' beliefs and practices usually have a rational basis, such as, in the area of dietary behaviors, optimization of protein intake. Morren favors a systemic approach that requires that every component of a reality is, or can be, linked to another (1986: 14), and is therefore open to the idea that a single property cannot account for a social behavior. Yet when looking for the explanation of a food taboo, his analysis turns out to be less cautious than what

---

22. There is no need to present here all the so-called materialist theories of dietary practices, of which Marvin Harris is no doubt the most zealous proponent. I have chosen to retain only one or two analyses representing this school of thought, which, moreover, have used ethnographic material gathered in New Guinea.

this methodological and theoretical position might suggest, rejecting as he does the idea that human behaviors might be dictated by nonrational factors (1986: 125–29).

Nearly twenty years later, Harriet Whitehead adopted behaviorist and cognitivist positions after having first distinguished herself in the American feminist line of thought.[23] Her book deals with the rules governing the consumption of meat (game and domestic pork) in a small community in the same part of western Papua New Guinea. According to this author, the prohibitions levied on meat among the Seltaman are the historical product of three interwoven sets of factors—ecological, psychological, and cultural: the availability of the flesh of different animal species, the psychological processes underlying the dietary habits, and the formation of disgust,[24] as well as local representations of proper social consumption, which is essentially dictated by rules of sharing (2000: 24–25). Whitehead's central thesis argues that the function of food taboos is to resolve problems involved in distributing game: prohibitions are a social response based on sharing and depend on the average rate at which hunting techniques make it possible to capture the game (2000: 243). This line of thought is in agreement with Morren but also with David Hyndman, two authors who have proposed a correlation between freedom to eat an animal species and its relative availability (Whitehead 2000: 117). But Whitehead goes further, suggesting the complementary idea that the more abundant a game animal is, the more people are accustomed to eating its flesh and the more numerous the categories of consumers that eat it. Conversely, she writes, the scarcer a game animal is, the less people are accustomed to eat it and the stronger the reactions of disgust regarding it. Because it is scarce, this game can only be distributed on a smaller scale, and it is highly likely that only a small portion of the community is allowed to consume it.

In addition to its patently functionalist dimension, which proves to be reductive, Whitehead's reasoning unfortunately fails to take into consideration some noteworthy counterexamples. For instance, how does she explain that the cassowary and the wild pig, the two largest game animals in the area, are forbidden to women and children, who make up the bulk of the population? Likewise,

---

23. See in particular the volume edited with Sherry Ortner in 1981, *Sexual meanings: The cultural construction of gender and sexuality*, now a Gender Studies classic in the United States.

24. See also Fessler and Navarrete (2003).

how does she account for the fact that the abundant *kwemnok* (*Phalanger gymnotis*) in the Seltaman territory was once reserved for older people? Far from being exceptions that confirm the rule, these examples show that an analysis of the symbolic representations locally attached to these animals, which the author rejects out of hand, would have enabled her to better account for the local system of food taboos.

What we already know of the prohibitions encountered among the Ankave is enough to convince us that they cannot be explained by this type of approach, which, while combining findings from developmental psychology and information on wildlife management, fails to listen to what local people say and to look for the implicit basis of dietary practices. Like the Seltaman's system, which clearly deserves an emic analysis,[25] the prohibitions observed by the Ankave would be incomprehensible if we were simply to assimilate them to a system of disgust formation and wildlife management. Although tropical forest peoples are finely attuned to their environment, it is highly unlikely that they adopted dietary practices with the explicit aim of conserving game resources on their territory. With all due respect to the defenders of peoples to whom they attribute the quality of deliberately and optimally managing their relations with the environment that feeds them, it is no doubt their small number that is the main factor in preserving their environment, which does not exclude their having intentionally developed complex and effective systems for managing it.

The authors of all these analyses tend to accept as self-evident the idea that a taboo is respected to prevent a negative effect on the person respecting it. And yet the Ankave system of prohibitions goes much further. Certain taboos are indeed designed to protect the observer: we saw, for instance, that children abstain from consuming those foods that grow too slowly so as not to impede their own growth. But at times in the life cycle marked by a ritual, it is no longer the individual who acts alone, but a specific set of related persons (mother, sister, husband), whose acts affect that individual. Bodies are thus connected by a sort of invisible fluid mechanics in which what one person absorbs finds its way into the body of another person. Body boundaries blur, and the analyst must then

25. As Jean-Pierre Olivier de Sardan writes, "the *emic* is centered on gathering native cultural meanings connected with the actors' point of view, while the *etic* is based on external observations independent of the meanings ascribed by the actors, and is defined by a quasi ethological observation of human behaviors" (1998: 153).

consider as much the identity of the persons concerned as the properties locally ascribed to the forbidden food. That was no doubt what Michael Lambek was saying when he wrote that what interested him was not the content of specific taboos but the fact that they were acts or practices that established and underscored important relations (1992: 246–47).

CHAPTER 7

Exchanges and prohibitions
A relational view

For the Ankave, banned foods do not have intrinsic properties that would complicate their inclusion in the system used locally to classify the world. No more than they are classificatory anomalies like those explored by Mary Douglas, which would not be among the components of the local ecosystem that members of this society are attempting to preserve by prohibiting their consumption, as proponents of a materialist or determinist outlook might suggest. Nor are they among the foods the group wants to protect by removing them from the younger members' diet so they will be unfamiliar with them and then reject them, as might be suggested by a psychological approach in terms of disgust formation. Lastly, the Ankave's food taboos do not act as identity markers in that the Ankave do not use them to differentiate themselves from neighboring populations.

I have distinguished two types of prohibitions: the few that a person respects for him- or herself, which apply only to children; and the majority observed for others in the process of making a person. How are the latter to be understood? To my mind, such prohibitions, whether they apply to foods or behaviors, are part of a larger set of social practices through which the Ankave express certain aspects of a kinship relation in the context of a series of transformations that accompany the normal course of life. In that, such prohibitions are comparable to the exchanges of objects and food that occur at fundamental points in the life cycle: birth, initiation, marriage, and death. Because of this, further pursuit of the goal I have set for myself—to understand how the construction of the male person is seen in the local context—involves a joint analysis of these two sets of ethnographic material.

In previous chapters we saw that, owing to the transformations they bring about in a person's status, certain moments in the lives of Ankave men and women are characterized by rituals requiring the presence of the entire local community, all clans combined. When a boy reaches the age of ten or there about, he and his companions go through the first two stages of initiations, during which the nose is pierced and the body is rubbed with red pandanus seeds; at this point he leaves behind his carefree childhood and his close relationship with his mother, forever. Over these weeks of ordeals undergone in the forest, a change of status occurs: he is not yet an adult, but he has become a young man aware of the future responsibilities he will shoulder when he takes a wife and has children—in particular, clearing a garden, building a house, procuring pigs, and in the past, defending his fellow tribesmen in the event of intertribal conflict. His new appearance attests to his transformation: he now wears a <u>pulpul</u> and no longer a skirt of flat bark fibers;[1] his back and buttocks are covered by a male bark cape, *ijiare*; diagonally across his chest he wears braids of orchid stems; and on his forehead he wears the shell and feather ornaments he has received from his father or a maternal uncle. Although he does not don this finery every day,[2] his silhouette has changed. He holds himself differently, more erectly, proudly. The movement bearing him toward adulthood, and that which will lead him to adopt the silhouette and the attitudes (control of the emotions, bravery) that are locally expected of a man, has begun.

This first change in the status of a male individual is thus the object of rituals in which different actors—men and women—take part, performing specific gestures, obeying prohibitions, uttering secret words in a strictly regulated scenography. Several weeks before the construction of the two big shelters where the novices' mothers and fathers, respectively, will stay, and which is the

1. Anga specialists have noted that, before their initiation, the boys' appearance resembled that of women (Godelier [1982] 1986: 63; Bamford 1998: 162).
2. On our first trip, in 1987, with the exception of one or two members of the group, all the Ankave were dressed like their ancestors; ten years later, this was no longer the case, and shorts and T-shirts prevailed. But most men and women still wear their <u>pulpul</u> and their grass skirt for ceremonies.

collective action marking the beginning of the ceremonies proper, numerous persons connected with the novices were already engaged in preparations. Aunts had already begun making little netbags; older brothers had gone to the high forest to gather the golden yellow stems of the wild epiphytic orchids that are braided to make the chest ornaments; other brothers had made bows and arrows; fathers and paternal uncles had prepared the shell headbands for their sons and nephews. In short, the community had set to work so that the boys of an age could be initiated.

These tasks are not compensated by a gift of pig meat or game because the kin tie that binds all these close relatives to the novices is enough to oblige them to participate in their nephew's, younger brother's, or son's graduation to a new status. These are part and parcel of the duties each one owes the boy. The maternal kin play a different role. First, one of the mother's brothers takes a direct hand in his nephew's initiation by accompanying, guiding, and comforting him during the ordeals he undergoes. And second, the compensations paid by the mother's brother or the maternal grandparents are not tied to specific tasks these relatives perform for their nephews and nieces or for their grandchildren, but are owed at regular intervals over the lifetime of every man or woman. The reasons advanced for these payments are much less pragmatic and run much deeper; they have to do with the role Ankave culture ascribes to the mother in making the child.

In other Anga societies, such as the Baruya or the Sambia, the role of the father's semen is charged with particular value because it not only contributes to forming the embryo to the same degree as the vaginal fluids but also, and above all, because it is the fetus' only food, which enables it to develop and to become a viable child (Godelier [1982] 1986: 90; Herdt 1981: 192–93). The mother's womb is merely a sort of netbag that holds a child fashioned and nourished by repeated contributions of semen throughout the pregnancy: "The Baruya woman can thus scarcely be regarded as her child's genetrix, since nothing passes from her body into that of the child, and her womb is merely a container for a body engendered and nourished by the man" (Godelier [2004] 2011: 234). But even if the father has the main role and the mother only harbors the child, another intervention is needed, because, as Maurice Godelier says "nowhere, in any society, do a man and a woman alone suffice to make a child" ([2004] 2011: 299). In this northern Anga group, the sun is the "supernatural father" of all children; he makes their eyes, nose, mouth, fingers, and toes (Godelier [1982] 1986: 51).

The Ankave's situation is different: the sun plays no role in procreation,[3] and semen comes into play only in forming the embryo, to the same extent not of the vaginal fluids, whose role is not mentioned, but of the uterine blood, which is nothing other than the menstrual blood retained in the uterus following fecundation. Not only does semen have a limited role, it is credited with having a harmful influence on the fetus. Here, sexual intercourse throughout the pregnancy is not encouraged; on the contrary, total abstinence from any sexual relations is the rule, thus allowing the mother's blood to do its job of growing the fetus. Since the mother's body provides her child with the blood it needs as well as fulfilling her own needs, she must consume foods that are believed to turn into blood when eaten. Sauce made from the red pandanus—which fruits for much of the year (from August to April, depending on the variety)—is, as we know, regarded as an actual vegetal substitute for human blood. Were we seeking the other element to add to the father's and mother's roles in producing a child, there is no doubt as to where we should look, for the origin of this bright red juice is described in a myth that makes it easy to assimilate to the product, and even to the life-giving substance, of a supernatural being. The events take place at the time the first men came out from a hole in the ground, near Obirwa, the place from which most of the Anga originate (Lemonnier 1981: 46).[4] Here is the story:

> The first man to appear in this world asked all those coming out of the ground to introduce themselves by their clan name. One of them remained silent; he did not have a name, and for this he was murdered by the others. His blood flowed out onto the ground. The part that hardened into a clot became the cordyline *oremere*; the red pandanus *perengen* appeared from the red liquid. Then this pandanus grew green leaves. People said to themselves that this tree had grown from the blood and that it was perhaps going to produce fruit. So they waited. A fruit appeared. And since this tree had

3.   For a comparison of the role of the sun in the conception of children and in initiations, see Lemonnier (2010: 213–16).

4.   The Baruya call this spot, located several hours by foot from Menyamya, Bravegareubaramendeuc (Godelier [1982] 1986: 143). From Beatrice Blackwood's account, the Kapau and the Langimar have a different story: the tree from whose trunk the Manki (Langimar), the Nauti, and the Ekuti (both people now speaking the Kapau kanguage) emerged was located in the Langimar district, that is between the Bulolo and the Upper Watut Rivers (1978: 156).

grown from the nameless man's blood, they decided that, thereafter, when they organized male initiations, they would forbid the consumption of this fruit. Some of the adult men wanted to taste the ripened fruit. They picked it and secretly took out the seeds and sucked them, taking care to hide the leftovers from the women. The seeds tasted good. They therefore took a shoot from the tree and replanted it. In those times, only men consumed red pandanus.

Afterward, many children were born. They pierced the boys' nose using one of the bones of the man-with-no-name, which they had kept. After having eaten red pandanus, the master of the initiations dreamed that the spirit of the man-with-no-name was telling him something: "After having pierced the nose, you will rub their body with red pandanus. This fruit came from my body; it did not come from nowhere. You will smear some on the boys' cheeks and on their shoulders. That will make them grow because the red pandanus will enter their body." That is what the man-with-no-name said. "You must smear my blood on their cheeks and on the front of their shoulders; it is my blood. It will mingle with the blood of your sons. It is not red pandanus, it is my blood. My spirit entered this fruit in order to make your children grow."

The storyteller added that, in those times, there was only the *perengen* variety of pandanus.[5] The man who appeared to the ritual expert in a dream had the particularity of being unable, unlike the others who came out of the ground with him, to tell what his name was, not because he was unable to speak—since other versions of the myth say that, on the contrary, he gave each Anga group a name together with the body decorations that characterize them—but simply because he did not have one. And it was for this reason that the Ankave murdered him. From this primordial murder and the blood spilled there grew (among other things, but there is no need to go into detail here) a tree that turned out to produce edible fruits with the capacity to produce growth. By rubbing the juice—or the seeds, but the myth, unlike the ritual (see pp. 83–84), does not say this—on the boys' skin, the men will make them grow through the action of the spirit of the man-with-no-name. The dream message detailed the ritual gesture they would have to perform. The man-with-no-name can be assimilated to someone with no

5.   For the full version of this myth concerning the origin of the red pandanus, see Bonnemère (1996a: 252–53).

identifiable clan. He is not an ancestor to whom some present-day Ankave could trace their descent to the detriment of others, but a primordial man endowed with supernatural powers, henceforth placed at the service of all the men without distinction. He brings them the means to grow their boys, to turn them into warriors, and to ensure survival by enabling the men to produce many children.

The question of whether the red pandanus juice consumed by the women during their pregnancy has something to do with the red pandanus juice the men now use in the initiations is tricky and demands a step-by-step reflection on the available ethnographic material. *On the whole*, the Ankave assimilate the bright red juice to human blood, which by definition comes from the mother. But this maternal blood was nourished by red pandanus juice during the pregnancy. The question is then: is something of the primordial tree, and therefore of the spirit of the man-with-no-name, present in each of the fruits of the trees that were planted on the territory over the centuries? A detail in the myth is of prime importance here: the first red pandanus was of the *perengen* variety. This is the first variety to fruit, opening the long production season of the species. During their pregnancies, women obviously consume the fruits that ripen during this period in their life, without distinction or preference for any specific variety. Alternatively, when the male initiations are organized, care is taken that they coincide with the fruiting season of the *perengen* variety. We can therefore suppose that this particular variety is more specifically associated with the man-with-no-name.

In all events, the idea of vegetative reproduction that these peoples retain from the cordyline implies that something of the primordial plant subsists in each new plant. This is in particular the case of the *oremere'* cordylines, which in myth has appeared in the place where the blood of the man-with-no-name had hardened into a clot. Two red plants then sprang from the two forms of blood—liquid and coagulated—and are used in the different stages of the initiation cycle (Bonnemère 1998: 108). Red pandanus also reproduces vegetatively, which plausibly suggests that every plant of the *perengen* variety contains a bit of the blood of the primordial man-with-no-name. In view of Godelier's affirmation that the intervention of a third agent is required to make a new human being, it would be hard to see the blood of the man-with-no-name as this third agent, since pregnant women do not have a preference for the juice of the *perengen* cultivar. But by way of a hypothesis, I would suggest that boys' bodies need to be infused with this supernatural substance, the *perengen* variety of red pandanus: the strength of the man-with-no-name is thus introduced into their bodies on several occasions during their childhood, first when, as small boys of five or six, they are fed some in secret (see p. 94), and then when they consume it between the two collective stages in order to ensure their growth, which as we have seen is modeled on gestation (see p. 104n7). Without being the third agent indispensible to making a new Ankave member of humankind, red pandanus juice of the *perengen* variety would thus carry a spiritual energy absolutely necessary to gradually attain adult male status.

THE MATERNAL KIN

Opposite to Baruya or Sambia views, this southwestern Anga group places great value on the mother's role, and through her on that of all the maternal kin. It is they who are the child's "real producers"; they are at the origin of its existence. That is why, as we will see in detail further on, for a long time in the life of both his sons and daughters, the father must make gifts in kind (game, domestic pig meat) to the members of his wife's family, of whom the brother, the children's maternal uncle, is the main representative. Such practices are common in New Guinea. Roy Wagner was no doubt the first to analyze, and in minute detail, a situation close to that of the Ankave. Among the Daribi living in the southwestern part of what is now Papua New Guinea, the maternal uncle, whom they call *pagedibi*, is a key figure in the life of every person. He is *"just the same as mother"* (Wagner 1967: 66).[6] And since he comes from the same womb as his sister, who as a mother transmits her blood to her children, he has the same blood as his nieces and nephews, but not as his own children, who inherit the blood of their own mother. Here, too, it is a view of the way children are made that founds the relation with the maternal uncle (Wagner 1967: 64). The sharing of blood, the equivalent of a bond with the common maternal substance, which makes the maternal uncle the true *"owner"* of his sister's children, explains the repeated gifts the *pagedibi* receives from his brother-in-law. These are "recruitment payments," which by no means cancel the bond of consanguinity each person has with his or her maternals, but simply allow the paternal kin to recruit

---

6.   Rupert Stasch likewise reports that, among the Korowai of Papua (formerly Irian Jaya), a man told him, speaking of his nephews and nieces: "oldest sister gave birth to them and therefore it is as if I had given birth to them myself" (2009: 116). On this particular topic, see also Bonnemère (2015b).

the children born into the community to their own group while acknowledging the maternal kin's rights on them. This relationship based on one blood and one substance lasts for the lifetime of those involved (Wagner 1967: 75).

However, that does not mean that either the Ankave or the Daribi are matrilineal societies where the maternal uncle ensures the recruitment of his sister's children into her group. And he is not the one who transmits his name or his land to his nephews and nieces. If the Daribi, or in this case the Ankave, sometimes give the appearance of matrilineal-descent societies, their rules of recruitment are quite different. That is why applying Africanists' unilineal descent models to the patrilineal societies of the New Guinea Highlands has come under constant criticism since the publication of John Barnes' seminal article (1962), even though he was not himself a Melanesianist. In this part of Oceania, there is very often no systematic correspondence between a clan and a local group (Bonnemère and Lemonnier 1992: 133–36). In the same hamlet or on the same land, alongside descendants in the agnatic line of a particular ancestor, we also find the husbands and sons of their sisters, even when the former are not in the majority. In New Guinea, principles of complementary descent are added to the recognized mode of descent reckoning (Barnes 1962: 6), enabling individuals to claim the use of a piece of land or access to a hunting territory. Eating food from a clan land and sharing it with members of a clan gradually contribute to turn an outsider into a fellow clansman (A. Strathern 1975: 33; LiPuma 1988: 100–101). Unlike some famous African societies (Nuer, Tallensi, Tiv), then, descent in this part of the world is not a necessary and sufficient condition for belonging to a group (Scheffler 1985: 3–4), since other criteria of recruitment can be the equivalent of the descent tie. Furthermore, in the case of the Ankave and the Daribi, a man can easily be given the temporary right to use the gardens of his maternal kin, just as he can reside in their village if he so desires (Bonnemère and Lemonnier 1992: 141, 145).

How is the recognition of the maternal kin's role in the life of Ankave children manifested in other areas of social life, and first of all in the exchange of goods? Over a lifetime, with key moments that mark the physical and relational development of each person, gifts of pig meat or game are made. Yet it would be hard to say of these gifts that they "circulate," since their beneficiaries, and therefore their path, is unidirectional. The gifts made for every child from the time of its birth all go to the wife's side, without exception. Her kin are both wife-givers—if we place ourselves at the level of the groups present—and the child's maternal kin—if we situate ourselves on an individual level. The child's father—with the help of his fellow clansmen—who offered goods in kind to "reserve" his future wife (see p. 145) and then paid a brideprice including money and half a pig,[7] must continue to give his brothers-in-law pig meat and game once his children are born. His wife's brothers are at once the representatives of the group of wife-givers and those who share their sister's blood, and therefore that of their nephews and nieces, as I have explained. It is because they share this life-giving substance that the maternal uncles have the capacity to inhibit the growth of their sister's children, and the gifts they receive are meant to both acknowledge a debt of life and prevent any malevolent action on their part. An individual's relationship with the maternal kin is thus fraught with deep-seated ambivalence.

A detailed account of the many prestations received by the maternal kin, all of which have specific names, will give us a better grasp of the important position of the maternal kin in Ankave society and in the life of each person in it. First I will describe the gifts made for all children, whether first or last born; those concerning only the first-born child begin much earlier in its existence, as I briefly mentioned, and will be analyzed later in this chapter. For all children born to a couple, *with the exception of their first born, whose birth enjoys a particular status*, an initial gift is made when the child begins to crawl. At that time, the father brings a piece of cooked pig meat or game to his oldest brother-in-law, who will redistribute it among the child's other maternal kin. Only the recipient of this gift, called *miaru'wa*, ensures its eventual redistribution. In other words, once the father has made this gift, he is not held responsible for the way it is shared, whether or not this follows local rules or custom. The matter is now in the hands of his child's maternal kin, who sometimes jokingly dispute its redistribution. A second gift, *noje nangwen*, is also composed of a piece of meat, and the giver and the receiver are, once again, the father and the maternal uncle who is supposed to redistribute the gift. The difference is that this gift is often indirectly asked for by the recipient, who points out that his nephew or niece has grown nicely.[8] In so doing, he is asserting his role in their proper growth and, when such words have been uttered, the gift is made as much to prevent a potentially malevolent act as it is to compensate an implicit service. In this way, the maternal uncle is pointing out that he and his group may deserve better—when childhood is over and the child's weight and height have visibly

---

7. In the past, shell-money was used, and marriage compensations were paid in lengths of cowry shells. This difference notwithstanding, the staging is the same today, where the money is laid on top of a half carcass of cooked pig (see p. 146).

8. As James Leach wrote concerning the inhabitants of Reite, who also make a series of gifts to the maternal kin while the child is young (2003: 133), these payments show gratitude for the child's growth.

increased—than the *miaru'wa* gift made some eight years earlier. These dis-
guised demands can be reiterated several times.

Another obligatory gift not left to the appreciation of the child's parents is
the *simo'e*. It is made up of a whole male pig, which is given uncooked after a
boy has been initiated. It is then cooked by the maternal uncle who received it
and shared with all his brothers and sisters. Some Ankave discuss this prestation
with reference to the fact that the maternal uncles and aunts helped make the
orchid-stem braids, others mention that the initiate's blood flowed during the
ritual, not following the nose-piercing, as one might think, but under the blows
meted out with cassowary quills, instruments that are both flexible and highly
resistant. And since it is this same blood that flows through the veins of his
mother's brothers and sisters, they must receive compensation. In all events, the
simo'e is the last of the gifts connected with a child's growth to be made to the
maternal kin. Remarkably, it is also the only one to be met with the *memia* countergift of a pearlshell, also called "the teeth of the maternal kin";[9] much later, the
initiate will wear this ornament around his neck (Lemonnier 2006a: 327–28).
Commenting on the *simo'e*, the Ankave underscore two different things: a payment for labor provided and a compensation for harm to a body whose blood is
shared by the maternal kin. Furthermore, the mother's brother, as his nephew's
sponsor, has received the same blows as the boy, which left him with bleeding
wounds, and the gifts he receives are no doubt compensation for harm done to
his own body as well. Finally, the gifts mean that, once initiated, the boy has
reached an important stage in his life: he has grown and is no longer as vulner-
able to possible malevolent actions on the part of his maternal uncles. A chapter
in his life has come to a close, as it were. And another will begin when he, in
turn, becomes a father and has to be generous with his brother-in-law so as to
ensure that his own children grow up to be healthy.

CONCERNING THE *SIMO'E* GIFT

In the Ankave's commentaries on the *simo'e* gift, doubts, approximations, and
even divergences between informants appeared, which has made it difficult to

---

9.   Unlike the inhabitants of Reite studied by James Leach, the Ankave do not say, "in
     the past a child was eaten by its maternal uncle" (2003: 148), but the expression used
     here might well evoke the same act.

develop a complete analysis. These discrepancies concern two points: the sex of the child for whom the gift is made and its generalization or not to all children (boys?) independently of birth order. It was only by observing what was actually done that I was able to resolve, almost definitively, these doubts, or at least to offer an interpretation of them. For a long time, the question of whether the *simo'e* was part of the gifts made to the maternal uncle of a niece did not occur to me since our Ankave friends associate the gift of a whole raw pig with initiation, and therefore with a boy. Then, one day in 1998, in the course of a discussion among women, one of them told me that when her younger sister's daughter had received a marriage proposal, her sister had chosen one of the grown pigs she had raised, and her husband had killed it and given it to the girl's maternal uncle. She added that it was a male pig that the many maternal uncles and aunts had shared: it was a *simo'e* gift. As the eldest sister of the girl's mother, my informant had received a share and remembered it well. Following this revelation, I continued my investigations and, there too, the answers varied: for some, more often the women, the *simo'e* pig is given also for a girl when she reaches puberty. "This time is the equivalent of initiation for the boys. The *simo'e* marks the end of the gifts for growing." For others, more often the men, "there is no *simo'e* gift for girls but it has an equivalent in the first gift made to ask for a girl in marriage. This gift always goes to the oldest maternal uncle, who shares it with any true siblings he may have. This gift does not have a special name. It consists of half a pig or half a cassowary, cooked."

How are these partially diverging comments to be interpreted? Everyone agrees that the *simo'e* pig has an equivalent for girls in the form of a gift of pig meat, which also marks the end of the gifts for growing made to the maternal uncle. Some take this equivalence further and call the first marriage gift by the same term as the gift given for initiation. Yet the two prestations differ in at least two respects: in the first case, it is half a cooked pig given by the future husband's family, and in the second case a whole male pig, raw, given by the parents of the initiate. Furthermore, the cooked half pig is given to the young girl's parents who personally take it to her maternal uncle.

There seem to be two cases, then:

1. If the girl reaches puberty but has not been asked for in marriage, it is her own parents who kill one of their pigs and give it to her maternal uncle. In this case, the gift is virtually identical to the *simo'e* pig given after a boy's initiation. In such a situation, the Ankave would tend to use the term *simo'e*.

2.	If the girl was reserved for marriage while still very young, or when she reached puberty, the half pig that her maternal uncle will finally receive (via the girl's parents) comes from her future parents-in-law. In this case, here too the parents bring the pig to the maternal uncle, but they did not raise the animal. It is as though the girl's future in-laws were making the final growth payment owed to the maternal uncle of their future daughter-in-law.

In view of the diverging interpretations offered by my Ankave friends, I came to think that the possible coexistence of these two situations made it hard for them to assign a specific status to this gift. As a consequence, they hesitate, as it were, about whether it is the final growing gift (equivalent to the *simo'e* for a boy and therefore called by the same term by some, which is regarded as sloppy usage by others), or the first in a series of marriage gifts, which we will soon discuss in detail. I therefore suggest that there is indeed, as the Ankave all say, a gift equivalent to the *simo'e* for girls but that, depending on her matrimonial status at the time of puberty, it is given by her parents (and in this case it is a whole uncooked pig) or by her future parents-in-law (in which case it is half a cooked pig). In both cases, the maternal uncle is the beneficiary and he shares it with his brothers and sisters, and in both cases it is the girl's parents who bring him the gift.

As for whether the *simo'e* gift is made for all children regardless of their birth order, or only for the first-born, this cannot be resolved independently of the question we have just been discussing. For girls, the marriage proposal entails a gift, and all female children are therefore concerned. The following comments were made about the boys: "The *simo'e* gift is obligatory for the first-born boy, and it is given for the other boys if their maternal uncles made ornaments for their initiation." Moreover, this task is often mentioned when real gifts are explained. In other words, this is not only the final gift for growing but also a compensation for the ornaments a maternal uncle is supposed to make for his sister's son. The fact that he forgets his duty of mutual aid in the case of a first-born will not keep him from receiving the *simo'e* pig. After Luke's initiation, I was told that some of his many maternal uncles had refused a share of the *simo'e* pig his father had given, saying that they would take their share when Luke's younger brother was initiated. This true case would tend to confirm the version that the *simo'e* gift is made for all boys.

We might ask then if the maternal uncle is obliged to make a countergift of a *memia* shell each time he receives this gift or if this ornament concerns only the first-born son. The information I gathered does not allow me to settle the question with certainty. When it comes to the girls, in any case, a countergift of a live piglet is systematically made. This is the *potiye'* gift, which the young woman may use as she wishes: in particular, she keeps the money she makes if she sells the grown pig when it is killed. This animal is usually the first in a long series of pigs raised by all married women over their lifetime.

The maternal uncles and aunts are the main beneficiaries of the growth gifts made by a child's father, but he must also give the *rwa'atungwen* to his parents-in-law. This is a gift of pig meat or game made to the maternal grandparents of his children while they are still small. It is given for all children born to the couple, but, unlike the *simo'e*, which must be paid to the son or daughter of the maternal uncle if he is deceased, no one can receive the *rwa'atungwen* in place of the maternal grandparents. It cannot be given to anyone else.

If the *simo'e* and the *rwa'atungwen* are the final prestations made during a boy's lifetime, a girl's life includes many more owing to a matrimonial practice that entails not only payment of a compensation in the form of money but also many gifts in kind called *tuage* (see below). These regular gifts over the girl's lifetime begin when the parents of a boy have chosen a little or a young girl for him and he approves. They then go to the girl's hamlet to present the marriage proposal. This visit has a special name, *igijinge'*, which means "to mark the path with a branch"—in other words, to tell others that he is not at home and they should move on.[10] If the girl's parents accept the gift of meat, it means they accept the marriage proposal. As we have seen, they are not the ones who will eat it but instead will take it to the girl's maternal uncle—a fact that led me to discuss the possible equivalence with the *simo'e* pig given at the time of a boy's initiation.

Above and beyond the gift that accompanies the marriage proposal, any marriage entails regular payments, made by the young man's parents, of goods in kind (domestic pig meat, less often game, and rarely bamboo tubes filled with *aamain* sauce) to the girl's parents. Spaced out when the future bride is still a little girl, these gifts, called *tuage*, become increasingly frequent as she approaches puberty and then taper off after the couple have had children, but they never cease entirely. The gifts are always received by the woman's parents, who redistribute them. The first *tuage* goes to her maternal uncle, and the following to the

---

10. For details see pp. 174–180.

respective kin groups, with a majority (70 percent) to her paternal kin.[11] These gifts are explicitly considered to be compensation for the care and education the young girl's parents have invested to make her into an accomplished wife. In addition to these regular gifts in kind, all marriages entail payment of a brideprice proper, locally known as *abare' nengwe'* (literally, "woman money"). Invariably composed of half a cooked pig and a certain amount of money (formerly lengths of shell-money),[12] this gift is always made once the young woman has definitively moved in with her husband, or even after the birth of their first child. In other words, the marriage must be seen to have settled down, the house built, and their first garden cleared. The Ankave say that today this gift of money, which can amount to hundreds and even thousands of kinas, refers essentially to the fact that the children born of the marriage should belong to their father's group. This is a classic case of a prestation that compensates a woman's own group for the recruitment of the children she bears to her husband's group. The money is received by the wife's father to be put aside to pay the future marriage compensation for one of her brothers (see p. 195).

In parallel to the *tuage* gifts in kind (usually pig meat) a man owes to his in-laws, on the occasion of the birth of each of his children, he gives his wife the marsupials he has hunted with those of his brothers and brothers-in-law who so desired. These are the *meemi tse'* ("birth marsupials") discussed in chapter 3 (p. 77), devoted to the ritual acts connected with this major event that is the birth of a man's first child. But unlike what happens on that occasion, the sisters of the child's parents are not forbidden to consume this game. Quite the contrary! When the hunting has been good and this strong-tasting game is abundant, the women, little girls, and not-yet-initiated boys of the family and neighboring families hasten to join in this meal. Initiated boys and adult men cannot take part in this properly female time of conviviality. One of them—in the example that springs to mind this was the new mother's uterine nephew, some twelve

---

11. These calculations are based on the analysis of the *tuage* gifts made throughout the married life of eleven now elderly women, whose matrimonial story is therefore over (Bonnemère 1996a: 108–10). See Wagner on "The contrasts between . . . wife givers and wife takers or between paternal and maternal lineality are not mysteriously 'given' facts, but differentiating social *assertions*" (1977: 641).

12. Among the Ankave, the shell-money is composed of cowry shells sewn on to a long strip of beaten bark. It is not, as is the case in other parts of Melanesia, attributed with an anthropomorphic character in local thinking (cf. Clark 1991: 317; Derlon 2002: 163–64).

years old but having already been initiated—takes charge of cutting up the animal, but the distribution of the pieces and the meal take place without him. If the hunting has been poor and only one marsupial was caught, it goes entirely to the new mother, because, it is said, she needs to get her strength back.

EXCHANGES AT THE END OF A LIFE

As might be expected, death is the final stage in this long process of exchanges and prohibitions punctuating the life of an Ankave person. When death comes, the deceased's close kinsmen gather in the house, where the fire has been extinguished and the stones and ashes of the hearth scattered, to watch over the body, which is propped up in a sitting position, in the case of a man, with the help of bows or fighting sticks planted in the ground and, in the case of a woman, digging sticks. If the man was married, his widow remains stretched out alongside the body for the duration of the wake. Over her everyday skirt, she has put on another one, called *itu'we'ge*, which she has made from one of her deceased husband's bark capes and which she will discard immediately after the burial. In the same circumstances, a widower sits silently beside his deceased wife but does not lie down.

The persons watching over the deceased express their sorrow in softly chanted laments befitting the circumstances (*nwabe'*), while smearing their face and hair with ashes and clay, and in some cases, scoring their forehead with their nails or a bamboo knife. The deceased's close relatives express their distress by destroying part of the plants in his or her garden and breaking some personal belongings: the bow for a man, the netbag for a woman, a lime gourd, et cetera. And as the Ankave believe that the *ombo'* cannibal spirits attracted by cadavers prowl around the place where the deceased lies, they chant to stay awake and to ward off their action (Lemonnier 2006a: 157).

A few days after the death, the time it takes family living in remote villages to arrive, a man, usually one of the deceased's cross-cousins, carries the body to the grave,[13] after having circled the house to throw the deceased's spirit off the trail and prevent its return. Before laying the body in the narrow slot dug in the ground (or formerly installing it on a platform), he removes the bark cape that

---

13. Until the mid-1970s, the body was laid out on a platform erected for the occasion in one of the deceased's gardens.

wrapped the deceased. In compensation for having been around "his stench," the Ankave say, this bearer receives a specific gift, formerly composed of shells and today of money, called *a'menge'*. This gift is unique in that it can be anticipated. In this case, two cross-cousins each decide to kill one of their pigs at the same time and to give it to the other. This reciprocal gesture implies abandoning all rights to the *a'menge'* gift when one of the two dies and the other is responsible for carrying the body to its final resting place.[14]

A long mourning period then begins during which the deceased's close relatives respect two prohibitions that invariably accompany any ritual marking an important moment in the life cycle: they cease consuming red pandanus juice and chewing betel. These taboos will be respected for a longer or shorter time depending on the closeness of the tie with the deceased. A husband and a wife often wait a year or two, and sometimes much longer, and lift the bans only after performance of the *songain* ceremony designed to definitively drive the deceased's spirit from the village. Children, sisters, and brothers also abstain from these two pleasures of Ankave life for many long months. A maternal uncle and uterine nephew respect these prohibitions for a shorter time, as do a woman's co-wife or sister-in-law, who do not belong to the deceased's family but in this way underscore the fact that "they had relations of mutual aid and support." For the more remote members of the deceased's kin, the length of time they respect the taboo is left up to them and it often lasts only a few days, enough to show the deceased that they are sad.

It is striking that women in mourning are more visible than men: their lamentations are louder, their *ajiare'*[15] ornaments more numerous, and they remain longer than the men in the state of empathy with the deceased characterized by abstention from "the good things [the deceased] can no longer enjoy."[16] Likewise, the lifting of taboos for women is more strongly ritualized than for men. We will come back in a later chapter to this differential involvement in the stages of the life cycle, but we can already indicate that, as in the case of birth, the "material" aspects surrounding death are a matter more for the women than for

---

14. For more details on this anticipated gift, see Lemonnier 2006a: 265–66.

15. The *ajiare'* mourning ornaments are made from fibers of the ficus, which are put together to make bracelets, knee bands, elbow bands, and even bib-like ornaments. They are particularly drab (see photo 12).

16. It will be remembered here that, if they so desire, men in mourning can actually consume red pandanus sauce in secret (see p. 50n6).

Photo 12. A woman in mourning, unlike a man, covers her whole body with the drab *ajiare'* ornaments and respects food taboos for a longer time. © Pierre Lemonnier (1987)

the men. In the past, in fact, it was the women who removed the skin of the deceased with their nails as it came away from the decomposing body.[17] The female cross-cousin or, in her absence, the sister or the wife who took on this unpleasant task, like the male cross-cousin who carried the body, received a compensation in the form of a gift of *a'menge'* shell money. The woman would first coat her hands with the yellow-orange *rwa'a omore'* clay the young mothers rub on their newborn babies and the experienced women smear on the initiates when they come down from the forest. This anointment and this particular clay are always present when someone graduates to a new status, when they pass from one world to another, and it is the women who do this. Carrying the body to the grave is a man's task, but many acts, behaviors, and gestures associated with death are still performed by the women, such as expressing the village's sorrow by rubbing their body with ashes, making the *ajiare'* ornaments, and wearing them for many long months before discarding them after the end-of-mourning ceremony.

The ceremony called *songain* is held a year or two after someone dies. It involves turning in a circle for ten or so consecutive nights, during which time the men sing, with some wearing a mask on their head or taking turns beating an hourglass drum, and the women sway their skirts and wave brightly colored leaves. The purpose of the *songain* is to bring the mourning period to a close and definitively drive away the deceased's spirit. Since Pierre Lemonnier has described it at length, in *Le sabbat des lucioles* (Lemonnier 2006a), I will simply discuss the gifts made at this time. The roles played respectively by the men and the women at this time that will allow people to return to normal life—insofar as individual and collective life deprived of relations with a loved one can be called normal—will be dealt with at the end of chapter 11 in pages devoted to the comparative analysis of the life-paths of the two genders.

The *songain* ceremony, which takes its name from the drums beaten on this occasion, closes with an exchange of pieces of smoked eel. The eels, which are plentiful in the valley's main river and its small tributaries, are caught in traps made of bark and rattan, the manufacture of which is a delicate job learned over a long time.[18] Several magical operations are also needed to make the eels

---

17. In Ancient Greece, too, it was the women who attended to the corpse, "which they viewed as their property" (Loraux 1989: 182).

18. To get an idea, the reader can consult the chapter on death and mourning in a bilingual volume by Pascale Bonnemère and Pierre Lemonnier (2007), *Les tambours de l'oubli / Drumming to forget*, which combines ethnographic text and photos, as well as Lemonnier's article (1996).

take the bait, which consists of live frogs caught at night by the wife of the trap-maker. Making and laying the traps are men's jobs, as are the smoking and cutting up of the eels, which are not in the usual diet of the Ankave because of their close association with the end-of-mourning ceremony. But it is a woman who puts the final touch on the trap, placing the spring, a gesture that is accompanied by a magical formula (Lemonnier 2006a: 246–47).

According to the norm—and as our observations confirm—the deceased's cross-cousins—in other words his or her father's sister's children and his or her mother's brother's children—are the beneficiaries of these eels, called *senge'*. All cross-cousins who express the desire receive some. For the man[19] who carried the body, or in the past the woman who flayed the corpse, this piece of smoked eel is added to the *a'menge'* gift of money already mentioned. When only a few eels have been caught or when someone expresses their preference for money (which is increasingly frequent), the *senge'* eel can be replaced by *kinas*,[20] but the gift will then be called *a'menge'*. It is therefore the nature of the thing given that makes the gift associated with death a *senge'* or an *a'menge'*.

Yet these two gifts are not entirely equivalent or interchangeable, as is shown by the analysis of the transactions I observed or reconstructed over nine *songain* ceremonies. It seems that smoked eel is never given to the deceased's "real" cross-cousins—the father's sister's children or the mother's brother's—in other words, persons linked to the deceased by an attested genealogical tie. In practice, those receiving a *senge'* eel are what anthropologists call "classificatory" cross-cousins, simple members of a terminological class. In the case of the Ankave mortuary exchanges, the distinction between real and classificatory cousins corresponds to a real difference in status, since only the latter receive pieces of eel.

We could interpret this difference in the type of gifts received depending on genealogical proximity with the deceased in the following manner: "being too close to the deceased and sharing a large part of the substances of which his or her body is composed (blood, fat, bone), [real cross-cousins] cannot eat the meat associated with him or her without symbolically engaging in an act of auto-cannibalism" (Lemonnier 2006a: 266–67). This hypothesis is consistent with a concern we already noticed in other contexts (see chapter 5, for example), where the theme of auto-cannibalism is likely to explain the taboos on food given at special moments in the life cycle of children or other kinpersons. Whatever

19. As we saw, this is usually a cross-cousin of the deceased.
20. This is a small sum of money (2 or 3 kinas, or not quite €1 in 2017).

this reason may be, let me conclude these remarks on the nature of the mortuary gifts by recalling that the burial (or deposing on a platform) and, until the end of the 1970s, the women's tasks involved in dealing with the corpse—in other words, all those tasks entailing contact with the dead body—cannot be compensated by eel meat. Only money (or, in the past, shell-money) is regarded as an adequate compensation for performing such tasks. The term *a'menge'* thus designates all monetary mortuary gifts, whether for the specific work in contact with the corpse or as the equivalent of the *senge'* eel when paid to classificatory cross-cousins.

Let us now turn to the interpretation of these mortuary gifts. Given the position the beneficiaries occupy among the maternal kin in the system of life cycle exchanges, it is relatively easy to make sense of the pieces of eel or the money received by the matrilateral cross-cousins. This is the last gift owed to these kinsmen for the role they played in the life of the deceased. It is, as it were, the final gesture acknowledging the life-debt owed to the maternal kin. In other words, the children of the deceased's mother's brothers and sisters receive the *a'menge'* gift on behalf of their kinsmen who would have received them personally had they still been alive. In reality, in a society where death usually comes early, this case inevitably arises; it is even the rule. The gift made to the deceased's *patrilateral* cross-cousins has an entirely different explanation, as Pierre Lemonnier showed in his book on death and mourning in Ankave society (2006a: 263–64). The latter gift is not, of course, an attempt to pay off the inextinguishable life-debt to the maternals,[21] but merely a countergift, which closes the exchange and marks the end of the payments made to ensure a child's growth. This exchange, as will be remembered, is composed of the *simo'e* pig given to the maternal uncle, for which he must in turn make a countergift, a *memia'* pearlshell if the child is a boy and a live piglet if the child is a girl. If a person dies before the maternal kin have been able to make the countergift, the maternal uncle or his children honor the debt with a monetary payment, *a'menge'*, to the deceased's paternal clan, in this case the patrilateral cross-cousins, for here again, it is unusual that the parents, uncles, or aunts are still living. This is therefore not a mortuary gift

---

21. See Godelier ([1996] 1998) and Lemonnier (2006a: 330, 334). When it comes to relations with the maternal kin, this debt never expires, even at death, as shown by Lemonnier's analysis of the actions of the spirits of these kin (2006a: 324–39). I follow the analysis of mortuary gifts proposed by this author (2006a: 261–64) but in another context than his own, that of assigning responsibility for misfortune and managing the mourning process.

properly speaking—since it is *on the occasion* of the death and not *because of* it that the gift is made—but a countergift in response to the final gift for growing received by the deceased, which should have been made earlier and which can no longer be put off.

The gifts for growing and the prestations made at the time of a death concern all siblings but additional gifts, of which there are four, are made for the first-born and are therefore associated with those ritual actions that are performed only when a man becomes a father for the first time. One of these, the *djilu'wa* gift, is made when the pregnancy is announced; it is the hardest to interpret because people's commentaries do not all coincide. The three others, which are distributed after the birth and on the occasion of the public phase of the ritual, are the objects of more general agreement.

What do the Ankave say about the *djilu'wa* prestation? That this gift of pig meat or game is made by the parents of a man to those of his wife whose pregnancy has just been announced. I said earlier that some add that this is compensation for having threaded the cord into the new bark cape the young man will have to wear until the child is born. The *renei onanengo'* ("pleasing the maternal aunt") is composed of one of the marsupials the men caught after the birth and is given to the sisters of the child's mother. The *nie'wa su'wa* gift ("showing the child") is made to the maternal grandmother for having rubbed the *omore'* clay on their first child and having transmitted to her daughter the knowledge associated with this gesture as well as the accompanying formula. As we saw in the description of the ritual actions performed during the public phase of the *suwangain*, this gesture and these words are intended to ensure the child grows properly, as quickly as the *tse' arma'* whose singed fur has been mixed into this clay. Finally, the fourth gift given for a first child—the lime prepared by the couple during the pregnancy—is given to those maternal kin who ask. The reader will remember that when the *me'we* fire fails to catch people say it is because this lime has not been correctly distributed (see p. 89). The ceremony ends with the general distribution of the *ogidje* cloth[22] that was prepared during the pregnancy; this is cut up into strips to be used as headbands by all those participating in the secret male ritual in the forest, but it is also given to parents of a young boy in the village—around two or three years old—whose age, according to custom,

---

22. Insofar as this gift is distributed to everyone, the pieces of the *ogidje* cloth are not among the gifts made to certain well-defined members of the family of a man's first child.

no longer allows him to go around naked. His mother will assemble the strips to make her son's first red loincloth. This is not a gift made within the kinship network but a collective way of expressing a tie between a ceremony marking the accession of a couple to parenthood and a little boy who, like the young father who has just gone through the *suwangain* ritual and all the men wearing the *ogidje*, will pass through a number of ritual stages before reaching manhood.

CHAPTER 8

Male metamorphoses

Now that we have concluded our analysis of the male initiations, which is particular in that it takes the women's involvement as seriously as that of the men and considers that the ritual stages cannot be envisaged separately, we can better understand local conceptions of maleness. We have seen in detail that to become an adult male and father in Ankave society requires the organization of a series of rituals in which several categories of a boy's kin find themselves closely associated. These stages correspond to moments in his life when his relationship with these relatives undergoes a change. This is the domain of practices and the concrete operations that enable a young man, at the end of his three-stage initiation, to achieve a relational status befitting his new condition as father of his first child. To arrive at this point, the ritual had first to act on the undifferentiated relationship between the boy and his mother, and then on that with his eldest sister. Only when these two relationships have been transformed is a man capable of, on the one hand, engaging with his spouse in a relationship of parenthood and, on the other, becoming a maternal uncle, a particularly valued status in this society, which expresses itself most plainly when he causes his nephews to be reborn during their initiations.

The Ankave approach this process by which boys grow up and move along from infancy to adulthood not only in the area of ritual but in other areas of social life as well. In other words, to understand the need to construct a male person (in contrast to the spontaneous passage from girlhood to motherhood) and to grasp the underlying logic, the anthropologist must also gather information from outside the ritual domain, be familiar for instance with the exchanges that circulate between a person's kin groups over their lifetime and even after death (see chapter 7). The anthropologist must also observe daily interactions or listen to what people have to say on topics as varied as how to care for newborns, spells cast by disgruntled maternal kin, women's inherent weakness, or the self-control men must demonstrate.

Oral literature is another idiom containing information on maleness. The Ankave corpus of myths is particularly abundant compared to that of other Anga groups and includes several kinds of narratives that the men and women like to tell their children. First are the *rodja'a meke*, a term that could be translated as "important words," which the Ankave consider deal with things that really happened. These are the myths that concern the origin of humankind and the identity of their group, which anthropologists customarily call "origin myths." Among the accounts handed down from one generation to the next are also the *pisingain tebo'o*, stories that come from the deceased, which, although they do not have the explanatory power of origin myths, nevertheless belong to a set of stories that offer keys to the local cosmology[1] and to the mental world of this people. Finally, there is a host of little stories associated with chants and songs that do not have a general name but are known by the context in which they are sung (initiation songs, wake songs, end-of-mourning songs).

If the origin myths refer to a past that really existed for the Ankave, this does not mean that this past comes down to a series of events connected by unequivocal relations. Only three stories are systematically told together and in an unvarying order: the first relates the origin of fire; the second, the way the genital organs were pierced and therefore the appearance of sexuality and procreation;[2] and the third, the origin of the male initiations. It is the last that interests us here inasmuch as it describes a series of metamorphoses leading to the birth of boys in possession of all the finery of the Ankave initiations, as they appear when they have just completed the ordeals of the collective rituals. Although this is a rather long story, it is worth transcribing in its entirety so as

---

1.   By this, I mean the ideas about the natural environment (animals, plants, minerals, heavenly bodies, rivers, etc.) and its origin as well as about the relations humans entertain with it.

2.   Let us recall here that among the Kapau-Kamea, this myth is also the one that relates how people got their first bullroarer (Blackwood 1978: 158–59).

to show the particular way the process of the production of initiates is depicted in the idiom of oral literature. It was told to us by seven different persons, four women and three men, all fairly advanced in years. I have chosen to reproduce the longest version here, which was collected by Pierre Lemonnier on July 11, 1987, from Erwa Nguye Patche, who at the time was already an "old man" of over seventy and who has since died.

In the past everyone lived here, but one old woman had her house near the headwaters of a river. One day a man came to her house with his dog. As the animal had run ahead, he asked the old woman if she had seen it. She answered, "No, my son, it didn't come by here. Perhaps it took the big path? Tell me, I don't have any children. How am I going to pick my breadfruits (*kwi'*)?" So the man climbed the tree. When he came down, the old woman struck him in the ribs with her stone adze. The man died and she ate him. She had tricked him.

Some time later, the man's younger brother went to look for his older brother and his dog. He asked the old woman if she had seen a man pass by. "No, my son, I haven't seen anyone take this path. Perhaps he followed the big path?" Then she added: "How am I going to pick my breadfruit?" He climbed the tree; she killed him like his elder brother and ate him as well. The third brother arrived in turn. As he was about to climb the tree, he noticed some blood and traces of dirt on the trunk. It was the dirt the two brothers had on their feet when they climbed up to pick the fruit. He continued to climb and said to the old woman: "Stand away from the tree so the fruit I am going to throw down doesn't land on your head." She stepped back a few paces and the man threw a breadfruit right into her eye and killed her.

He quickly climbed back down and noticed that the old woman had hidden a stone adze in the waistband of her skirt and that it was stained with blood. So he went into her house and saw a dry bamboo suspended from the roof. He caught hold of it and withdrew the plug of leaves. It contained human bones. Having put the plug back in, he took it away, and took the old woman's adze and cut her body into pieces to be buried. He then dug a hole, gathered the pieces, and covered them up with dirt and grass.

Then he emptied the bamboo full of his brothers' bones into a pool and went home. Their bones were in the water. Several years later, he returned to the spot where he had buried the pieces of the old woman and then went to the pool. He saw some tadpoles in the water, but nothing had grown on the woman's grave. He went home and stayed for several seasons before returning to check the pool. The tadpoles had grown and had become frogs with four legs. When he came back again, he saw human arms and legs. A small *e'ire'* cordyline had begun to grow on the woman's grave. Once again he went home. When he returned to the forest, he saw that some boys were playing with *ika'a sipiare'* fruits (a Ficus). Then he went to the grave and distinctly saw several plants with red-veined leaves: two kinds of cordyline (*e'ire'* and *yauya'we'*), *ndaya'a* plants (*Acalyphy grandis*, a Euphorbia) and *tewiba* (*Plectranthus*, a Lamiale). He also saw some *wawi ore'* ginger and some *ime'* croton alongside the grave.

Then the man went to pick some yellow orchid stems and some reeds used to make the pulpul and gave them to the women to prepare. They made ornaments to be worn across the chest, small netbags, pulpul, and when everything was ready, the man went to the pool. There he saw many boys, because each bone had given birth to one. They were all singing. Then the man went to cut some wood to make bows, after having secretly counted the boys while they were sitting around warming themselves in the sun, to see how many pieces of wood he needed. Then he began to make bows in a house set to one side, all the while keeping an eye on the boys and eating what the women gave him. He placed the bows above the fire and went to find the bowstrings. Each time he tried to string a bow it would break. He said to himself that he had to wait until the wood dried some more.

His wife then approached the house where her husband was living and saw the broken bows left there. She thought he had gone about it wrong. She turned the bow around, strung it, and it worked perfectly. She strung all the other bows one after the other. Her husband then arrived and told his wife that he had not managed to keep the bows from breaking. She explained that they had to be turned around first.[3] He took her advice and drew the bow. Then she told him to shoot it: "You hadn't thought to turn it the right way around? See, that way the bow doesn't break." When all the bows were ready and laid above the fire, the man went to get the netbags, the pulpul, and the chest ornaments, and told the women to go dig tubers for

---

3.   The myth does not go into detail about this "evidence," but the woman places the string—in this case a long strip of bamboo—inside the curve of the bow, and not on the outside as the man was doing.

the preparation of a big meal. The man took some to cook in the forest and set out, while the women went to look for something to eat. The following morning, the man took the pulpul and the ornaments and told the women to cook all the food they had gathered. They wondered why so much was needed. The man intended to give the boys the bark capes that cover the buttocks (*ijiare'*).

When he came to the pool, he saw that one of them had been struck in the eye and the others had hidden in the water. He asked the wounded boy to come closer, then he dressed him in the pulpul and the cape and adorned him with the chest ornaments. Then he told him: "I am your father. Show yourself to your companions so they can see your new ornaments." The boy called the others, who all approached, admired their companion, and asked to be adorned like him. The man dressed them in ornaments and pierced their nose. Then he gave each one an additional cape to hang on their netbag, a bow, some bird feathers, and some ginger. When they were all adorned, the man led them to the village.

While he was coming down from the forest with the boys, his wife handed out *e'ire'* cordylines to the women, while the men took those called *oremere'*. The man also gave the boys some plants from the latter variety. All the cordylines had grown on the grave of the old man-eating woman.[4] The women who had received plants sat down out of sight. The boys arrived holding their cordylines in the air and whistling. The women waved theirs in the same way. When the men got close to the women, the latter began a song the men did not know. It came from the women. Now they sing it at the same time as the women, before the nose-piercing ceremony. This happened near Menyamya. At that time there was only one language [Anga].

Before proceeding with the analysis of the myth concerning the origin of the male initiations, let us note that all the other versions we collected feature five brothers, and not three as in the present case, but otherwise the scenario is identical. None mentions either the plants that, in the present myth, grow on the old woman's grave and are waved by the men and women when the boys come down from the forest following the rituals. Among the shorter versions, some do not contain the passage where the hero's wife teaches him the right way to string the bows he has made so that he does not go on breaking them

4.   Like the ginger the boys receive at the same time as their ornaments.

one by one, nor do they mention the songs that accompany the initiates' return, which the women are again said to know. Others do not mention a wounded boy among those playing with the fruits of the *sipiare'* Ficus tree. Finally, three of the four women who told me versions of this myth did not mention that the man pierced the boys' noses before dressing them and decorating them with the ornaments characteristic of the first-stage initiates.

Beyond these variations—including the logical problems they raise, such as the origin of the red *oremere'* cordylines that another myth associates with the death of the man-with-no-name—all the accounts furnish material that allows us to discuss the questions of interest to me here: How are the male initiations staged in Ankave oral literature? How is boys' physical growth represented in the narratives?

Let us begin with the second question. In the myth transcribed here, as in the various other extant versions, the boys result from a series of metamorphoses in which the bones of murdered adult men—two or four depending on the version—slowly change, in the water of a pool, into tadpoles, then frogs, then small boys.[5] The youngest brother found the bones of these siblings when he had gone in search of his older brothers; they were the remains of an old woman's cannibal feast,[6] which she had kept in a big bamboo tube. Thanks to the youngest brother's actions, the bones are reborn as boys after having gone through the two developmental stages of an animal with which the Ankave are familiar: the frog. Furthermore, in the symbolic world of the Ankave, the frog is associated with female figures, as shown in the story that Onorwae, a woman of around fifty at the time—one of those delightful "informants" who has since disappeared and to whom this book is dedicated—told me on April 24, 1993:

---

5. This story is not proper to the Ankave. In fact, all specialists of Angans mention a version, which varies more or less from others. Among the Kamea, for example, a man has been killed, not by an old woman but by his two wives—who are sisters—because he tricked them by adding feces to the bark where he placed the marsupial he hunted to be cooked. They prepared ornaments for the boys that had changed from tadpoles (themselves having come from the bones), but upon their return to the pool they saw that the boys had "performed initiation upon themselves, and that each now sported a hole in his nasal septum" (Bamford 2007: 37). The men then entered a tree. The women finally found them, cut the trunk, and gave group names to all the men who came out as well as allocating them a piece of land. "This is how human beings came to be in the world" (2007: 38).

6. This is not the case in the Kamea version, briefly related in the preceding note.

An old woman went to weed her bean garden. A white cockatoo came and perched on a piece of wood that was holding up the bean plants. The old woman took a piece of *yore'* setaria, threw it, and killed the bird. Another cockatoo flew up shortly after and she killed it too. Then a parrot (*inge'paa*) flew up and landed on the beanpole. She killed it as well. Later, another cockatoo flew up, and she killed it using a setaria. When she had killed them all, she burned the birds' feathers and then went to cut some bamboo. She cut up the birds and filled a bamboo of the *sere' pia* variety with the pieces and some leafy vegetables. When she had finished cooking them, she set the bamboo filled with the birds on a platform inside her house. Then she went to pick some leaves of *ara' sijiwi'*, *kwiape*, and *teperepi*, and collect some *i'tugwe* and *onu'wa* bark. It all smelled wonderful. Meanwhile, five young men had been shooting arrows at the old woman's house. The first four missed, but the arrow shot by the fifth hit the bamboo full of birds dead center. The first four young men all found their arrow, but the fifth couldn't find his. He therefore decided to go into the old woman's house and there saw that his arrow was stuck in the bamboo tube. He pulled it out and smelled the aroma of the game on the arrowhead. The fifth man went to tell his brothers, who sniffed the arrow. They emptied the tube and ate the flesh of all the birds except for the three heads, which they set to one side. They put them back in the tube with their own excrement, placing the three heads on top. When the old woman had finished gathering the fragrant leaves, she returned home, took the bamboo, and saw it contained excrement. So she took a digging stick—*roju'wa* (name of the stick) *tuwi'we'* (name of the tree)—and followed the footprints of the five young men. Then she heard five birds (which were the young men who had been changed) crying "*atsi!* [grandmother], here we are, here we are!" They were perched on the branch of an *ayo'o* palm. She followed their footprints and said: "How am I going to climb the tree where you are?" So they each threw down a vine (*unanengwa*), but the vines of the first four didn't reach the ground. The fifth young man, the one whose arrow had hit the bamboo tube, threw down a vine that touched the ground. They continued to call out to the old woman to climb up the vine and join them. And so the old woman began climbing up the tree. The young men had stuck rattan thorns in the ground all around the tree. The old woman fell down because the fifth young man cut the vine. She broke apart: her torso became a *tse' rwatse'* echidna (this animal's nose is the digging stick she had put in her mouth in order to climb); her buttocks turned into a *menenge' menepuwe'* frog. As for her fingers, the thumb became the insect *pisingain ubrere* and the fingers became *pugwe'* insects. These insects are eaten, including by adults in the case of the second. Her big toe became a *pisigain suwewa*, also edible, and the four other toes also became *pugwe'*. The young men turned into *tsitsa* birds.

This narrative describes several metamorphoses of humans into animals. I will return later to the men changed into birds, but I would like first to look more closely at the multiple changes undergone by the body of the old woman who fell from the vine that the last of the five brothers had thrown down from the tree where they were hiding. They had taken care to scatter rattan thorns on the ground at the foot of the tree. The dismembered body of the old woman produced several animals: an echidna, various insects, and a frog. The frog came from a very particular part of her body, her behind, whose local lexical usage suggests it included her genitals. The metaphor that associates frogs and women is thereby charged with a gendered, if not actually sexual, meaning that can be found on other levels as well. For instance, if a man spots a frog nearby, as Pierre did during one of our stays, he will immediately be told that he must expect a woman soon to make a pass at him. The trapping of eels, which Ankave mythology says appeared following the transformation of a man, or his penis depending on the version, involves the trapper's wife collecting frogs the night before the traps are placed in the water. It will be remembered that the live frog attached to the spring of the trap serves as bait for the eels, whose association with men and the male member is entirely explicit (Bonnemère 1996a: 318–21). Ankave symbolism does not associate frogs with femaleness and women in general but with a particular category of women, those with an explicit capacity and desire to seduce and attract men or animals with whom the latter are clearly associated. These are all reasons to think that the present representations account for the prohibition on consuming frogs that young men are enjoined to obey, or more precisely, those who do not yet have children.

What can we say about this metamorphosis of (male) human bones into boys related in the first myth reported here and which appears as a growth process in two intermediary stages, materialized by the appearance of the tadpoles and then the frogs? First of all, the story no doubt stages a rebirth entailing a prior killing. This killing takes the form of a murder committed by an old woman on the person of young, married men, followed by the consumption of their flesh. Then there is the fact that their rebirth takes place in an aquatic medium that enables the slow and gradual transformation of the young men's bones into soft shapeless matter from which the legs of a frog emerge, which will later turn into human arms and legs. In view of the strong association between frogs and female sexual organs, can we venture to suggest that the intermediate stage in boys' growth is conceptualized as female and that the development of a boy implies passing through such a stage?[7] This is no doubt not an exaggeration, based equally on what the Ankave say when comparing the way the little boys look in their shapeless loincloth with the women, whose skirts do not have the characteristic triangular shape of the male pulpul. In this case, masculinity would be conceived as an ultimate stage of development of which a feminine stage would be a prerequisite. Likewise, this female stage in the development of the male person could be seen as the metaphorical equivalent of pregnancy, the moment when the body of the boy is contained in that of a woman. This is difficult to assert insofar as the Ankave do not make an explicit connection between specific elements of the myth and specific ritual actions, but the impossibility of offering any certainty should not prevent us suggesting hypotheses. Such a hypothesis would concord with the representations of male maturation and the ritual practices during which this occurs, since we find metaphors in which women's procreative capacities are underscored and enlisted.

Another series of metaphors can be detected in the vocabulary used for certain pieces of specifically male clothing. After a boy has undergone the ordeals of the first two initiation stages, which are collective, he is given a bark cape called *ijiare'*, which hangs by a string from the back of his neck and is attached at the waist with a belt of braided orchid stems. The term *ijiare'* also designates the not-yet-unfolded wings of the butterfly; we could therefore posit that the boy's transformation into a man is like that of the chrysalis into a butterfly. After he has undergone the first two stages of his initiation, he is like a young butterfly barely out of its chrysalis, whose wings have just begun to unfold. In giving the same name to the cape that covers the men's buttocks and the wings of the new butterfly, the Ankave may be trying to express the idea that the young initiate is now in a new physical state, free of the—maternal—envelop that had until

---

7.   Note in passing that we could not say the same thing of the Kamea myth, as Sandra Bamford does not mention frogs, only tadpoles—she even uses the expression "tadpole-men" (2007: 37). And there is no ambiguity when she reasserts a hundred pages later: "bones become tadpoles, which become human beings" (2007: 137).

then served as a symbolic container.[8] His infancy spent in a largely female world
had not yet allowed him to break this bond with his mother, which the Ankave
see as being symbiotic. By calling on the image of an insect breaking out of
its chrysalis, the Ankave are expressing the idea of a *radical transformation*, for
nothing in the butterfly stage recalls the insect's earlier encased state.[9]

As we saw at length, it is the male initiation rituals that act on the fusional
character of the mother-son relationship and transform it. More generally, these
rituals effect a series of transformations bearing on the content of the relations
the young boys entertain with certain categories of female kin, in this case, as
we have seen, their mothers and their older sisters. The oral literature expresses
the boys' physical development and maturation as a series of metamorphoses in
which nonhuman figures play a key role.

In all events, these metaphors make it possible to account for the complete
transformation of the boys' bodies during the initiations and their new physical
state. In this way, ritual practices and oral literature, each in their own idiom,
help explain what is at stake in this key moment in the life of male children:
it involves at once a relational transformation, operated and staged during the
initiations and associated with a transformation of their mental state through
learning to control their emotions in the face of unexpected and stressful events,
and a physical change evidenced in the altered silhouette of the boys dressed
in their new clothing and ornaments. The first requires the presence of persons
involved in the relationship to be transformed, for we know that, in the minds
of the Ankave, the nature of a relationship cannot change without the participation of both terms. The second calls upon the animal kingdom for the means
to express the extent of the modifications in the boys' body: from tadpole to
frog to grown man, from chrysalis to butterfly, more than mere growth is involved. We are talking about a metamorphosis: adult men are not simply boys
that have grown; the physical and psychological ordeals they have endured have
produced a radical transformation; they have become other. What is expressed
here is that the difference between an uninitiated boy and an adult man is of the

---

8. Cf. Bamford's already mentioned extended use of the word "containment" to
    describe the mother-son relationship before initiation.

9. For the Baruya, it is the tadpole's transformation into a frog that symbolizes the
    boys' growth; the image is just as radical as the one chosen by the Ankave. And
    the cape that falls down over the boys' buttocks is called "the tadpole's tail" (Pierre
    Lemonnier, pers. comm.). In both cases, the transformation—a metamorphosis—is
    complete.

same magnitude as that between a chrysalis and a butterfly.[10] Drawing a parallel between the boys' development and animal growth characterized by a radical morphological transformation is the means the Ankave have found to satisfactorily express the major effects they ascribe to the male initiation rituals. In using animal metaphors to express a change in the novice's body and in directly involving in the ritual those women with whom the novice entertains a relation whose nature must be transformed, the Ankave are clearly expressing the idea that the maturation of male children occurs on several levels: a relational level, which is played out in ritual, and a bodily level, accounted for in the oral literature through references to the nonhuman world and expressed in the ornaments worn by the initiates returning from the rituals and their various ordeals.

OF BIRDS AND MEN

In order to better grasp the representations of masculinity and the construction of male personhood, we need to stay with the world of the forest and its inhabitants. Among the occupants of this forest world omnipresent for the Ankave in the Suowi Valley, birds have pride of place: the feathers of some species are worn by the men as ornaments during rituals; their blood is "transfused" to males[11] suffering from anemia; the consumption of their flesh is subject to numerous taboos; their songs and calls are the object of interpretations that, in a ritual context, govern the participants' behavior, and their names are invoked in certain magical healing ceremonies; lastly, they play a role in several myths. Analysis of these different ethnographic data shows that the relationship humans,

---

10. In a chapter in the catalogue of the first anthropological exhibition at the Musée du quai Branly, Anne-Christine Taylor and Eduardo Viveiros de Castro contrast the Western and the Amazonian representations of metamorphosis: "Our cultural imaginary as illustrated by the writings of Ovid or Kafka conceives metamorphosis as the involuntary transformation of an individual's bodily sheathe whose core—the soul, the consciousness—nevertheless remains human. . . . Metamorphosis as conceived by the Indians refers to a reverse process: it is the interiority that is transformed in the first place, which then dictates a bodily change expressed more or less literally. . . . It is more a matter of undergoing a modulation of the subjectivity" (2006: 192). Further reflection would be needed to reach a more detailed understanding of how the Ankave envisage the actual process of metamorphosis.
11. Women and girls cannot benefit from such a "transfusion" of bird blood, nor can they eat their flesh (see pp. 49, 168).

and especially men, entertain with birds is a very close one. There is therefore reason to take a closer look at the elements indicative of this relationship and to establish its nature.

Among the stories the Ankave tell, the one Pierre and I usually call the "myth of the man-with-no-name" (see pp. 136–37) is especially rich, recounting as it does the origin of most of the plants and other natural elements that feature prominently in the initiation rituals. But that is not all: one April day in 1998, in Aix-en-Provence,[12] our Ankave friend Simon was helping me translate the dialogues recorded in the films Pierre had made four years earlier, when he told me a piece of the story I had never heard of before. Here are his words:

> When the man-with-no-name was killed, his spirit turned into birds. They tried to drink this blood: first the *ajine* bird tried to drink, and then the *pitongwen* bird drank some. That is why they are red. That is a story you must not repeat to Ankave women: The *paa* bird did not drink the blood, but some splashed onto his feathers and so he also became red. The *ika'a rwa'ne* tree[13] also came from the spilled blood of the man-with-no-name. The birds drink the juice of its fruits. The *ajine* bird is the first to have drunk this juice, when the sun was setting.

What else do we know about birds? In the main, that close attention is paid to their vocal manifestations during the initiations, and especially when the novices are eating. If the call of a bird of good omen is heard, such as one of the three featured in the myth, during a meal in the forest, the news is good: the bird has used this means of expressing its concern for the boys, it has indicated to the men present that the boys have positive personalities. The qualities of the bird that emitted a signal are transmitted to the young men undergoing the initiation ordeals. Inversely, it is said that when a bird of ill omen is heard singing on the same occasion, its failings will be transferred to the boys if they do not immediately spit out the food they are chewing. The *topa* bird, for instance, is the incarnation of a food thief: any novice hearing its call but failing immediately to spit out what he is eating would be in danger of becoming a thief, too.

---

12. Like other Angans—in particular our Baruya friend Koumain—Simon asked to "make the acquaintance of your family in France." At the close of a short "humanitarian" visit in March 1998, Pierre came back to France with Simon and the three of us left three months later for Papua New Guinea, where we stayed for several weeks doing our jobs as anthropologists.

13. See p. 49n4.

In some sense, the bird recognizes those like him and so sings out. And it is the duty of human beings to change the course of events by blocking the action of the bird that emits a message of ill omen.

The Ankave thus regard birds as beings capable of communication, which follow the course of human affairs and sometimes meddle in them. The idea that birds are capable of intervening in the lives of humans governs certain taboos that pregnant women, and even all women of childbearing age, are required to respect. As we saw (see p. 116), the flesh of the *newimbere'* bird of paradise is not eaten by women of the Ngudze clan for fear that any children they might have would become bald as adults. Likewise, we know that the women of the Idzadze clan do not eat duck so that their children will not be born with webbed feet—certainly less frequent than baldness, but something that worries the Ankave since such a person would have something of the cannibalistic *ombo'* (Lemonnier 2006a). Sometimes it is enough that a woman out walking in the forest disturbs a bird; it will show its displeasure by causing her future children to become bald later in life.

Like frogs, marsupials, pigs, dogs, and birds have a particular aptitude for communication. Yet only birds are able to talk to humans and have their actions interpreted by them, whereas the intelligible world of the other animals mentioned above is usually confined to their own species.[14] No doubt the origin of the birds' special aptitude to enter into relations with humans, and sometimes to harm them, is to be sought in the fact that they came from the spirit of the man-with-no-name, the primordial being whose blood gave rise to most of the components handled in the male rituals and which certain birds drank, hence their red feathers. These birds, *pitongwen'* and *ajine*, and the men who have undergone the rituals share the fact of having ingested the blood of the man-with-no-name: the birds drank directly from the murdered man's blood and today drink the juice of the fruits of the *ika'a rwa'ne* tree that grew on the spot where this blood spilled out;[15] the initiates secretly consume the juice of the *perengen* red pandanus, a tree that also originally grew from the blood of the primordial man, which literally contains this blood, owing to its vegetative

---

14. This does not stop hunters trying to influence their behavior by tricking and coaxing them to make them easier to catch (Lemonnier 2006b).

15. The eagle did not drink the blood of the man-with-no-name but it scattered his remains after tearing apart his body with its talons. Note that the ritual expert holds an eagle feather when officiating in the initiations.

mode of reproduction. The red feathers of the two birds are among those used to decorate the initiates' head.

No doubt it is this shared ingestion of the original being's life-giving substance that makes it possible to "transfuse" the blood of the birds into the body of men who need it. In chapter 3 (pp. 48–49), we saw that the parents of a man whose wife is expecting his first child and who therefore strictly abstains from red pandanus sauce, which normally helps ensure his health, tell him that, as long as he is discreet about it, he can still drink the blood of the two red birds, *agidji'we* and *pitongwen*, after having cooked them lightly so as to preserve the blood in their flesh. And if a child or an adult does not have enough blood, which can be seen from their white fingernails, a shaman will cut up a bird that has been caught by a close relative, collect the blood on a leaf, dip his finger into it, blow over it, and apply it to the person's body. The bird's blood thus mixes with that of the ailing person and becomes human blood. It is because of this practice and the discourse surrounding it that it seems legitimate to use the term "perfusion" in accounting for it. In all events, the compatibility between the blood of the birds in question and men's blood is total, which is not the case for the other animals.

I also need to say that the proximity between birds and humans sometimes extends to identification and entails the possibility for men—but not women—to become birds. Several myths thus tell the story of young men who, in an attempt to escape their enemies, change into birds and take refuge in the branches of a tree, out of their assailants' reach. Sometimes this proximity concerns personality traits, as shown in several short narratives featuring birds that adopt behaviors that could be easily transposed to humans: in one case, a bird of paradise steals a taro that a cockatoo has just cooked in the ashes, because of which he will henceforth and ever after have a disagreeable cry. In frustration, the cockatoo rubs his feathers with the ashes, giving them their characteristic color. Another story depicts the *newimbere'* bird of paradise as a secretive animal that encourages *noye'* (*Paradisaea rudolphi*, the Blue Bird of Paradise) to coat his tail feathers with soil, omitting to tell him that he himself had dipped his own in red pandanus sauce. When they show each other their plumage, the feathers of *newimbere'* appear bright red and, in local opinion, much prettier than that of *noye'*, which the soil has dyed blue, a color the Ankave appreciate much less and which they do not use in their feather ornaments and never in the necklaces of tiny plastic beads that some wear today. Each of the birds then goes home: to the headwaters of the rivers and thus to the high forest for *noye'* and to the lower altitudes, where the red pandanus grows, for *newimbere'*. A third story describes the same at once facetious and cruel attitude of a stubby bird with a short tail (*yama*) that tells another bird (*tenge'*) that he has put his tail into the fire. *Tenge'*, who is too gullible, does likewise, thus mutilating his feathers and shortening them forever. Furious, he strikes *yama* on the top of the head, which ever since has no feathers there.

With perhaps the exception of the cassowary—which the Ankave also classify as a bird (Bonnemère 2006) and which will be discussed shortly—no other animal stars in a myth. And above all, when animals are mentioned, they act like their modern-day conspecifics and not, as here, in the way ill-intentioned humans might behave. This peculiarity would tend to confirm the special place of birds in the life of human beings, and particularly of men: here they intervene, negatively, on the offspring of the adults who have eaten their flesh or disturbed them in their habitat, or prompt novices and their mothers to react in a fitting manner if the bird that has manifested itself is regarded as a bad omen.

When the men come down from the forest after having completed the initiation ordeals, they appear magnificently adorned with plumes of the most beautiful birds found in the area. From time to time they also discreetly drink the juice of the fruits of the *ika'a rwa'ne* tree, just as certain birds do (see p. 49n4). It is hard to say whether or not, in adorning themselves in this way and consuming the same sweet juice as the birds whose colors they adopt, they may be expressing a desire to identify with them. No doubt, in any case, these male individuals entertain a relationship with these birds whose only equivalent in the female world is the relation between women and the cassowary.

The next chapter, devoted to the female life cycle, will give us the opportunity to discuss the symbolic contiguity the Ankave establish between women and this large, flightless bird. This will not lead us too far from our main subject of inquiry, since the relationship governs a certain number of practices also having to do with the women's sons and husbands, which in turn will allow us to pursue our exploration of the relational dimension the Ankave ascribe to most of their actions, including those that, from our Western point of view, are the most individual.

CHAPTER 9

Women's lives: A path unmarked by rituals? Part I
Daughters, nieces, sisters, "fiancées"

The earlier chapters talked so much about men's life-paths when examining the various rituals that mark the stages between childhood and adulthood that one might rightly assume that in comparison women's life-paths are less than spectacular. The present chapter and chapter 11 will attempt to remedy this altogether relative insufficiency, as we see female figures turn up at every stage of the male life cycle: As mothers and sisters, they are closely involved in the growth of their sons and brothers; as future mothers, they are required to observe a number of partially parallel behaviors that are entirely complementary to those demanded of their husbands. This means that focusing on the representations of men's accession to adult status and fatherhood in no way signifies the women have been forgotten, owing to the Ankave's view of personhood, which foregrounds the relationships that bind each person to others, the very conception that is staged through the rituals, is constantly transformed and reshaped. And yet it is useful to consider the way women's lives unfold in themselves, which will enable us to better understand it in contrast to the specificity of the male life cycle.

A woman's life plays out in the absence of large-scale, organized ceremonies: no ritual is performed when a girl menstruates for the first time and, as we will soon see, when she moves in with her husband, the strictly codified gestures that accompany her first night in the home of her parents-in-law are performed within the close circle of the immediate family (the woman, her husband, and their respective parents), and concern her no more or no less than her husband. There is nothing in common here with the emphasis on the need for boys to go through ritual ordeals on several occasions in order to become full-fledged men. Nevertheless, it has been amply shown that a woman must respect taboos and specific behaviors on various occasions, which concern not so much her personally as other persons with whom she has close ties. As a consequence, what strikes the anthropologist in these situations is the contrast between the woman's position with regard to a brother, a sister, a son, or a daughter, whom she accompanies at important times in their life, and the position of the men, who in most cases merely undergo the action of someone else and only rarely act for someone other than themselves. Women, on the other hand, are only slightly influenced by the actions of someone else. We must now attempt to understand why this is.

The birth of a girl does not occasion practices significantly different from those that accompany the arrival of a boy. Nothing is said about why it is a female and not a male fetus that develops in the womb, unlike other societies, which imagine that the paternal and maternal substances are in a struggle for dominance and see in the child's sex the sign that one or the other is the more powerful (A.-C. Taylor 2008: 97–98). For the Ankave, the only influence a fetus might undergo can be read on its skin: if it is light skinned, it will be said that the parents made love in the daytime, and if its skin is dark, that their lovemaking took place at night. And the determination of its sex obeys laws that have nothing to do with the intervention of the parents via the substances each produces at the time of conception and about which nothing is known.

Yet as soon as the child is born, certain gestures that accompany its development will differ depending on its sex, for the new human being has to be integrated into a world where the activities of the men and those of the women, whether ordinary or extraordinary, are largely distinct and where the life-path of each person follows a very different course depending on their sex; and this is true from the very moment of birth. First of all, the placenta and umbilical cord are placed in the hollow branch of a tree whose variety depends on whether the baby is a girl or a boy: in the first instance, it is an *ika'a suje'* (*Castanopsis acuminatissima*), which bears fruit that is consumed occasionally after having been cooked in bamboo tubes together with leafy vegetables; in the second, it is an *ika'a robe'* (*Lithocarpus celebicus*), a tall tree whose fruit resembles a big acorn and which is the systematic object of jokes among the Ankave because of its cap, which looks like the glans of a penis. In the same vein, when a mother eats some palmgrass (*Setaria palmifolia*), or *yore'*, after having abstained from them throughout her pregnancy, she deposits the skin at the foot of a different variety of the same plant depending on whether she has borne a boy or a girl. In the first case, it will be an *a'ki' kura'te'* or *a'ki' ore'*, the leaves of which are used to thatch the shelter of the initiates of the first two stages; in the second, it will be an *a'ki' pungwen*, whose leaves are used exclusively for the roof of the temporary hut of a mother and her newborn child (see p. 69). The difference refers directly to an event that will deeply mark the life of each one, according to whether it is a boy or a girl: initiation and childbirth.

On the other hand, the initial care and the magical gestures performed on the body of the infant are identical for all children. As I have said, in their first days of life, mothers smear their baby's body with a mixture of orangish-yellow clay and ashes mixed with the singed fur of one of the marsupials caught by the men immediately after the birth (see pp. 77–78). Later, when the baby is dunked in the Suowi River for the first time, its mother will be holding different objects depending on the child's sex: a *wiamongen* nut (*Mucuna albertisii*)[1] if it is a boy, and a banana stalk and a *kama'a* cowry if it is a girl. The aim is to ensure that, in the future, each will carry out correctly the tasks and duties incumbent on their sex. The banana stalk refers to gardening activities, and the *wiamongen* nut to hunting magic, in which it is commonly used. The *kama'a* cowry may refer to marriage, by way of the cowry shell-money that was used not so long ago in the bridewealth paid by the husband's family. Then the hair from the first haircut and the first baby tooth lost are placed at the base of a green cordyline for children of both sexes, and the leftovers from their first solid meal are placed on the threshold of a house full of people, for it is said that reference must be made to the large population dreamed of for one's own group so as to encourage the fertility of the generations to come and thus ensure the group's survival. This time as well there is no differentiation according to the child's sex.

Then comes a long period during which no magical intervention is performed on the children designed either to install them in roles specifically associated with their gender or to strengthen them and make them grow in good health. That being said, their respective activities are already clear, since small girls go to the garden with their mother and help them by carrying home a few

---

1.   This is the magic nut, par excellence. Men use it in particular in hunting magic; it is a component of the magic bundle the ritual expert always carries for initiations.

leafy vegetables in their little netbags, while the small boys spend most of their time playing or shooting <u>pitpit</u> arrows with their miniature bows. Puberty will separate the life-paths of boys and girls more radically: as we know, boys undergo collective initiation rituals lasting several weeks, while there is nothing equivalent or even similar for girls. A girl is reserved for marriage at a very young age by the family of a man who is usually ten or so years older.[2] The Ankave do not have a wedding ceremony as such, simply the marriage proposal (*igijinge'*), which is formally made by the young man's parents after having consulted their son.

THE MARRIAGE REQUEST

In the past, the family would come empty handed, "to talk, that's all," and also "to avoid shame in the event the girl's family refuses." Today, the formal aspects of this request increasingly resemble the features of the visits that, in the event of an agreement, will be paid regularly and in which gifts in kind (*tuage*) are presented to the family of the future bride. The girl is not consulted and can only guess at the fate promised her, for to tell her the identity of her future husband would make her feel ashamed when they chanced to meet. Ideally, she should learn his identity only once she reaches puberty but this is hardly ever the case for, children being very fond of meat, it is extremely hard to distribute the meat offered on behalf of the little girl while excluding her without telling her why. In effect, it is forbidden for a girl to eat the *tuage* meat given for her; therefore, when she soon understands she has been reserved for marriage, all she has to do is watch to know which family has made the request.

To give an idea of the formal character of the *igijinge'* marriage request, I will describe that made for Sari beri, at which I was present on January 20, 1988.

At around 10:15 a.m., Tumnuki, the mother of Philip, left the village of Ajakupna'wa for Olale, home of the parents of little five-year-old Sari beri, the only daughter of Iwadze Dzadze (Josef) and Idzi wiei. Widowed a month earlier, Tumnuki wiei was accompanied by her younger sister, Obe wiei, and their respective daughters, Sani, twelve years old, and Opi beri, six. The two women were heavily loaded: Tumnuki wiei was carrying her last-born in a big netbag, and Obe wiei had on her back a big piece of pig meat,

---

2.   Note that the practice still exists although it is less systematic than in the past.

which she had bought the previous day for 30 kinas, when Sa'andziwo's sow had been put up for sale.

An hour and a half later (as often happens with Ankave women, we dawdled along the way!), we came to Olale, and everyone passed through the cordyline and croton enclosure surrounding Josef's house. Those present were numerous, for a plentiful meal of tubers accompanied by red pandanus sauce was being prepared, and we all sat down in silence near the girl's parents. At noon, the pig meat was still on Obe wiei's back in the netbag, concealed under her bark cape.

Around 2 p.m., the girl's mother and the two sisters from Ajakupna'wa were deep in discussion, but the piece of meat was still invisible. They were just coming to the subject of the visit, but Idzi wiei murmured that her daughter was too young to be "betrothed" to Philip (who was fourteen or fifteen). The discussion then started up among the men, in this event, between Josef and John, a distant relative of Philip but a neighbor of Tumnuku wiei in Ajakuna'wa, who had come for the meal. Josef pointed out that the people of Ikundi were still fighting with those of Olale not so long ago.

OBE WIEI. "The conflicts are over now."

JOSEF. "Before he died, my father told me we must help and defend our affines."

He went on to say that if little girls were promised to boys older than they, the boys tended in the end to choose more mature women, even before the betrothed had reached the required age.

TUMNUKU WIEI. "Perhaps you would rather have Ngudze Erauye's son, who is better with words than my own son?"

JOSEF. "We have many affines in Ikundi, but they are always trying to pick a fight with us. Erauye wia, for example, he's my affine; well, I'm still waiting for him to give my wife a *potiye* pig."[3] [Erauye wia is the maternal uncle of Idzi wiei, Josef's wife.]

TUMNUKU WIEI. "Omadze wo [from Olale] recently beat his wife, Ikundi akwa'ei [from Ikundi]. Are our children going to act like that?"

At 2:30 p.m., people seemed to relax a bit. But Obe wiei suddenly began shouting at the men who had come from Olale: "Why are you throwing up obstacles like that?" Then, turning to his eldest sister: "Why did we come here anyway? Come on, let's leave!"

---

3.   See p. 145.

TUMNUKU WIEI. "If Philip's father weren't dead, he'd be here with us. I had to come all alone to pay a visit. Unfortunately my son doesn't go to the forest; he spends his time playing cards. I scold him but he doesn't listen to me. I tell him to go gather areca nuts, pandanus fruit, but in vain."

JOSEF. "Listen! Since my daughter is little, don't feel obliged to bring *tuage* often. This will do [in the meantime, the meat had been discreetly unveiled.] But why didn't Nguye padzerwa [young Philip's paternal uncle] come with you? If he had come, we would have taken you seriously and accepted the meat right away. You women, you don't know how to ask or to speak right. We will follow you home."

Josef added that the brother of Erwaje Omadze (from Olale) had already asked for his daughter and brought vegetal salt. "He left it at our house in our absence. Only children were there. Now we are going to give it back."

TUMNUKU WIEI. "The salt they brought, you should tell them to come for it."

Throughout the discussion, Sari beri, the little girl in question, was present.

TUMNUKU WIEI. "So this pig, I'm supposed to take it back home?"

JOSEF. "No, you'll leave it here."

JOHN. "We're going to take this kid [Philip] in hand, we who are his maternal kin."

JOSEF. "Philip sometimes forgets I'm his *nengwo* and doesn't always behave as he should toward me. That is why I made a fuss a while ago."

TUMNUKU WIEI. "This pig meat, should I take it back for Ikundi? There are nothing but already grown girls there, so I preferred to come here."

At 2:50 p.m., Josef said that the man who had left the salt (Erauye Nguye) had just arrived.

JOSEF. "I lectured you, but I'm going to take this pig. And if I hadn't intended to accept it I would not have used the harsh words I did."

The girl's parents finally decided to follow Tumnuku wiei and his sister home and then to go on to Itsewobene to give the pig meat they had just received to Rodze akwiye, Sari beri's maternal grandfather, because it was the first *tuage* gift and the girl had no maternal uncles left.

The example I have used is not altogether representative of the rule regulating the identity of the beneficiary of the first gift of meat the future husband's family makes to that of his betrothed. In effect, insofar as it is possible, it is always given to the girl's oldest maternal uncle, who then shares it out to his own brothers and sisters (see pp. 145–46). In the present case, the absence of maternal uncles and aunts led the girl's parents to pass the gift on to Sari beri's closest maternal relatives, in this event, to her mother's father.

A few years later, when the first signs of puberty appear, one of the girl's maternal uncles rubs her chest with the orangish-yellow clay (*rwa'a omore'*) applied to the body of those who need to be fortified or who have not finished growing. As one Ankave friend told me, with few illusions about her kinsman's aim: "My maternal uncle had rubbed me with clay so that I would grow and he could eat a lot of game before dying" (see chapter 7). For the faster his niece grows, the earlier she marries and has children, which brings her in-laws to give more *tuage* game to her parents, who redistribute part of it to her maternal relatives.[4] In reality, the *tuage* gifts in kind never cease completely, at least in theory, for in practice an aging husband no longer makes gifts to his wife's family.

To what extent can this marriage request be said to be a ritualized event, and if it is, precisely who is concerned: the little girl or the young man for whom she has been chosen? The fact of going into detail about this step in a chapter devoted to analyzing the female life-path could lead us to consider it as a stage in this unfolding. But insofar as it is the first moment in a series of exchanges that bind two families, it is as much an event in a woman's life as in that of a man. However, since marriage entails a change of residence for the wife, it is perhaps more life changing for her than for her husband.[5] In all events, that is the way the Ankave seem to see it, since the moment when a girl changes her place of residence is the occasion of a set of acts and ritual gestures meant, it is said, to lessen her anxiety. The young man, on the other hand, does not need to be accompanied in this way. Before describing this event regarded as essential in the life of a woman, I will attempt to answer the first part of the question by asking what the elements are that would allow us to consider the marriage request as a ritualized event.

As one of my interlocutors told me, this type of meeting always entails the kind of conflict observed during Tumnuku wiei's visit to Olale. It is customary

---

4. I would like to make it clear, however, that, apart from the first gift, which always goes to the maternals of the bride, her paternal relatives receive up to 70 percent of the subsequent *tuage* gifts (Bonnemère 1996a: 80).

5. Everything is nevertheless relative, since, owing to the small numbers in the group, it is unusual, although not exceptional, for a woman to marry far from home. Nevertheless, it is she who leaves her family while she is still very young.

to evoke, however fleetingly, relations between the potential couple's clans or villages, and in particular the tensions that may characterize the relationship. It is also common for the girl's family not to accept outright the offer made by the young man's family—in other words, to stall, to present a few arguments against the union, in short, to feign reluctance. A girl is not given without signifying, by expressing hesitation and doubts, that a woman is a valuable gift that should be compensated by repeated gifts in kind. To be sure, this ritual is not seen as a collective event involving the entire community. But a marriage is not contracted in a few minutes; it supposes a commitment on the part of two groups that can only be based on relations of trust and good will. The unfolding of the consultation and the discussion is thus established according to an immutable scenario. It is in this sense that the marriage request can be said to be a ritualized event. Another step in the long process leading from the request to conjugal life corresponds even more closely to the criteria that would define an action as a ritual; it is the day the girl, who was betrothed years before, is led by her parents to the home of her future husband where, if all goes well, she will remain.

A RITUAL OF ADJUSTMENT

The moment chosen for a girl to move to her new home depends on how close to puberty she is. One morning, the fiancée is taken to the home of her future husband's parents by his sister, who has come for her. If the young man's family lives far away, the girl's own parents go with her. When the time came for her to move, Taweri, who had been betrothed to a man from Sinde (a valley a day's walk from Ayakupna'wa), was thus taken by her parents, who even stayed with her for two weeks and began to clear a garden for the young couple. In the same circumstances, when the time came to move in with her in-laws, Taweri's little sister, Taweri padzerei, betrothed to a man from Ayakupna'wa, was left in the company of only Idzadze beri, who here played the role of her future husband's mother,[6] and her daughters, who had come for her to Subu, her parents' village located upstream from Olale (see map 1).

When the families of the future couple set a date for this change of residence, the girl's father prepares three capes from the bark of the *ika'a kwi'we* (*Gnetum gnemon*), while her mother makes two netbags from fibers obtained by

---

6. This man did not have a sister, and his mother had died many years before.

beating the bark of the *ika'a erwa*, a ficus (*Ficus hesperidiiformis*). They will also take with them lengths of braided orchid stems for the young man. They set out late in the afternoon, for if they were to arrive in the middle of the day, it is said that the girl would feel ashamed or embarrassed. Such an emotion is also forestalled by a brief ritual performed by the father using three plants: cuttings from the *a'we* taro (*Colocasia* sp.) and sugarcane taken from the family garden as well as a short-leaved yellow cordyline. The girl walks between her mother, who goes in front, and her father, who follows her. The father takes advantage of his position to gather a bit of earth on which his daughter has just stepped, to which he adds a stone. He also uproots a green-leaved cordyline, which he hides with the three other plants until they arrive. When they are within sight of their future affines' house, he plants the three specimens he has taken from his garden. The visitors then settle down outside, with the exception of the father, who enters the house. Everyone chews betel and smokes while congenially talking about this and that.

When the sun has set, the girl's father deposits the earth he collected on the way on top of the stone that he also picked up, then he plants the green cordyline while uttering a formula and watching the path the future spouses will later take and into which the magic power has rushed.

When night falls, everyone goes inside and sits down in strictly codified places, which will determine each person's position for the night. The girl sits between her two parents, facing her future husband, who in turn is seated between his mother and his father. The talk goes on until everyone falls asleep. Earlier, the girl's father had made her a bed with the bark capes he had prepared, while pronouncing a special formula he had learned from a mature man who already has a married daughter. The bed is composed of his own daughter's cape, in which she wraps herself, the cape that will be given to her future husband and which serves as her mattress, and finally the cape that will cover his back and buttocks (*ijiare'*), which she uses as a pillow.

Once the young people are fast asleep, their parents discreetly move so that, upon awakening, the couple will find themselves together. Only the young man knows about the stratagem in advance, which is meant, it is said, to reduce his fiancée's apprehension. In the morning, the new bark capes are distributed in front of the girl, who is somewhat shaken by the idea that not only has she spent the night unaware next to her husband but also that she pillowed her head on the *ijiare'* cape that will now be given to him. With this gift of capes goes a magical practice that says, "the young woman must now be with her husband as a bark cape is on its wearer"; in other words, closely bound to him. The various ritual gestures are performed only if the marriage has been preceded by a "betrothal" (*igijinge*). If for one reason or another the alliance was concluded without a prior request, nothing is done to prepare the future couple's married life. Talking about these practices, the Ankave say they are meant to overcome the girl's apprehension and create solid and durable relations between the spouses. If the girl should be overcome by fear, the new capes are moistened in the river just before nightfall. They gradually dry as the girl sleeps.

The association of the bark capes with water obviously makes one think of the initial stages of the male initiations when these pieces of clothing made for the occasion are presented to the novices and their mothers who, as we remember, will dunk them every day in a stream close to their respective places of residence. We will soon have the occasion to come back to this, since these two components repeatedly appear together in several of the rituals connected with the life cycle. But already I would like to say that this practice refers to events related in a group of myths that depict a people of women. Here is the version told to me by Tenawi wiei and Ikundi beri on September 10, 1987:

At that time there were supposedly only women. They all slept in a very big house and had cleared a single huge garden. One day, the oldest woman saw a man; she told her sisters to plant sweet potatoes, sugarcane, and a large number of other foods. There were five men, who were brothers, and there were also five women, all sisters.

Some time later, the oldest sister, who had stayed home, saw that her sisters' bark capes had been borrowed by the men. Under the first cape was a black-skinned man. Under a second cape was a lighter-skinned man, and so on. The capes of the dark-skinned women had been borrowed by men with lighter skin and vice versa. It was raining.

The eldest sister wanted to put her own cape near the fire, but a man was hiding under it. She soon saw her sisters arriving, bearing food as well as firewood. They set down their netbags and then took their capes to place them next to the fire. The eldest sister then sang: "*wia bonge bonge wige, beri bonge bonge wige*" ("light skin, dark skin, all are under the capes").

Hearing their eldest sister singing, the four sisters asked her what these words meant. The eldest sister replied: "It's my song, only mine." The other sisters said: "Alright, but we would like to hear it." But the sister had stopped singing. So the four others took their capes under which the men were hiding. And the five women ate with the five men.

The youngest sister then went out to pick some *daka* leaves to consume with areca nuts. The youngest of the men saw that this woman's buttocks and breasts were very dirty, and when she tried to take her bark cape, he struck her on the bottom with a stone axe and told her she was dirty. The man's brothers then made it rain, which washed the youngest woman's breasts and buttocks. Then the youngest of the men married her. And then all of them got married and all the women became pregnant.

Although there is no mention of bark capes, another version also features cleansing water and enables contact—sexual contact in particular—between men and women. It was told to me on October 14, 1987, by Idzadze onexei:

A man from Ikundi who was out hunting marsupials with his dog a day's walk away came to a spot where there were lots of houses and women who were clearing gardens on their own. He saw a woman. They did not speak to each other. The woman was dirty, and as she wanted to sleep with this man, she went home to wash, and told the other women, her younger sisters: "I'm going to spend the night in my garden shelter." She went and spent the night with the man from Ikundi. In the morning he returned home after having told the woman to cook some sweet potatoes. So she prepared ten sticks, wrapped them up and gave them to the man so he would remember to come back with nine other men. The women prepared a meal of pig meat and sweet potatoes cooked in an earth oven (<u>mumu</u>). The man had told the eldest sister: "When you hear a whistle, the women must come and prepare food."

Lots of men arrived. The <u>mumu</u> had not yet been opened. The women understood why their eldest sister had told them to prepare a big meal. They climbed onto the roof of their house with bamboo tubes they had filled with water. After having made an opening in the roof, they poured the water into the house. If all the women had not done this, the men would have died upon entering the house. The women then picked leaves from various trees and made beds for the men to sleep on. They shared the food cooked in the <u>mumu</u> and that night they all slept together.

When she had finished her story, Idzadze onexei added that, in this house no one had ever made love and that, as a consequence, if the men had lain with the women without water having been poured beforehand, they would all have fallen ill. The women, on the other hand, had nothing to fear because they already slept in this house.

In both versions, women living alone are a potential source of danger for the men who encounter them for the first time. The erogenous zones of their body—at any rate, those of the youngest—are dirty and must be washed before the men can touch them. In the first account, the men therefore make it rain; in the second, it is the women who pour water into the house so that the men can enter without fear.

Even if the Ankave do not spontaneously associate the realms of myth and ritual, it seems to me that, without doing violence to the ethnographic material, we can find correspondences between these accounts of a first carnal encounter between five until-then self-sufficient sisters and a group of five men and the ritual of the first night in the home of the parents of a future husband, which they told me about in detail. That day, the future spouses are in a way prepared for their coming sexual life by the ritual staging of the main material components—water and bark capes—featured in the myth in which is expressed the primordial dirtiness of women, which must be, if not eradicated, at least diminished if men and women are to live in closer proximity. That is the condition of the possibility of a shared life.

From the moment of this ritual onwards, a new conjugal couple exists in fact, even if they have not yet built their own house or cleared their garden and are, for the time being, still living with the husband's parents. This transitional period can last several months, since building a house is a lengthy endeavor in this society where cooperation does not extend beyond the conjugal couple (Lemonnier 1999b). The husband works alone to gather the necessary construction materials (wood, vines, and sometimes bamboo), then patiently and single-handedly erects the structure over many long weeks. His wife intervenes at the last minute, gathering the bamboo leaves or armfuls of long kunai grass, which, once she has made them into bundles, her husband will use to thatch the roof, which is round or—as is more often the case today—pitched. They will also soon have to clear a garden and, here too, it is customary that no one, including close relatives, comes to lend a hand. To the extent that, when it sometimes happens that two brothers decide to clear a piece of forest located on adjoining lands, each will work his own plot with his wife. Only the moments of rest and relaxation are shared.

And so several months will go by before a young couple stops depending on their elders, has their own home, and produces their own means of subsistence.

In return for this temporary hospitality, the young wife will accompany her mother-in-law to her gardens, thus contributing to the daily harvest necessary to the household; she helps her prepare meals and sometimes takes on the chores of fetching water and gathering firewood. It is said that a mother-in-law replaces the mother the girl had to leave when she moved in with her husband; and it is the mother-in-law who continues her education, teaches her garden magic, and explains how to conduct herself with her husband. She also advises her on how to raise the piglet her maternal uncle has just given her, and which is, as will be remembered, compensation for the first *tuage* gift he received at the time of the marriage proposal.[7] This pig has a special value, for it is the first in a long series that every married woman raises over her lifetime. If all goes well, it may also be the ancestor of a productive line! Together with shell-money and now currency, which unfortunately do not reproduce, pigs are the Ankave's primary form of wealth.

It is also certain that a girl who has left her family at the early age of fifteen or so can find her mother-in-law to be an important source of moral support. With the exception of rare cases of marriage in a distant village, a married woman's family is not more than a few hours' walk away and, in all events, ties are never broken, if only because the rules of matrimonial exchanges require the husband's family to make regular gifts of game or pig meat to the family of the wife; these are the *tuage* gifts we have already discussed (see pp. 145–46). In the early years of a marriage, each time a pig is killed in a valley and its meat is put up for sale,[8] the young husband buys a piece to be given as a *tuage*. He immediately takes it to his parents-in-law, and his wife comes with him to visit her family. These gifts become less frequent when several children have been born and have grown up, but theoretically, at least as long as the protagonists are alive, there is no reason for the gifts to cease altogether. The Ankave's situation is close to that encountered in some other New Guinea societies, besides their difference in other domains. In Hagen, for example, women maintain ties with their natal kin, formally and informally (M. Strathern 1972: 294). As M. Strathern observed, "many sisters these days prefer to live at their father's or brother's

---

7.   This is the *potiye'* gift (see p. 145).

8.   According to what we have been told, this practice of putting meat up for sale had "always" existed; at least it long precedes "contact" with the outside. The only changes are in the form of money used (shell-money in the past, currency today) and in the prices, which have gone up.

place rather than their husband's" (pers. comm., July 5, 2017). As for an Ankave woman who loses her husband, she returns to her village and can decide, after the mourning period, not to follow the custom of levirate, which dictates that a widow marry one of her husband's brothers. Finally, her own brothers often take her in and spontaneously side with her if she is fighting with her husband; the husband is then obliged to give his brothers-in-law a bit of pig meat or game so they will agree to return their sister.[9] Men's loyalty to their sisters is an important aspect of the bond between them. If her brothers may sometimes try to convince her to go back to her husband, they never reject her, and they systematically take her side, at the risk of spoiling their relations with their brothers-in-law, with the dangers of feuding that such a break once implied.

This protection is a reminder of how important a sister, and especially an older sister, is in the life of a boy and then a future father, first of all because she accompanies him closely in these key moments that are his initiation and the first-birth ritual. These significant events of the male life cycle are the theater of several relational transformations and as such, as I have shown and said several times, require the presence of all the persons involved in the relationship concerned (see also Bonnemère 2017). It ensues that, even if this ritual is not organized for the woman who takes part in it as the sister of the young initiand, it consumes several weeks of her life and has a direct impact on her relationship with her brother. The major transformation in this relationship occurs when her brother becomes a father for the first time. It will be remembered that she has been associated with the young parents-to-be ever since the pregnancy was announced and, like them, has respected prohibitions and worn a new bark cape. At dawn on the day of the ceremony, she accompanied her sister-in-law to the big river, then they waited together for the men to come down from the forest in their finery and later joined them on the village ceremonial ground for the public phase of the ceremony. Finally, she stood with the new mother and her baby as the *me'we* fire was lit and her brother handed her some areca nuts. Thus, at the close of a feast ending the ritual performed for a first-time father, a parental couple has come into existence, and a new relational situation has been established that will henceforth obviate the ritualized presence of the husband's

---

9.   On this particular point, the Hagen situation differs: "brothers do not always come to the sister's aid and may side with their brothers-in-law" (M. Strathern, pers. comm., July 5, 2017). This may well have to do with the importance of relations between affines in large-scale, ceremonial exchanges.

sister when the following nephews and nieces are born. Last of all, in order for a man to attain the status of maternal uncle, with its highly valued capacity to act for others, his sister must have children.

Attaining full manhood thus depends closely on the life-path of the man's eldest sister, and I have sometimes wondered—and this might be a further and future line of reflection, even if the Ankave say nothing that points in this direction—if the ritual gestures she must perform for her brother in the collective stages of the initiations may not also impact on her as well, enabling her, for instance, to attain the status of mother. In effect, when they go and fetch tubers to feed their mothers and brothers, do they not take on a responsibility that was the mother's one as well as anticipate their own future? The question is all the more relevant here, since the Ankave stress that the ideal sister to accompany her brother during his initiation is a childless elder one.

In any event, the relationship between a brother and his sister lies at the heart of men's access to parenthood. Finally, let us recall that the interwoven destinies of a man and his sister extend beyond their generation; it is a maternal uncle who causes his sister's children to be reborn during initiation and he has the capacity to harm them, in virtue of the power of life and death of the maternal kin in general, of whom he is the principal representative.

A woman's eldest sister also plays a role when she has just given birth to her husband's first child (see p. 80). On the day of the public ceremony, her eldest sister accompanies her to the river with the other women and scrubs her body with lemon-scented leaves and then soap. When they have returned to the outskirts of the village and have hidden behind a thicket of trees, it is also she who cuts her younger sister's hair and draws the red lines on her forehead.

An elder sister, so important for her brother, the Ankave say, that the rituals punctuating his life would not be effective without her contribution, thus also intervenes in the life of her sister. This involvement is much less marked, however, and someone from another kin category could easily replace her, whereas a classificatory sister would absolutely have to be found for the male initiations.

In a previous chapter, we discussed at length the food taboos and obligations imposed on a pregnant woman and the behavior required of her at this time. As we saw (p. 115), these are meant to protect the baby she carries by abstaining, for example, from consuming game having physical or behavioral traits she seeks to avoid transmitting through the food she eats. On the contrary, the red pandanus sauce she is supposed to consume in large quantities turns into blood, which directly benefits the baby. Throughout her pregnancy and during the several days following the birth, a woman is therefore in an altogether special relational situation that imposes the adoption of appropriate behaviors. These consist in acts that are part of the ritual for constructing a parental couple, which includes many other acts as well. This is neither a female nor a male ritual, but instead a "ritual of parenthood," which includes a phase for each sex, with their own gestures, which are not revealed to the other, as well as a shared collective phase. The ritual is organized for a man on the occasion of the new relational situation created by the future arrival of their first child, which the community is duty-bound to both celebrate and accompany.

This new relational situation is a further stage in a woman's life, in which she is first a wife, then a mother, and then as time goes by, a grandmother. This second period in her life is marked by as many rituals as the preceding stage, and here too the key moments seem to concern her less than other persons connected with her. But before discussing these statuses characteristic of the second period in a woman's life, let us pause to examine the brother-sister relationship and its temporal displacement in the form of the relationship between a maternal uncle and his sister's children. These two relationships play an important role in Ankave social life at the same time as they help us understand how the society views the construction of the male person.

CHAPTER 10

The brother-sister relationship through the years

We must now temporarily leave the description and analysis of first-hand ethnographic material and turn to the issue of the brother-sister relationship as
it has been approached in the literature on Melanesia. This relationship is the
centerpiece of the Ankave rituals for the construction of personhood, and so
a side trip through the work on this topic is indispensable for gaining a better
understanding of any specificity the situation as studied in the present book may
have. The excursus necessarily affects the written style, and if readers are somewhat put off by the difficulty of the pages that follow, I can only assure them
that the book resumes its normal course in the following chapter.

In the early 1950s, when the first postwar anthropologists discovered the
New Guinea Highlands, one ethnologist chose to base himself in a coastal zone,
Bogia Bay, located on the northern coast of the island northwest of what was
then called Madang District (and today is called Madang Province). Kenelm
Burridge had trained at Oxford and had become the first anthropology student
at the Australian National University of Canberra,[1] where in 1953 he received
a doctorate from this young institution.[2] Like most of his colleagues, he also

---

1. If I am to believe the pages written by John Barker in the *ASAO Newsletter* 78 (Spring
   1991, pp. 20–22), today available on the Association for Social Anthropology in
   Oceania's website: www.asao.org/pacific/archives.htm#news.
2. The Australian National University (ANU) was created in Canberra in 1946 by an
   act of the Federal Parliament.

penned numerous articles on social organization and kinship, with the result that, between March 1957 and March 1959, the journal *Oceania* published six of his articles of variable length, each devoted to an aspect of social relations among the Tangu, namely: friendship; *gagai*, a hard-to-translate concept of group; descent; marriage; adoption; and siblingship.

The plainly entitled article "Siblings in Tangu" (1959) contains a series of intuitions and hypotheses concerning the role of the brother-sister relationship in structuring social organization, today a popular topic of research in a world where the two key concepts in anthropology of kinship are still descent and alliance. Burridge, a precursor not cited by the proponents of an approach that gave as much importance to the brother-sister relationship as to these two pillars of the field, had already added marriage rules, as continues to be done.

Raymond Jamous' more recent research in northern India shows that "these two categories [consanguinity and affinity] do not represent the whole domain of kinship. The notion of metasiblingship is made necessary by the need to designate a social reality which cannot be reduced to either of the two categories" (2003: 185). He uses his neologism *metasiblingship* to "speak of a level of value which transcends the distinction between consanguinity and affinity" (2003: 42), and consequently, the derived term *metasiblings* to express the fact that Ego's generation does not always make a distinction between consanguines and affines. The terms *consanguineal* and *affinal* kin are reserved for contexts in which distinctions of this order are necessary. This proposition implies the existence of two levels: "a global one, which recognizes only metasiblings *bhai* and *bahin*, and a more restricted one, which includes marriage ties in which the same principle of metasiblingship is applied when one starts with a brother-sister relationship, whereas the consanguine/affine opposition is meaningful only if one starts with the brother-brother or sister-sister relationship" (2003: 42).

More specifically: among the Meo, studied by Jamous, an as-yet unmarried person, whether male or female, has siblings only in their own generation, "brothers/*bhâî*" and "sisters/*bahin*." Contrary to the Iroquois-type kinship systems to which the Ankave belong, here no distinction is made between parallel and cross-cousins, and therefore none between those whom one is allowed to marry (usually cross-cousins) and others. This is the reason for the term metasiblingship: it underscores this terminological specificity wherein consanguines and potential affines are placed in the same category. Things become more complex after the marriage: new terms, different for a male and a female Ego, appear, and terms constructed from *bhâî* and *bahin* are used in the case of marriage by sister exchange. A man's sister's husband is a *behnoï* (and not a *jija*, as he would be if he were an "ordinary" brother-in-law), and the *behnoï*'s sister is a *bahin*. For a woman, her brother's wife is a *bhâbî* and the *bhâbî*'s brother is a *bhâî*. Phonetically close to those designating the opposite-sex metasiblings, "brothers/*bhâî*" and "sisters/*bahin*," *behnoï* and *bhâbî* do not designate affines as opposed to consanguines but metasiblings by marriage (Jamous 2003: 49). This is not the common situation, in which kinship vocabulary changes with matrimonial status, but the result of a metasiblingship revealed by a specific affinal relationship linking two brother-sister couples. Metasiblingship is thus closely bound up with a particular form of marriage.

This terminological feature does not exist among the Tangu, but other "pillars" of kinship are so weak that Burridge refrains from asserting from the outset that the descent system is patrilineal, matrilineal, or bilineal, since whether the stress is on one side or the other depends on the context. We have here a now-classic case in this part of the world where the official residential pattern is continually violated and where it is difficult to associate a clan with a territory (see p. 140). Burridge thus takes a strong interest in the brother-sister relation, which he believes to have a role in structuring the society he is studying. In terms of attitudes, he compares it to the conjugal relationship, with the obvious exception of the sexual component. When her brother is a baby or still small, his sister takes care of him, comforts him, carries him around, and is like a second mother to him. Before his marriage she may cook for him, and the logical consequence, eating food prepared by a woman, implies intimacy, which exists here without being accompanied by sexual contact. Finally, according to Burridge, the Tangu ethnography shows that a man's idealized or spiritual partner is his sister (1959: 131). The brother-sister relationship is not reciprocal in childhood, and it is only much later that a boy is able to fulfill his role as his sister's protector, precisely the only one the husband can never perform: that of protecting her from her spouse (1959: 132). There is thus a time lag in the support one provides the other: the sister takes care of her little brother when he is a child, and as an adult he sees that his sister is treated well by her husband. Or at least he intervenes if his sister's marriage is marred by violence. In New Guinea, a married woman often takes refuge with one of her brothers in the event of conflict; among the Ankave, we have seen that she can stay with him until her husband brings his brother-in-law a piece of game or meat to compensate for his bad behavior and sometimes for his wife's blood he has spilled. Theories concerning the transmission of blood are not far away here, for a brother and his sister share the same blood,[3] which they inherited from their mother by virtue of their stay in her womb, bathed in this precious fluid and nourished by it. It is thus a blood shared by the brother-sister couple that the husband and brother-in-law compensate. In this, the brother is affected by the violence almost as directly as his sister.

Burridge suggests, "one might say that in Tangu social life is possible, and individuals reach maturity, in terms of adequately resolving the sibling to marital relationship" (1959: 131). For if "the substitution of wife for sister, and husband for brother, are mental or psychic processes [because all Tangu participate in varying degrees], [they] are also sociologically relevant" (1959: 133). For the Tangu of Bogia Bay, the (first) ideal marriage for a man is with a woman in the category of mother's brother's daughters, but never his real matrilateral cross-cousin (1958: 46). Formerly, the betrothed would enter her new house accompanied by a brother of the mother of her future husband[4] together with one of her brothers who, for the occasion, would make a show of hostility toward their future brother-in-law; he, in turn, was supposed to feign fear. That is one way of making clear the relations expected between them: "the groom is not only beholden to the brothers for exchange relationships, but will have to beware of them if he maltreats his wife" (1958: 49). A deflowering ritual, "presumably, a coitus interruptus" (1958: 49) followed, after which the semen was recovered and mixed with certain grasses, some of which were taken from the girl's skirt. The mixture was finally introduced into the milk of a coconut that had been cut in half and given to the groom to drink by his (classificatory) maternal uncle and future father-in-law. It is said that this is a fertility rite designed to ensure the birth of many children and productive gardens (1958: 49, 50). Such a marriage with a woman from the category of mother's brother's daughters, accompanied by ritual gestures, creates welcome exchange relations between two brother-sister pairs and divides the community into two equivalent—or nearly equivalent—halves in a relation of reciprocal exchanges of goods (1958: 51).

---

3.   Cf. Sandra Bamford's ethnography in which she suggests that, although the Kamea term used to refer to a sibling set may be glossed as *one-bloodedness*, "neither a woman nor a man is considered to be 'one-blood' with their children; the term refers exclusively to having issued from the same woman's womb" (2007: 61).

4.   Given the marriage rule, for the fiancée, this classificatory mother's brother is a "father" (1958: 49).

Among the Tangu, access to land is transmitted in the paternal line, but filiation is characterized by stress on the maternal line, Burridge writes. Children born to the same woman are known as *mwerz ungunwan* ("one womb"), and very often the same term designates those born to two sisters who themselves have the same mother.[5] The womb is the deciding factor in speaking of identity and difference between two individuals of the same sex and generation. So, "though *mwerz ungunwan* may select and unite for a variety of purposes certain individuals within a uterine line, it by no means defines a permanent and known group of matrilineal kin" (1957: 62). Another term, *ringertiam*, built on the root *ringer* and used to speak of the source of a stream, is particularly suited to opposite-sex siblings born to the same parents, but also extends to a mother's brother when speaking of his relation with the son of his real—and not classificatory—sister.[6] The "real" mother's brother entertains an affectionate, tutelary relationship with his sister's children, something that is not the case of those in this kin category who did not have the same parents as their mother.

In all events, here is expressed the important temporal dimension entailed in the brother-sister relation, which is at the origin of the avunculate, whose value anthropologists have demonstrated in kinship systems the world over (Lévi-Strauss 1963a). When it comes to society as a whole, all siblings in Ego's parents' generation are at the origin of the division between Ego's paternal and maternal kin, but the brother-sister couple has a particularly strong impact inasmuch as the children born of the two members of the pair are sometimes Ego's preferred spouses. More often classificatory cousins than the real children of the brother and sister, they are nevertheless regarded as belonging to the sister's or the brother's side. It is also for this reason that research specifically devoted to cross-siblingship has studied it in conjunction with forms of marriage. But contrary to kinship studies that stress descent or alliance, Jamous looks not only at the marriage model but also at the ritual functions resulting from the brother-sister relation, in particular those attributed to the paternal aunt. In so doing, he

---

5. The Ankave place similar stress on matrilineality, however the accompanying term does not mean "womb" but "breast" and "mother's milk" (*amenge'*). It is also used as a term of address between persons whose maternal grandmothers are—or more often were—sisters. Here, as among the Tangu, this term does not create a recognized matrilineal group but underlies a nonexplicit but strictly respected prohibition on marriage (Bonnemère 1996a: 144–46).

6. Burridge speaks in terms of "mother's full brother in relation to full sister's son" (1957: 62).

has discovered a "double movement entailed in this marriage which separates the sister from her brother and then returns her to his family to ensure, by ritual means, the continuation of the generations" (2003: 186).

Could we then suggest a symmetrical interpretation of the intervention of the mother's brother among the Tangu as a return of the brother to his sister's family, in order to ensure her children's fertility? The proposition might also hold for the Ankave. But then marriage rules would not matter, since they are given different expressions in these two New Guinea societies while perhaps manifesting themselves concretely in similar ways: no marriage between first cousins and tolerance of polygyny with sisters. As Burridge writes, "men and women have sisters and brothers irrespective of marriage and descent" (1959: 136). Same-sex siblingship is the model for relations of cooperation; the brother-sister relation is the model for relations of exchange. Finally, "so long as the basic unit remains the household and not a corporate descent group, siblingship provides a sufficiently flexible principle on which to base marriage and the consequent relations between households" (1959: 154). It is on this note that Burridge ends his article on "Siblings in Tangu."

COMING BACK TO THE ANKAVE

We now come back to the Ankave, enlightened by what we have learned about the potential importance of the brother-sister relationship for the organization of society. Reading the authors cited in this chapter led me to wonder why my analysis of the sister's role in life cycle rituals did not spontaneously gravitate toward the marriage alliance. There are no doubt several reasons for this: first of all, contrary to the Tangu in the 1950s, the Ankave explicitly reckon descent patrilineally when it comes to clan belonging and the transmission of land and stretches of river for trapping eels. This appears clearly in women's names, since they are, without exception, built on the name of the father's clan or that of a river or mountain located on his clan lands (see p. 224). Men's names are constructed differently, and it is as if women, who marry out of their birth group, carried the memory of their clan belonging and the local descent rule (Bonnemère 2005).

When it comes to uterine kin, even if these relatives have a primordial value, it is not activated in the domains we have just been discussing. There was therefore no call to look to the social organization proper for any structuring principles other than those of descent and alliance. The importance of the brother-sister relationship and its development over time, and the bond between the mother's brother and his sister's children appear clearly only in the domains of ritual and life cycle exchanges. The approach I have taken in this study therefore focuses on the person and his or her development, while considering marriage as the means of access to reproduction and parenthood rather than studying its formal aspects.[7] In a sense, I have adopted an *emic* point of view, which emanates from within the society and reports what its members have to say. But that is not a reason to neglect the *etic* point of view, that of the anthropologist who stands outside the local viewpoint, who looks beyond what his or her friends have to say for the implicit representations that might explain certain practices (see p. 130n25). I will return to this point when we look at marriage forms in Ankave society.

As the preceding chapters described at length, an eldest sister plays a key role during her brother's childhood. As among the Tangu, she is sometimes a second mother for him, consoling him, carrying him on her shoulders, and feeding him. But her accompanying role extends well beyond his early childhood, since she is the element articulating—enabling—his transition from the status of young boy now released from the symbiotic relation he had with his mother to that of father of a first child. At this time in his life, the cross-sibling relationship looks something like a one-way street. As Burridge writes, "formally, the relationship is one of respect expressed in services. In reality the onus is almost entirely on the sister to provide for her brother" (1959: 130). For the Ankave, the brother assumes his role only once he is an adult and in exceptional circumstances (in the event of marital strife a sister will take refuge with her brother). It is as a maternal uncle that he exercises his responsibility and lends his sister's children the support he had enjoyed from her. When his nephew goes through the ordeals of initiation, he is the one who most often acts as his sponsor; he carries him on his back through the corridor of branches and he receives some of the blows meted out with cassowary quills; he stands behind his nephew and holds him when the ritual expert pierces his nose; he

---

7.   To be exact, I must add that, in an earlier publication (Bonnemère 1996a), I studied marriage alliances from a normative standpoint—marriage rules—and from a practical point of view—analyzing all marriages in one clan, or a little over 600 unions.

is with him again when important secrets are revealed around the fire in their rudimentary shelter. As his "partner of pain," as Gilbert Herdt puts it, he is also the boy's chief support during these trying physical and psychological ordeals. Vis-à-vis his sister's daughter, he is there to guarantee her physical growth and fertility. When she shows the first signs of puberty, as I have already said, he rubs her chest with clay while muttering a formula designed to ensure she will have many children when she marries. And, as we have seen, it is to him that the girl's parents will deliver the gift of half a cooked pig that accompanies the marriage request. Last of all, by giving her first piglet to her, he helps his sister's daughter become a good wife; in other words, a woman who works hard in her gardens and raises many pigs. Pigs are an important source of income insofar as from time immemorial they have been killed and cooked so that pieces may be sold in the village. Having pigs also enables a married man to fulfill his obligations to his in-laws by the regular gifts of meat, *tuage*, discussed above (see pp. 145–46).

While the maternal uncle's support of his sister's children is the temporal extension of the relationship between a sister and her brother, the two relations are not entirely comparable, for the sister's support for her brother is unconditional whereas a mother's brother's support for his uterine nephews and nieces depends largely on good exchange relations between affines,[8] and in this case on the gifts he receives from his brother-in-law. If he deems the gifts of game or pig meat he is owed until his nephew's initiation and his niece's marriage are insufficient, he can transform his life-giving powers to convey illness, hinder the growth and fertility of his sister's children, and even cause their death. The relationship with the maternal kin is thus marred by deep-seated ambivalence, and it is on good relations with them that a person's physical development, good health, and fertility depend. When a person is sick, when a couple is unable to have children, suspicion inevitably falls on the maternal uncle of the sick person or the supposedly barren woman; in this case, the remedy will be to make him an additional gift, in the hope that he will cease his spiteful actions. It is easy to understand that such a situation is a likely source of tension between brothers-in-law, since a father is always afraid of not having done enough to satisfy his child's mother's brother, and thereby having potentially endangered

---

8.   Except for his role as his nephew's sponsor during initiation that he will take on anyway.

the child's health. Relations between affines and relations with maternal kin are thus intrinsically intertwined, since a man's brother-in-law is at the same time his children's maternal uncle. Therefore getting along with one's brother-in-law and fulfilling one's obligations to him ensures he will be well disposed to one's children.

The asymmetry between a person's paternal and maternal kin is thus central to Ankave social life; it regulates the life cycle exchanges; it explains the ills afflicting a person; and finally it ascribes exorbitant powers to the maternal kin, leaving those on the other side with no choice but to try, through their gifts, to elicit benevolent actions and to moderate their always-to-be-feared malevolence. The maternal uncle is thus a close relative whose feelings must be taken into consideration because if one is in good health and has a large family, it is in part thanks to him. Being the source of the fertility of his sister's daughters, the mother's brother enables the society to perpetuate itself. And any dissatisfaction he may feel with the number of gifts received during his nephews' and nieces' childhood can have dramatic consequences, since he is able to make them seriously ill and even to cause their death. Let us also recall that the capacity to harm does not cease with the death of the maternal uncle, since his spirit can continue to harass his sister's children (Lemonnier 2006a: 324–25). The mother's brother acquires these powers of life and death at the close of a gradual and lengthy process involving a series of ritually orchestrated transformations in his relations with his closest relatives and in their presence. As we know, the figure of the sister, who enables him to become a maternal uncle and thus to exercise his powers, plays a key role in these transformations.

For a man, having a sister also guarantees he will be able to get married. In a system where bridewealth must be given to obtain a wife, it is the sum received by the betrothed's family that will be used to acquire the girl her brother has chosen. A man without a sister finds himself in a difficult situation: he will have to get the money by some means other than simple redistribution within the family—for instance, by leaving the valley to work on the coastal palm-oil plantations. A man's sisters not only enable him to become a maternal uncle, they also enable him to become a husband. A man's fate is thus closely bound up with that of his sisters. Could it be said that the reverse is also true—in other words, that a woman's fate similarly depends on that of her brothers?

Indeed, we might wonder if the ritual work a sister performs for her brother at the time of his collective initiation as a small boy and years later when he is about to become a father for the first time[9] does not also operate a ritual transformation that enables her to advance on her life-path and to become a mother. Ideally, as we know, it is an older sister who has not yet borne children who accompanies her brother in the life cycle rituals. When she puts a new bark cape over her head, like her brother and her sister-in-law, is she merely accompanying this couple, or does this behavior have an effect on her own future? Could the triad formed by these figures not be seen as two couples in which the male component occupies a different position in each: future father in one case and future uncle in the other? Fatherhood would thus also be the anticipation of both the man's future status as maternal uncle and his sister's motherhood. Her presence alongside her brother when he becomes a father for the first time thus prefigures this highly valued social status. In short, the man's pregnant wife makes him a future father, and his sister makes him a future maternal uncle. The physical presence of both women is indispensable when he goes through the final stage of initiation after the birth of his first child; the brother-sister couple is a prefiguration of the avuncular relationship that will fall into place when his sister has a child.

The brother-sister relationship and that between a maternal uncle and his sister's children are both characterized by an ingrained asymmetry, but the direction of this relationship has changed in the course of the process by which the brother has become a maternal uncle. Initially the beneficiary of his sister's actions, he has become someone who has the capacity to act for or against her offspring. At the same time as transferring this capacity, over time the cross-sibling relationship also effects a reversal of the action's direction. The sister loses her capacity to act on her brother when she becomes a mother, at which point he acquires this agency over his uterine nieces and nephews. But, whereas the sister's action on and for her brother was always positive, that of the maternal uncle can be either positive or negative. It is the quality of the affinal relations,

---

9. As with the boy who, when his nose has healed, adopts behaviors that differ partially from those of his mother, whereas they were patterned on hers at the start of the rituals (see p. 107n15), there is also a difference in the behaviors respected by the initiate and his sister that intervenes between the end of the first stage initiations and that of the second stage. Without going into detail, we can posit that these now-different behaviors relate to the practices connected with consumption of the *tuage* pig meat or game (Bonnemère 2015a).

and in particular those between the brother and the sister's husband, measured by the number of gifts the first receives from the second, that influences the benevolent or malevolent use to which a maternal uncle puts his powers.

In the previous chapters we discussed these affinal relations in terms of the rituals and gifts that accompany marriage, the future wife's change of residence, and the birth of children; in the next chapter we will examine them from the standpoint of the wife as mother and grandmother, as her life as a woman continues to unfold.

CHAPTER 11

Women's lives: A path unmarked by rituals? Part II
Wives, mothers, grandmothers

At different times in her life, a woman must adapt some of her behaviors to the life-path of others than herself: her brother, her sister, but also, in a case we have not yet discussed, her husband, and last—and above all—her children. She takes part in the collective stages of her sons' initiations; however, as we will see, this is not the only time a mother is involved in her children's life. But let us look first at the situation that requires a married woman to play a ritual role in her husband's life.

HUNTING CASSOWARIES

Some men become great cassowary hunters, and the effectiveness of their snares is proof of a particular ability to catch this animal associated in the Ankave imaginary with women (Bonnemère 2006). The first four cassowaries a man catches are always eaten among men. The women and the trapper himself are barred from this meal. For the hunter, this prohibition is lifelong (a hunter is not allowed to eat any of the game he has caught), but the ban on cassowary is ritually lifted for women on the occasion of the fifth capture. Here is what happens, as told to me by two women who had experienced the event;

When a man has trapped a cassowary for the first time, he leaves the animal in the forest somewhere not far from his home and then tells a male member of his family—a brother, father, or paternal uncle—who goes to cook it there. The fire is always lit "in the manner of the ancestors," that is to say by friction, failing which, the hunter may never catch another cassowary.[1] When it has been cooked on a fire lit in this way, the cassowary is laid on a bark cape and eaten by the men, with the exception of the trapper and any children who may be present, both boys and girls alike. No married woman may eat this meat. The remains are not left lying around but are thrown on the fire, once again for fear that later traps will not be effective. The next three cassowaries caught are cooked and eaten in the same way. None of these can figure in the *tuage* gifts paid over the lifetime of a marriage.

When a hunter has caught his fifth cassowary, his wife is called to take part in the event. Idze Mowoni tells the following story:

> Barabas, a man of experience, told Andrew, my husband, that this was his fifth catch and it was time I ate some. Andrew went to get the cassowary he had caught, put it in the water to preserve it, and came to tell me. Together we went to the spot in the forest, and pulled the cassowary out of the water. I am the one who carried it to where it was customary to cook this kind of game. Barabas joined us; he plucked the bird and cut it up. Then he prepared the earth oven, gathering wood and stones. My husband and I watched. While the cassowary was cooking, Barabas pierced my earlobe with a cassowary-bone awl that belonged to him and then placed a small piece of bamboo in the hole. He told me I was supposed to refrain from eating certain foods such as leafy vegetables that become soft when cooked, so as to encourage the wound to heal. The cassowary's liver had been cooked separately, in a piece of bark. Barabas opened it, cut up the liver, and then spit some vegetal salt onto it. He gave me a piece of liver and I gave the rest to my sisters, who had come. The meat itself was eaten by the men, with the exception of my husband, of course, and the children.

---

1. Even though they now use matches and lighters, the Ankave still know how to make fire in the traditional manner. The technique they apply uses the heat obtained by sawing a length of rattan back and forth through a piece of hard wood that has been split to form a sort of clip. The tiny sparks ignite a wad of beaten bark fibers and dry leaves.

The story Onorwae told me is more or less identical, except that it was her husband who plucked and cut up the animal. The man of experience who had pierced her earlobe and given her a piece of liver to eat had told her: "That hurt, eat this liver, then." The meat was then given as *tuage* to Onorwae's brothers. Several days later, when the hole in her earlobe had dried, the man who had done the piercing inserted a cassowary quill (*siru'a*) ring into the hole. When the hole gradually becomes enlarged, it is possible to insert several quills, which is what most women do.

It was not without pride that my two women friends told me how they had attained the status of cassowary hunter's wife, stressing that women whose husbands do not catch cassowaries do not wear earrings, and when you see a woman wearing them, you think her husband knows how to catch cassowaries. I must say that as I was reading the English version of this chapter prior to its publication, I was struck by something that did not occur to me with such clarity at first sight. As seen, the first consumption of cassowary meat by the wife of a talented hunter is highly ritualized. An experienced man officiates, piercing (of the earlobe) is involved, taboos on leafy vegetables are imposed to help the healing, the liver of the animal is cooked separately in a bark and then cut in pieces and prepared by the same experienced man by spitting vegetal salt, as in other taboo-ending contexts. Finally, from what the woman cited said, but I do not know whether this is the usual practice, she was given a piece and gave the rest to her sisters who came and joined them, which gives a collective tone to an otherwise individual or conjugal ritual. All this made me think of the piercing of the boys' noses, although I plan to pursue the comparison another time. As for the meat of the cassowary, it was eaten by other adult men but not the husband, since he was the hunter. And no children were allowed to have a share. In the other case, the meat was given as a *tuage* gift.

This big, flightless bird is no ordinary animal.[2] It is endowed with physical attributes—large size, strength, extreme endurance, powerful and dangerous

---

2.   There are three species of cassowary, which are distinguished by size and habitat: the Dwarf or Bennett Cassowary (*Casuarius bennetti*), whose height does not exceed one meter, lives deep in the forests covering the hills and high mountains. This is the cassowary most commonly trapped by the Ankave. The second species, the Southern or Double-Wattle Cassowary (*Casuarius casuarius*), is bigger, up to 1.5 meters in height and up to sixty kilograms or more, and lives in the lowlands. The Ankave encounter it only rarely. The third species (*Casuarius unappendiculatus*) falls in between—measuring between 1.2 and 1.5 meters—and lives in the lowlands of northern New Guinea (Beehler, Pratt, and Zimmerman 1986: 45–46).

claws—that are as impressive as they are strange: the presence of quills rather than feathers, the absence of knee bones, and the inability to fly. Furthermore, the bird displays what are considered to be ridiculous and even repulsive behaviors: it has a huge appetite and minimal control of its sphincters and it eats windfall fruits and excretes them undigested: "They [cassowaries] do not chew the fruits, they swallow them whole then expel them through their cloaca, like the females expel their eggs," explain the Kasua, a population living on the southern slope of Mount Bosavi in southwestern Papua New Guinea (Brunois 2007: 88). The potential consequence is that they may eat their own excrements, thus scandalously violating the distance to be respected between food and excrement, emphasized by the Maring, a Highlands people (Healey 1985: 156) or the Sulka of New Britain (Jeudy-Ballini 1995: 222).[3] Naturally nervy, the cassowary is sensitive to changes in its normal environment and can be very dangerous if cornered or deprived of its young. Its behavior with its offspring is also out of the ordinary: the males, which are smaller than the females, incubate the eggs and raise the young (Beehler, Pratt, and Zimmermann 1986: 45; Brunois 2007: 88). The females can be polyandrous, mating with more than one male per season and laying each clutch of three or four eggs in a different place (Majnep and Bulmer 1977: 148). The Sambia say that cassowaries do not make nests (Herdt 1981: 134). All these features set the animal apart for numerous New Guinea groups, who do not include it in the class of birds, as a famous article says: "Why is the cassowary not a bird? A problem of zoological taxonomy among the Karam of the New Guinea Highlands" (Bulmer 1967).

This is not true of the Ankave, for whom the cassowary is indeed a bird, and, unlike other regions of New Guinea (Feld 1982: 47), there is no ambiguity or lack of agreement among informants on this point. Yet the myths in which this animal appears tell of a double transformation, that of a woman into a cassowary, and that of the cassowary into a woman (Bonnemère 2006). Only some of these accounts provide any details on the situation prior to this substitution. Simply, a wife is mentioned who did not behave "properly." She would defecate anywhere, forget to fetch firewood and water or to light the fire, or would give her husband half-cooked food. At this point a double conversion occurs, by

3.   The Ankave, like other peoples in New Guinea, often mention the role of cassowaries in the germination of certain fruits. For instance, the Kasua say that barely has it been excreted, "the fruit is already sprouting because kasua's belly is hot" (Brunois 2007: 88).

which some of the myths begin. The transmutation is sometimes related in great detail, as in the version in which, as a couple was going to the forest, the husband saw his wife eating shoots of a favorite plant of cassowaries. He then loses sight of her and goes back home. The wife returns only later and spends the night outside. When dawn comes, the husband notices that his wife has left, abandoning her skirt next to a few cassowary quills. He goes to look for her and is present at his wife's definitive transformation: she is eating fruits from the trees and the bamboo knife she had taken with her has become a quill (*siru'a*). Even though she sees her husband coming after her, the changed wife continues on her way deep into the forest. The man returns home and—some time later—a woman arrives from the forest. She performs all her household chores perfectly but does not wear a bark cape, explaining to him that henceforth he will have to make traps to catch cassowaries but must never eat them himself.

This version of the myth shows the reciprocal transformation of the cassowary into a woman at the same time as it designates the animal as potential game. The storytellers often add—with a charmingly enigmatic air that reminds the anthropologist that she cannot hope to understand everything—that all men and women descend from this transformed cassowary, just as cassowaries were engendered by the imperfect wife from the village.

Transcribed in its entirety below, another myth clearly shows the equivalence between women and cassowaries,[4] and gives more details on the representations attached to this animal:

A man and a woman met in the forest while each was on the way home to their village. They decided to walk together and talked along the way. Not far from them, a female cassowary was eating *ara' torwamonge'* [not identified] shoots, but they did not see her. The female became pregnant following her meal and gave birth to a boy instead of laying an egg. She did not know what to do with her offspring. They slept side by side. The baby grew and had a happy nature. A few months later, he sat up. He had nothing to

---

4.   For the Sambia, too, the "cassowary is fundamentally 'female'" (Herdt 1981: 134). As for that other northern Anga group, the Baruya, they designate cassowaries throughout their lives using the same words as for women: "The young, with their light plumage, are called *bwarandac*, little girl. The 'little girls' then grow and, when almost adult, become *tsindraye*, pubescent girls. The adults are called 'women' or 'old women,' depending on their age" (Godelier [1982] 1986: 127).

eat and slept a lot. His first tooth came in when he began to crawl. Then he was ready to stand up and walk. The cassowary-mother took him with her, pushing him along with her beak, and both spent their nights in the forest. One day, while her child was still deep in sleep, she left to eat fruits and gathered some for the little boy. She gave them to him, but he refused them. Wondering how she was ever going to feed him, she decided to visit the humans' gardens. There she noticed some ripe bananas and took two away with her into the forest. Her child was asleep: she woke him with her beak and held out the bananas. He took them, peeled them, and ate them. Then the cassowary-mother realized that this was a food that suited him and she continued regularly to take bananas from the gardens. And so her son grew.

One day, the cassowary-mother entered a village. She came to a house whose door was closed and rapped sharply with her beak to open it. She went in and took an adze, a loincloth, and some ornaments, which upon her return she placed next to the sleeping boy. When he woke up, he tried to cut some wood but he was still too little. His mother watched him and then went out to find something to eat in the gardens. She used her feet to harvest some tubers; she also took some sugarcane, and brought it all back to her child. He tried to drink the juice of the sugarcane and to eat a raw taro. He peeled it but, after tasting it, threw it aside. Then he broke out in sobs and tried to bite into a raw sweet potato, which this time was edible. Nevertheless, he still cried and the cassowary mother was very worried. And so she returned to the village where she opened the door of the house once more and entered. There she took some dry bamboo to light the fire. Her son was out walking nearby and when he returned, he saw what his mother had brought back; he asked many questions and tried to use everything. Smoke rose up and poured into the cassowary-mother's beak. Flames sprang up, the boy blew on them, and the fire grew stronger. Then he placed [on the fire] the raw taro he had tasted earlier and thrown away. The cassowary-mother watched him, then, while the food was cooking she went off to find something for herself.

Later the young boy took up the adze and set about cutting some trees to build a house. Then the cassowary-mother returned to the gardens to take some cuttings to plant. Back home, she saw that her son had finished his house. He planted what she had brought back, then lit a fire in the house and fell asleep. The bird spent the night nearby, outside. The plants grew well. Then he built a fence around them.[5] His cassowary-mother was wondering a lot about what would become of her child and she returned to the neighboring gardens. There she saw smoke, approached, and saw a woman planting. She touched her gently with her beak. The woman turned around, saw the cassowary's prints, then went back to work. The bird touched her more roughly and the woman straightened up once more. Then the cassowary pointed her beak at the netbag, the bark cape, and the bamboo knife of the woman, who, trying to understand what this animal wanted, decided to follow it. Together they walked to the young man's house. The cassowary pointed to the door with her beak. The woman approached, saw the man inside, and went in. The cassowary-mother made sure the woman was not timid and that the couple got along well.

Time passed. Food was plentiful and the household aged. The young woman's parents believed her dead and had prepared *ajiare'* mourning ornaments. But they had gone to her garden and had noticed the cassowary's prints. One day the young couple and the cassowary-mother went to see the woman's brother. When they saw her, everyone threw away their *ajiare'*. Then they noticed she was accompanied by a man and a cassowary. That night everyone went to sleep. Only the cassowary stayed outside. The woman remembered that she had been asked for by this bird, and she spoke of it saying: "This is my *atsi'* [female Ego's mother-in-law]" and the man said, "Here is my mother."

The next morning, the cassowary-mother opened her eyes very early and went to wake her son, who was fast asleep. She told him she wanted to leave, and her son asked her to stay a while. Finally, he followed her, taking with him only his knife, even though his cassowary-mother had told him to stay with his in-laws: "I found you a wife, you must stay with her." They arrived home and fell asleep. The next morning the female cassowary rose and set out on the path to the forest. Her son followed her. She gathered tree fruits while trying to persuade her son to return to his in-laws. She penetrated deeper and deeper into the forest with her son still behind her. At one point, he caught her by the foot, but she shook him off and kept climbing. They spent the night in the thick forest and the next day the young man tried again to retain his mother by her foot. She had defecated the fruits she had swallowed. The son wept as he continued to follow her.

---

5.   As is sometimes done to protect the gardens from the animals they attract.

The cassowary-mother did not want to go back to the village. She was returning to her wild state. Her son had not eaten and begged his mother to turn back. Then she came up to him and, because she wanted to leave for good, gave him a few of her quills, saying: "You will use these to make magic when you build traps where you have seen cassowary prints and fruit on the ground."[6]

After listening to his cassowary-mother's words, the man went back to the village. He was so sad and dismayed that he could not eat a bite for two days. The following day, the picture of his mother began to fade, and he began eating again. The cassowary had told him to forget her and to think only of the wife she had found for him. She had added: "When you get back to the village you will see a tall man. It is your father and you must call him Papa." A year passed. The man hardly thought of his cassowary-mother any more. The couple now lived in their own house. Another year passed. The man went out to hunt marsupials and, when he came to the forest, noticed a great number of the fruits that cassowaries eat. So he went to cut some rattan ties to make a trap. He slept in his house for two nights and then went to inspect his trap. A big cassowary was caught. He took it home and gave it whole to his affines as a *tuage* gift. They took it away and ate it.

Rather than an exchange between a woman and a cassowary, this myth concerns a being that has something of each: the cassowary in question looks and behaves like this bird, but it has given birth to a human baby.[7] The myth recounts the efforts of this cassowary-mother to raise her child (who does not resemble her), to socialize him and to introduce him into the world of humans. After the cassowary found a wife for her son, she teaches him hunting magic, and the first *tuage* game he brings his affines is a cassowary.

The tale is a perfect illustration of the enigmatic statement: "We are all the offspring of the primordial cassowary," which underscores the idea of a descent relationship between this animal and human beings in general. The cassowary's ability to give birth to a human child is no doubt to be attributed to the fact

6.   Cassowary snares are set near trees bearing fruits they like.
7.   Bernard Juillerat notes that, in the case of the Yafar, the cassowary "has been ascribed quasi-human traits, whence its role in cosmogonic mythology, in which it appears as a maternal, nurturing entity" (Juillerat [1986] 1996: 200).

that women and cassowaries are interchangeable, they are beings endowed with the same reproductive capacities. This interchangeability between a cassowary and a woman depicted in several myths is also present in the terms of address: the term a man uses to call his wife is a paronym of the term that designates the cassowary (respectively: *apianga'* and *apienge'*).[8] The Ankave say that if they call women by this term, it is because the first woman once lived in the forest as a cassowary.

No doubt this set of representations concerning women and cassowaries is to be associated with the ritual piercing of the earlobe of the great cassowary hunter's wife. In addition to the skill required to make the traps, success in capturing this animal attests to the ability to establish a relation with a being closely associated with women and therefore perhaps with women themselves. This proximity can also be seen in dreams, for when a man who has set a trap dreams a few days later that a naked woman is touching him or that a potential new wife introduces herself, he is sure that a cassowary has been caught. Capturing this animal is therefore a bit like seducing a woman, and the involvement of the trapper's wife attests to this metaphorical relationship between the cassowary and a certain category of women, precisely those who are potential marriage partners and objects of desire.

The practices surrounding eating this peculiar animal are not restricted to the married couple, since the mother of a cassowary hunter is included in the permanent ban affecting the consumption of this game bird. In effect, a woman may never eat the cassowaries her son has caught, whereas, with the exception of eels, which are discussed below, she can eat the flesh of any other game animals he may catch.[9] The Ankave say that if she were to eat a cassowary caught by her son, he would never catch another one, which is also what they say when trying to explain the prohibition on a hunter himself eating the game he has caught. The Ankave do not comment on this perpetual ban, but it is tempting to interpret such a situation with reference to the mother-son relationship, which, despite its transformation in the first stages of the initiations, has not totally lost its previously symbiotic or undifferentiated character (see pp. 104–05).

---

8. Other examples of paronyms among the Ankave can be found in Bonnemère 1994. For a definition of the term, see p. 54n9.

9. Insofar as he has been actually initiated, for if he catches any game whatsoever before having his nose pierced she must absolutely abstain from consuming it.

CATCHING EELS

The eel is a sort of "symmetrical" male counterpart of the cassowary, since it results from the transmutation of a person, but this time of a man.[10] Here is the myth old Ibua akwoningi told me on October 24, 1987:

> I'm going to tell you the story of a man who turned into an eel. Two brothers lived together. The elder was never in a hurry to come home; he would dig in the riverbed and always came home when night had fallen. The younger wondered where he went. The elder brother's wife would cook food, but her husband would not come home. He told her: "Make me some ornaments." She braided orchid stems into chest ornaments and made a pulpul. Then he asked the two women and his younger brother to fetch some sweet potatoes. Which they did. Together they went down to the river and cooked the tubers. The elder brother then told the two women: "One of you must stay up here, the other must go down there, and I will stand in the middle." Then he told his younger brother: "You, watch carefully; I'm going to put on my pulpul." They wondered what he was going to do and watched him. The older one said to his younger brother: "When I enter the water, don't cry." This man slipped on a new pulpul, new chest ornaments and feathers, and entered the water: "You, go home."
>
> The older brother did not warn his brother he was going to turn into an eel. The older brother's wife became an *ara' temi* grass, the man entered the water, and became an eel. The second woman became an *ara' sijiwi'* grass. The younger brother was left alone and he wept for his older brother and the two women. He went back home to sleep and had a dream in which his older brother told him: "You mustn't cry, I have become an eel. Take a trap and place it where I entered the water." Ever since, we make eel traps. The younger had another dream. In his dream, his older brother told him to catch some frogs and to make a trap: "If you see a very big eel, you must not eat it because it is me; you must give it to others to eat. If you catch small ones, you can eat them." He also taught his younger brother the charm for catching eels, and it is this formula that we use today.

---

10. There is another myth, which I will not relate here, that tells that it was the very long penis of a man who was importuning a woman in her gardens that changed into an eel after she had cut it off (Bonnemère 1996a: 318–20).

In another version, which Wite Peete akwiye, a young man living in a hamlet in Sinde Valley, told me on March 21, 1993, the story begins the same way, but the ending, which I have transcribed here, contains more details:

> Before, there did not use to be any eels. The younger brother of the man who had changed into an eel went down to the pond and saw one. He hit it with a stick to kill it. But when he tried to catch hold of it, it slipped out of his hands and returned to the water. So he told himself that he had to strike harder. Which he did. He took the eel he had caught home and cooked it. But he did not eat it because he remembered it was his brother. Other men ate it. They all found it very tasty: "Where did it come from?" The younger brother returned to the pond to see if there were any more eels. There were a lot of them, little ones and big ones. So he went to catch some frogs and put them in the water. He watched what happened and saw that all the frogs had been eaten. He said to himself that he had to make traps of bark. He carefully attached the vines and then went back to catch some frogs and placed them in the trap. He went home, slept for a night, and came back. He saw an eel, caught it, killed it, brought it back to the village, and cooked it in an earth oven. From that time on everyone made eel traps. And since then we eat eels.

Making eel traps is exclusively a man's job, which takes a long time to learn (Lemonnier 1996). But placing them in the stream and the magical practices surrounding this operation require close cooperation between the sexes, which may have an equivalent in the magic performed by the wife of a cassowary hunter when his trap remains empty.[11] When a boy catches his first eel, his father, paternal uncle, or big brother seizes it and strikes the boy with it, pronouncing a formula known only to the men. As in the case of the cassowary, consumption of a man's first eels is governed by very strict rules: the first three times (or four, according to one of the stories I collected) he catches an eel, all the trapper's close male relatives eat some, and if he is married the men of his wife's family join in. The fourth (or fifth) time he catches one, he eats some for the first time,

---

11. One woman told me that, in this case, she went to the place where the cassowary her husband had previously caught had been cooked and deposited some *nenge'* leaves on the cold ashes. Her husband then succeeded shortly thereafter in luring a cassowary into his trap.

in the company of women, after having cut up the eels and prepared the bark tubes in which they will be cooked. His sisters, mother, and maternal aunts gather leafy vegetables to cook with the eels. Again, it is the trapper who cuts up the eels; he chops their tails into small pieces that are given to the women present to bite into, and then spits onto the rest a mixture of fragrant-smelling leaves, ginger, and vegetal salt before distributing the pieces and eating some himself. The Ankave stress that, like him, a man's mother can eat the eels he has caught only after the fifth time. They do not offer an explanation for this practice but spontaneously mention the restrictions on a man's consumption of the cassowaries he has trapped. Yet the two cases are different, since neither the hunter himself nor his mother can eat a cassowary he has captured.

THE IMPOSSIBILITY OF BREAKING THE SYMBIOTIC BOND WITH THE MOTHER

Let us retain that these practices corroborate the idea that once she is a mother, a woman is ritually involved in different stages of her children's life. This is particularly true in the case of her son, since, as I have shown at length, she must be present at two important rituals that constitute the first collective stages of his initiation. But the nature of the bonds between a mother and her offspring can also be seen in the rules governing the consumption of *game* (see also Bamford 1998: 161–62). They are identical for a mother and her son in the case of two animals depicted in myths as the result of the transmutation of human beings: the cassowary is never consumed by either the trapper or his mother; and the eel caught when a man sets his traps for the fifth time is eaten by himself and by his mother at the same time as by other women. The need to model the behavior of a mother on that of her son and vice versa shows that the symbiotic bond that united them when he was small did not totally disappear with his initiation.[12]

---

12. Among the Kamea, the taboo that unites a mother and her son—and concerns only "smelly game" (marsupials?)—is different in even more ways than this one. First, the taboo falls on any (smelly) game and not particularly on that caught by the boy. Second, once he is initiated, he can start to eat some while it was forbidden for him before for fear that his mother "would sit in the house all day long where she would eventually die" (Bamford 2007: 94). On the contrary, she was able to eat game when he was still a child but stops eating it—and forever—from the time his initiation begins since it would be harmful *to her* if she did (2007: 93). In short, whereas the first taboo is for another, the second falls into the category of the usual taboo situations (see chapter 6).

The relation between a mother and her daughter is of the same nature, as indicated by the practice dictating that neither may eat the *tuage* game given for the girl's marriage. The mother can do this only once her daughter has grown up and married; in other words, when she has definitively changed her place of residence.

When her children have their own children, a mother retires from the scene, as the analysis of the rite for the birth of a man's first child has shown. The Ankave often recall this: "She already received the *meemi sare*' when her own son was born and therefore cannot receive it today when it is this son who has had a child"; or "The mother of the young father cannot eat the meat of the *meemi tse*' marsupials her son caught when his baby was born because she already had some when she gave birth to him." That being said, the reason behind this prohibition cannot be entirely contained in these statements, for in this case it would be hard to understand why the mother of the young woman who has just given birth can eat the marsupials, whereas she too had some *meemi tse*' when her daughter was born. This asymmetry must be somehow linked to the difference in the nature of the relation between a mother and her daughter, on the one hand, and a mother and her son, on the other, a difference that no doubt has to do with the parallel character in the first case and the crossness in the second. In the case of her daughter, a mother can take part in the meal of birth marsupials that her son-in-law and his close relatives have caught, but when it is her own son who is the hunter, she must abstain. In this case we are tempted to explain the taboo in the same way as the restrictions already discussed on consumption of the cassowaries and eels caught by a man, which he and his mother must obey in the same way, owing to the vestiges of symbiosis their relationship still contains, despite its transformation in the first initiation stages. In all events, the paternal grandmother of a newborn is excluded from the gestures and ritual exchanges performed on the occasion of the birth. Only the maternal grandparents receive a gift of pig meat, the last it is said, called *rwa'atungwen*, to be made during the childhood of their grandchild (see p. 145).

Now that the practices punctuating the life of a woman have been presented in detail, we are better prepared to compare, and therefore to understand, the life-paths of a man and a woman. The most striking feature concerns the different position each occupies in their kinship network. Briefly, with respect to a man, an Ankave woman is more often called on to exercise *agency on behalf of someone else*: as the sister of a man, she is involved in the collective stages of his initiation and then, above all, when he is expecting his first child; as the sister of

a woman, she accompanies her to the river to bathe and adorn herself in preparation for the public phase of the *suwangain* ritual; as the wife of a cassowary
hunter, she is subjected to a ban on the meat of this animal so that her husband
may continue to catch it; as a future mother, she consumes red pandanus sauce
so that the child in her womb may grow; as the mother of a boy, she partici-
pates in the first two collective stages of his initiation and does not consume
the cassowaries or the first eels he catches; and as the mother of a prepubescent
daughter, she abstains from touching the *tuage* meat paid for the girl's marriage
so as not to hamper her growth; finally, as a paternal grandmother, she cannot
take part in the meal of birth marsupials caught by her son for the birth of his
first child.

This "capacity to act for others" includes various practices: rubbing performed on the body of someone else but also obeying prohibitions on food or
behaviors, or on the contrary consuming a food, not for oneself as might be
expected but for someone else. This special aptitude of women to affect other
persons seems to come to them spontaneously, whereas men acquire it only
when they prepare to become a father for the first time, at the close of a gradual
process that placed them first of all in the position of being *the object of the actions of others*. Only then, as the ethnographic material related here has already
shown at length, are they capable of acting for someone other than themselves:
for their pregnant wife, when they abstain from red pandanus juice in order to
reduce the risk of a hemorrhage that might occur during the birth; for a uterine
niece when she reaches puberty and, as a maternal uncle, he rubs her chest with
clay to stimulate her development; and finally, for a uterine nephew when he
goes through the initiation ordeals with him.

This agency is thus exercised by men in the framework of two relations only:
a conjugal relation but only in the context of procreation; and an avuncular
relation, at the time his sister's daughter and son see their body changing and
assuming the aspect it will have when they become fertile. One could venture to
say that, on the contrary, the capacity to act for others is characteristic of wom-
en, whatever position they may occupy in the kinship network of the person on
whom their action is exercised. This is not to say that women are in any way endowed with a specific property that would make them more gifted for relations
than their male counterparts. Rather than a personal attribute that only women
might possess because they are born female, it is the specific and prime place
they occupy in the process of generation and the nurturing role they have with
regard to their offspring that, for the Ankave, determine their capacity to act for

others. What characterizes the maternal function in this society is a woman's aptitude to affect other persons by her own actions.[13]

We have seen that this specific relational capacity is expressed throughout a woman's lifetime since, at different stages in the life of those to whom she is tied, she finds herself in a position to accompany them and to act on their behalf. But she is only exceptionally the object of another person's action, notably during childhood and when she changes her residence upon marrying. In the latter context, and although the Ankave claim that the first-night ritual is designed to vanquish the girl's apprehension and possible fear, it is clear that it also aims to bring the two members of the new couple together. In this case, the magical gestures performed by the betrothed's father and the shift in position during the night concern the young couple and not only the wife. As for the absence of any large-scale rituals for girls, an observation that already opened the two chapters devoted to the unfolding of a woman's life, it attests primarily to the fact that there is no need to transform the relation between a mother and her daughter for the latter to grow up. It also shows that, in the world of the Ankave, to be the object of someone else's action is decidedly not a relational position befitting adults of the female sex.

---

13. Cf. Kamea ethnography according to which women have a spontaneous capacity as well—here, that of acting as a container (Bamford 2007: 63), as Bamford glosses it. Both of us thus agree on the fact that women are endowed with a capacity—linked to their position in the procreation process—that men do not have. My point for the Ankave is that the whole ritual sequence lead men to acquire this capacity to act for others, which they use as mothers' brothers.

CHAPTER 12

A few other relational figures?

The analysis of the rituals and exchanges accompanying the Ankave life-course reveals the importance people lend to the relational dimension in their conception of personhood. In every human society, since humans are eminently social beings, others are the humus and the world of meaning without which no one learns to live like a human being; to this self-evidence, the members of Ankave society add a few special twists.

As they underscore, when talking about the final ritual in the cycle organized for a living person, the—classic—ultimate goal of Ankave society is to perpetuate itself, and each must play their assigned role in this endeavor by becoming a parent. This is not an individual choice; it is a social obligation each person owes, as it were, to society as a whole. By punctuating the gestation period that leads to the birth of a man's first child with ritual gestures and behaviors, Ankave society accompanies the individuals and makes an event that the Western world tends to see as a private affair into an eminently social and collective concern. But that is not all, for if we focus on the individual's access to parenthood, the role played by others is equally fundamental. The Ankave's conception of the person places such emphasis on kinship relations that it is not even conceivable that someone might grow up and reach maturity merely as a result of the passage of time and living in society.

In all societies the world over, persons could of course be described as "relational" inasmuch as they live in relation with others. But it seems to me that the Ankave concept has a feature not found elsewhere. This resides in their conception of the male life-path as a succession of transformations in the nature of the relations he entertains with several female figures, and in making this an indispensable condition of his access first to fatherhood and then to the status of maternal uncle. Over this ordered series of transformations, the collective ceremonies transform the mother-son relationship to enable the son to become a father and then by transforming the brother-sister relationship to become a maternal uncle; in other words, a person capable of acting on behalf of someone else.

In a way, it is as though the relations were not external to the person but actually contributed to defining him or her. The Western view would tend to say that people have relations with others—these relations being therefore external to them even if they affect their interiority and have a great impact on their well-being—and that their maturation is a process to which close relatives must obviously adapt; but I do not think the Western view considers it necessary to act on these close relatives in order for young people to reach adulthood. Among the Ankave, on the contrary, growth and changes of status require, as we have seen, an intense ritual work in which several close relatives are intimately involved.

Furthermore, Ankave culture stresses the difference in men's and women's positions with regard to reproduction and access to parenthood. In the case of men, this difference is expressed in the need to ritually transform the nature of their relationship with their mother if they are to become fathers, whereas women become mothers without the need for any ritual action.[1] The Ankave conception of the conditions of access to fatherhood requires that first of all, a man's relation with his mother, who has fed and raised him throughout childhood, be transformed for all to see, and ritually staged with the participation of its two constituent poles. Then it demands that his relationship with his sister be transformed in turn by the same process.

---

1. The Ankave—and the Kamea—do not have female initiations, whereas the northern Anga organize them when a girl menstruates for the first time. Maurice Godelier analyzes these as a being complementary to the male rites inasmuch as they ensure the women consent to their domination by the men ([1982] 1986: 49–50; Lemonnier 2004: 147).

A man's relations with his two closest female relatives are thus associated, through ritual practices, with specific moments in his life. To move on to a new stage in the eminently social process leading to fatherhood—in other words, for his life as a man to unfold—the content of these relations must change. Or to put it yet another way, when a man becomes a father, he cannot *still be* a son in the same way he was previously. For the Ankave, parenthood reconfigures kinship relations as a whole. To be sure, there is nothing very original in this, if not the local way of conceiving this rearrangement as, not the automatic outcome of the birth of a first child in itself, but as that of the deliberate visible and ritualized action of the human group.

This conception, which sees the coordinated action of the individuals composing the two terms of a relation as the only possible means of its transformation, and this relational transformation as the source of a modification in the person is marked from the outset by a distinction between the sexes. As I showed at the end of the preceding chapter, men and women are not equivalent in their capacity to act for others, and they do not occupy the same position in this world governed by the notion of mutual influence that is at the heart of Ankave practices designed to construct a person over a lifetime.

LEENHARDT AND KANAK PERSONHOOD

According to Maurice Leenhardt ([1947] 1979), the Kanak's relational conception of personhood excludes the idea that a human being (*kamo*) might exist outside the role they play and the positions they occupy in a social world that saturates, as it were, their existence. The problem with this view is that it implies that the Kanak do not have what could be called a "feeling of individuality." Yet, clearly beyond the many and varied conceptions of personhood found the world over, whether these emphasize the social fabric in which each person is a thread or, instead, value individual autonomy, each inhabitant of this world experiences themselves as distinct from others while sharing a typically human way of living, thinking, feeling, acting, and experiencing (Théry 2007: 443). In his article "A category of the human mind: The notion of person; the notion of self" ([1938] 1985), Marcel Mauss called attention to the importance of distinguishing between awareness of self, which is universal, and the normative conceptions of personhood, which are cultural conventions. Moreover, several social scientists rightly stress the need, when using the term *individual*, to distinguish the empirical agent present in every society from specific modern representations embedded in the history of the Western world that place a social value on individual autonomy in respect of social conventions.[2]

When he drew his famous diagram representing the Kanak view of the person ([1947] 1979: 154), Leenhardt forgot about the empirical human agent, or rather he supposed this figure to have disappeared into the fabric of social relations.[3] But by definition, the (living) empirical agent never disappears. In this sense, his critics are right in saying that the Kanak, like all human beings, are aware of being individuals, but their criticism nevertheless goes too far when they reject the totality of Leenhardt's analysis, since in so doing they question the possibility that there might be some variability in the normative representations of the person. And consequently, they amalgamate the descriptive level (in which the individual exists universally) and the level of the analysis of a conception held by a particular world (where the individual is or is not a culturally recognized value), whereas there is no correspondence between the two. In a way, Leenhardt forgets the empirical individual, while his critics forget that this individual is not everywhere held to be a social value.

REVEALING LANGUAGE FORMS

In support of his interpretation of the Kanak person as eminently "relational," Leenhardt advanced the existence of dual forms in the languages of New Caledonia in general and in that of Huailu in particular. The forms he cites are, on the one hand, dual pronouns ("both of us," for instance) and, on the other hand, nouns designating couples or pairs and probably stressing locally valued social ties. This was Leenhardt's point of view when he wrote: "it is customary in Melanesia to never hold only one view of people and things but always to see them from the standpoint of a symmetrical relation or a participation" (1930: 13). In other terms, as Michel Naepels says, when Leenhardt brings dual linguistic forms into his theory of the participations involving the individual, he

---

2.   I am thinking here in particular of the anthropologist Louis Dumont (1978), the philosopher Vincent Descombes (2003), and the sociologist Irène Théry (2007).

3.   Here, in Maurice Leenhardt's own words: "The *kamo* is thus poorly delineated in the eyes of others.... Nor is the *kamo* himself better delineated in his own eyes. He is unaware of his body, which is only his support" ([1947] 1979: 153).

is using "an ontological interpretation of the language, as though it reflected the most basic characteristics of Kanak life" (2007: 76).

Is it possible to infer from linguistic features in general and from grammatical forms in particular the existence of a particular cultural representation? Most linguists think that no conclusion of a conceptual or even cognitive nature can be drawn from a grammatical feature. The question of the relation between a language, a perception of reality, and concepts is not recent, as we know from the discussions sparked by Émile Benveniste's famous text, "Categories of thought and language" ([1966] 1971), and the no-less famous "Sapir-Whorf" hypothesis, which holds that, "reality is to a large extent unconsciously constructed by the linguistic habits of the group. Two languages are never sufficiently similar to be regarded as representing the same social reality. The worlds in which different societies live are distinct, not simply the same world with different labels" (Détrie, Siblot, and Vérine 2001: 138).

I do not claim to bring anything new to this theoretical debate, which is largely beyond my competence and the scope of the present book, but I would defend the idea that, in a specific domain like the normative conception of the person, it is legitimate to think that the various uses of kinship, whether in language or elsewhere, are likely to be significant when taken together. At any rate, that is why I thought it would be useful to mention the existence of lexical terms that might attest to the importance given certain kinship relations in a study analyzing male initiations as moments in which transformations in the content of the mother-son and brother-sister relationships are staged and effected.

The Ankave have special terms for particular kinship relations (see table 1 below). Not all relations, however, have a specific term: some are missing, as though they had been forgotten in this naming system. Although they have not been the object of many studies by specialists of kinship terms, those terms that do not designate a position in a kinship system but rather a relation between two categories of person are often found in the Australian Aboriginal languages. They are what specialists call *dyadic kinship terms*,[4] and are always what anthropologists call *reference terms*. In other words, they are not used by the partners of a relation to address each other but by a third person talking about them and thus

---

4.   Here is Francesca Merlan and Jeffrey Heath's definition: "By dyadic term, we have in mind an expression of the type '(pair of) brothers' or 'father and child,' in which the kinship relationship is between the two referents internal to the kin expression" (1982: 107).

underscoring the tie between them. Among the Ankave we often find such terms in myths, in their plural rather than dual form, for the story usually concerns a set of sisters or brothers confronted with misadventures from which only the youngest escapes unscathed and takes an action that changes the course of the story.

What precisely are the relations covered by such terms? In the first place, and as the following table shows,[5] they are more frequently relations between men than relations between women. The second striking feature is that, with the exception of the opposite-sex, conjugal relationship, all relations designated by a specific term in the Ankave language concern persons of the same sex.

Table 1. Ankave terms for kinship relations

Relationship	Dual form	Plural form
Between a man and his younger brother(s)	rera'rongwau'	rera'rongwa'wa
Between a woman and her younger sister(s)	renabe'renanengi'pau'	renabe'renanengi'wa
Between men married to sisters	roare'roarerwawau'	roare'roarerwawa
Between a man and his son-in-law	rene'reneangwau'	rene'reneangwa'wa
Conjugal*: a man and his wife/wives	oramberayau'	oramberayo'wa
Conjugal*: a woman/women and her/their husband(s)	riembe'riangwayau'	riembe'riangwayo'wa
Same-sex filial (male Ego)	rane'wamerau'	rane'wamero'wa
Same-sex filial (female Ego)	renemie'i'bau'	renemie'i'bo'wa
Between cross-cousins	roaye'roayawau'	roaye'roayawa
Between brothers-in-law	rambe'rambawa'u	rambe'rambawa
Between a man and his uterine nephew(s)	riame'wamerowa'u	riame'wamero'wa
Between a man and his grandson(s)	reria'wamirowau'	reria'wamiro'w a

*Whether the couple is monogamous (in which case the dual is used) or includes several wives (plural form).

---

5. For the most part, the table is based on information contained in the unpublished "Angave Anthropology Sketch" written by Richard and Marilyn Speece from the Summer Institute of Linguistics (SIL), who lived with the Ankave for nearly fifteen years (Speece and Speece 1983: 172–73). See also p. 17.

We note, for instance, that of the sibling ties, only those between brothers, on the one hand, and sisters, on the other, are designated by a special term. When the Ankave want to talk about the relationship between a man and his sisters or a woman and her brothers, they do not use a specific term but a periphrase meaning literally "her oldest brother and his (younger or older) sisters," depending on the case (*raro te'ne renanengi te'ne* or *rangwo' te'ne renangwi te'ne*). The same goes for the relationship between a man and his daughter(s) and a woman and her son(s); here, too, the Ankave must use a periphrase. How are such practices to be explained?

First of all, I would point out that it would be hard to say only ritualized relationships are designated by a distinctive term, since I showed at length that, during initiations, it is precisely relations between persons of the *opposite sex* that need to be transformed and that the mothers and sisters of the boys are extensively involved.

Instead, what appears when we examine the list of those relationships the Ankave designate by their own term of reference is that some of them are based on the notion of "transmission," whether of rights on the land (between a man and his sons) or magical knowledge—for example, between a woman and her daughters. Same-sex siblings can be regarded similarly, inasmuch as two brothers share land rights, which they inherited from their common father, and two sisters received the same knowledge from their mother, in particular concerning childcare and gardening. Other terms express (male) relationships involving exchanges of goods. For example, the relationship between a maternal uncle and his nephew, which, as we saw, is punctuated by regular gifts from the boy's parents to his mother's brother, requires using a specific term, whereas the counterpart between a paternal aunt and her niece, which does not entail exchanges, is designated by a periphrase.[6] Another example of a relationship marked by exchanges of goods and for which there is a specific term is that between cross-cousins. It is expressed particularly when one of them dies. In effect, it is in this kin category that a man is chosen to bear the body of the deceased to its final dwelling place, for which he receives the *a'menge'* gift. As we saw in chapter 9 (see p. 148), this gift has the particularity of being able to be anticipated, in

---

6.   As we have seen, a father's sister plays no role in her nephews' and nieces' life: she merely helps make the body ornaments for her brother's son at the time of his initiation, like the other family members, and does not have any particular social role in the life of her niece.

the form of the reciprocal and simultaneous exchange of a domestic pig, which results in abandoning any claim to receive the *a'menge'* when one of the two dies and the other is called to bear the corpse.

Finally, the other relations for which the Ankave have special terms all refer to male affines: a man and his son-in-law, brothers-in-law, and men who have married sisters. As affines, these men are in a relation of which exchanges of goods or mutual aid are a key-component: a son-in-law makes regular gifts in kind (domestic pig meat, game) to his father-in-law; the wife's brother goes with his brother-in-law to hunt marsupials at the birth of each of the latter's children; two men married to sisters have the same in-laws to whom they owe bridewealth and *tuage* gifts in kind (see pp. 145–46). It sometimes happens that they make each other gifts of pig meat, as I observed one January day in 1988, on the occasion of the sale of a pig belonging to an inhabitant of Ayakupna'wa, when two men married to sisters each bought four kinas worth of meat, which they gave to each other.

In view of these different ethnographic observations, we are justified in advancing the idea that relations designated by a special term carry a social value that other relations do not. This relationship is based on exchanges: of goods, knowledge, or labor, which are reciprocal when they concern persons of the same generation and asymmetrical when different generations are involved and the older generation transmits knowledge or land rights to the younger one.

Perhaps some readers will find that none of the above substantiates the hypothesis of a relational conception of the person. Yet, disposing of a word to designate a relational configuration rather than having to use a periphrase juxtaposing two kin terms (for example, "a brother and his sister") implies a mental attitude in which the very fact of the relationship is apprehended before the reality of its components.[7] A single word designates a social and mental reality in which the components of the relationship form, as it were, an inseparable whole, for it is precisely the combination and not the separate existence of each component that is relevant. As Rupert Stasch, an anthropologist who worked with the Korowai of West Papua puts it: "dyadic ties are represented as basic, and persons are represented as pieces of dyads" (2009: 76). When the term for

---

7. There are other lexical details too that point to the priority of relations: here I am thinking of so-called sex-relative kin terms, which are not found among the Ankave but which have been thoroughly investigated in a variety of other ethnographic contexts (Alès and Barraud 2001).

the dyadic kin tie is pronounced, the speaker's mind apprehends *at one and the same time* the relationship itself, the exchange entailed, and the social context in which the exchange takes place. The individuals bound together by such a tie become, in the present context, secondary, obscured, as it were, by the overall organizing image of the whole. Joel Robbins writes about the use of such terms among the Urapmin: "setting aside the dyadic/triadic issue, I am inclined to call them 'relational terms' and to use them as evidence of the relational image of the social world that is central to Urapmin culture" (2004: 301).

More specifically: does this mean that those relations—and the social facts comprised in them—for which there is no specific word are less important to the Ankave? This would be hard to sustain, since there is no special term for certain relations that are central to the male rituals, such as that between a mother and her son, or between opposite-sex siblings. Instead, we need to en-visage the hypothesis already advanced when discussing the mother-son bond that the Ankave do not see these relations as linking autonomous persons but rather as creating an entity characterized by a certain lack of differentiation. It can also be said that the common quality Ankave culture ascribes to these two relationships is the fact of being unstable: a male individual can become an adult man—a father and a maternal uncle—only if his relationship with his mother and then his sister are radically transformed. We are therefore led to posit that it is not possible to designate by a single word a relational configuration that, while retaining the same components, over time undergoes a complete internal modification. By contrast, relations indicated by a special term all share the fact of not having to be ritually transformed in order for an individual to become an adult, and therefore a parent.

PERSONAL NAMES

Even personal names, which might spontaneously be thought to be associated with a unique individual, are marked in Ankave culture by their relational con-ception of the person. Several rules govern the construction of personal names, which differ according to whether the name is being chosen for a woman or a man. The names of men are built according to an unspoken rule that the father's clan must be mentioned. In names composed of two terms, by far the most frequent case, the father's clan comes first and is usually followed by the name of the mother's clan. A male personal name thus designates an individual as the product of the association of the two clans from which he comes. As a consequence, many boys have the same name, since individualization does not prevail over that which makes each person a member of the group contained in a social universe circumscribed by clan membership (Bonnemère 2005).

Women's names look different. First of all, they are always composed of a single term. And this term is less often the name of a clan than that of a river, a stream, or a piece of forest located on the territory of the little girl's paternal clan. This is a hard-and-fast rule: a woman's name never refers to a territory on which the girl-child's mother's clan might have rights, but that does not mean that some women do not carry a name that does not refer to the father's clan. In this case, it is the mother who, having been struck by something at the time of the birth or shortly after, while she was isolated on the outskirts of the village or in the forest, suggests to her husband that he give the baby a name connected with the situation in question. This can be the cry of a bird heard during the delivery, a grass encountered on the path or a song she remembered at the time of the birth. In short, mothers have some leeway in choosing their daughters' names.

As in the case of male personal names, those given to girls are meant not only to individualize their bearer but also to enroll them in a social world—this time not by making direct mention of the father's clan name but by giving her the name of some feature of his clan territory. In both cases, women's names are vectors for expressing the patrilineal descent rule found in this society. It is the second situation, in which the mother chooses to name her baby girl after something that happened at the time of the birth, that might be most connected with a principle of individualization. In all other cases, which are in the majority, an individual's personal name does not express anything more than clan belonging and therefore their position in a social network composed of kin groups.

To these main terms is added a sort of affix that indicates the person's birth order within the group of siblings. There too we find a distinction between men's and women's names. It is as though male children were named without considering the possibility of girl siblings. And this is also the case of the affixes of female names. In other words, the names of boys and girls all carry terms indicating birth order, but the sequence within the group of same-sex siblings is independent of the group of opposite-sex siblings. Here are a few examples: Idzadze Nguye is the eldest son. His personal name is made up of his father's clan (Idzadze), followed by his mother's (Nguye). His sister, born three years later, is called Obeni, after a river that flows through her father's clan territory.

The third and fourth children, both boys, received the names Idzadze Nguye akwiye (2nd) and Idzadze Nguye padzerwa (3rd). The last child, a girl born in 1987 who died prematurely, was called Obeni akwaei (2nd). It is thus impossible to know the boys' relative position with regard to their sisters and vice versa. Alternatively, we know for sure that Idzadze Nguye akwiye is the second son in the family and Idzadze Nguye padzerwa the third. Likewise, we are sure that Obeni is older than her sister Obeni akwaei, but nothing tells us the number of years, or brothers, between them.

Those are the main principles for forming personal names. How are they used? Although these names are used more often than in the past when the Ankave call out to each other, in the majority of cases kin terms are still the first reflex. Having lived for several generations with a minimal though constant level of women arriving from the outside (whether they live in the two other Ankave valleys, Angae and Sinde, or come from the neighboring Iqwaye group), marriages have created networks of particularly tight kin ties, with the result that everyone, or nearly everyone, is a consanguineal kinsman or an affine. In situations involving close relatives—the most common case—the kin term prevails. Sometimes, if the context leaves no ambiguity, only the birth order name is used to hail someone. A younger child will thus hear the call: "Akwiye!" Furthermore, when a father or a mother asks a child nicely to fetch some object, they will use what I have called, following Mimica, a "name of endearment" (2005: 184–86, see also Bonnemère 1996a: 146–47), the equivalent of "darling" but more specific than the latter inasmuch as the child's sex and the mother's clan determine the nickname used.[8] Two persons of the same sex whose mothers are from the same clan will thus be called by the same nickname. And this applies to all the clans in the valley. But a boy and a girl whose mother is from the same clan will be called by different nicknames. Adults also use these nicknames among themselves in convivial contexts so that they could be translated in Tok Pisin by something like "please, you whose mother is an Idzadze, give me this or that."

Aside from the prevailing use of kin terms and nicknames, which are basically of a relational nature, the Ankave often use teknonyms in addressing each other. For instance, a woman with children will more often be hailed by "mother of Idzadze Nguye!" than by her personal name. In other words, what the Ankave

8. The terms in question are all borrowed from the plant kingdom: they refer to wild plants or cultivars of sugarcane, areca palm, red pandanus, banana, taro, or sweet potato (Bonnemère 2005: 190).

privilege once again is the use of a term indicative of a relational status ("mother of a given boy") rather than the personal name.

Without seeing these naming practices as an actual "proof" of the existence of a relational conception of the person in which an individual can become a parent—a fundamental stage in life for the Ankave—only through acting on the relations binding them to certain categories of women, we are obliged to note that they point in the same direction as the expressions designating a specific relationship or as the dual terms. These ethnographic details attest that the Ankave are particularly attuned to relations as constitutive components of the person. They also confirm the findings of the study of life cycle rituals showing that, over a lifetime, a person, in this case a man, graduates from one status to the next and acquires the capacity to act for others—which, as we have seen, is central to the Ankave culture—only once his relations with certain close relatives have been transformed.

CHAPTER 13

"The Melanesian person": Debates

> *Social persons do not reach what we would call completeness until they have participated in all the rituals of Orokaiva society, including their own funeral.*
> —André Iteanu, "The concept of the person and the ritual system"

In the Ankave-Anga society of Papua New Guinea, all men must go through a set of rituals commonly called "male initiations," which combine mental and physical ordeals, learning the behaviors required of an adult man, seclusion, and promiscuous living conditions. Although the literature defines these rituals as being based on the exclusion of women, we have seen that in the case of the Ankave, the participation of the novice's mother and sister is indispensable to their efficacy. The analysis of the forms of this female involvement I proposed in the foregoing chapters shows that the first two (collective) stages of the ritual act on the boys by transforming their relationship with their mother. Later, in the first-birth ritual, it is the young father's relationship with his sister that undergoes its own modification, thus yielding to the conjugal and parental relation. This ritual is thus much more than the third and final stage of the male initiations, since it involves the whole community and establishes the couple in their parenthood. At the close of the public phase, which marks the end of the rite, the new parents know the gestures and magical formulas they will need for the birth of their other children. They have become parents.

The analysis of this set of rituals also revealed the precise steps entailed in accomplishing the relational transformations: first, reiterate the earlier state of the relation to be changed, which requires the presence of its two terms; second, once the ritual has been performed, signify that the nature of this relation has changed by means of a gesture emblematic of the new relational state.[1] In the collective stages of the initiation rituals, both mothers and novices are secluded in their respective spaces and perform the same gestures, thus staging the symbiotic relationship that bound them during the pregnancy and then, in a different way, throughout infancy and early childhood. When the first-stage ritual is over and a differentiation between the novices' behavior and that of their mothers has been established (see p. 107n15), the boys return to the village and present their mothers with some small game; this gift shows that the formerly symbiotic bond between them has become a relationship between two persons in which exchange is possible.[2]

A final lesson to be drawn from the analysis of the Ankave ethnographic materials concerns the sequential and indivisible nature of the rituals that make up the initiations. Indeed, we cannot understand how the process of constructing a male person is locally conceived if we view the different phases of the initiations as independent of each other. Likewise, it is impossible to limit the first-birth ritual to the day of the actual celebration. The prohibitions, gifts, and specific behaviors required throughout the pregnancy are an integral part of this final male ritual. To reduce it, for example, to the day the young father is led into the forest to the small altar representing the primordial ancestor would be purely and simply to truncate the information available for the analysis of such an event and to ignore the ordered succession of the rituals within which this secret male rite takes on its full meaning.

---

1.   The result was obtained by adopting a viewpoint similar to that of Martin Holbraad, even if the Cuban Ifa cult he describes is not an initiation of the same kind as that analyzed in these pages and the transformation it operates cannot be described as an organized accumulation of relationships (2008: 231). Recalling the banality of the idea that initiation makes neophytes into different persons and the lack of novelty in establishing a distinction between internal and external relations, he asserts that what matters is to develop the logical framework that makes it possible to account for these self-evident ideas (2008: 255).

2.   As we saw (pp. 104–05), the Ankave do not seem to see the mother-son dyad as a relation but seem instead to view it as an indistinct entity.

Having set out this argument with its various components, we now need to try to see how it fits into the existing theories on the person and life cycle rituals in this part of the world. For beyond ethnographic description and regional comparisons, anthropology consists in producing theoretical hypotheses capable of accounting for the diversity of existing social and symbolic productions. Does the analysis of the Ankave ethnographic material tend to validate or, on the contrary, invalidate these theories? Does it point us toward a more measured path that would suggest accommodations? If the research on ideas about the person in Melanesia and the practices to which they give rise was marked by the publication in 1988 of Marilyn Strathern's major book, *The gender of the gift: Problems with women and problems with society in Melanesia*, a large number of earlier studies also deserve our attention. First of all, M. Strathern drew inspiration from them and, too, they are today still among those references consulted directly, and not only through the work of other commentators, in support of various points of view.

AN UNPRODUCTIVE QUARREL IN THE END

The controversy that crystalized around the writings of the missionary anthropologist Maurice Leenhardt, who worked in New Caledonia from 1902 to 1926 and published a detailed analysis of the Kanak notion of the person, is a good illustration of some of the antagonistic positions on the validity of his interpretation that continue even today to divide the anthropological community. Seen from the outside, this controversy seems clearly to oppose specialists of this part of the world, who cast doubt on the validity of Leenhardt's theses, and other anthropologists who, attracted by the originality of his analysis of the Melanesian person, use it as a particularly relevant example of a major difference between Western thinking and that of those "remote populations" that in Leenhardt's time were referred to as "primitive."

To be sure, in the past few years Leenhardt's work has undergone a certain rehabilitation, well after the English translation of *Do Kamo* ([1947] 1979) and the publication of James Clifford's book on this author's work and view of the Melanesian world (1982). Recent research on "the relational person," inaugurated by M. Strathern's comparative study *The gender of the gift* (1988) and continued by what was subsequently called the New Melanesian Ethnography, followed on the ideas advanced by Leenhardt. New Caledonia specialists do not recognize the Kanaks with which they were familiar from Leenhardt's writings and consider there is no reason to oppose one form of thought to another, for which the notion of individual does not have the same value.

Aside from the fact that affirming a difference in ways of conceptualizing the world does not mean supposing a relation of inequality between them—as shown recently by Philippe Descola in *Beyond nature and culture* ([2005] 2013) or Irène Théry in *La distinction de sexe* (2007)—comparative research of the scope of that conducted by M. Strathern may remind New Caledonia specialists of the early-twentieth-century work on the "primitive mentality," and in particular the work of Lucien Lévy-Bruhl, a close colleague of Leenhardt, who is also enjoying a certain comeback in anthropology after long decades of neglect (Keck 2008). Lévy-Bruhl did not see what he called "primitive mentality" as a colonial view of the other but as "a real problem for philosophy when it attempts to describe human practices in terms of its own discourse" (Keck n.d.). How can one account for a practical mind that tolerates contradiction (see the famous expression "The Bororo are Arara"), whereas, ever since Aristotle, logic has been governed by the principle of noncontradiction (Keck n.d.)? For Lévy-Bruhl, the practical mind, which accepts that contradiction is possible, and the theoretical mind, which does not, exist side by side in every person and in every society, but in proportions that vary. In so-called primitive societies, collective representations affect perceptions and cause people to perceive beings that are imperceptible and yet real, analogous to dream phenomena (Keck n.d.). Lévy-Bruhl uses the term *participation* for the action of the collective representations in individual perception, which "is not to be understood negatively as a state of mental confusion, but positively as an attempt to rehabilitate the place of affectivity in the life of the mind" (Salmon 2008). Even with Lévy-Bruhl there was therefore hardly any question of inequality or anteriority in an evolutionist sense between two ways of viewing the world.

Nor do we find such a mindset in Marcel Mauss' 1938 lecture, which could rightly be regarded as a "founding moment in ethnology of the person" (Tarot 2008: 22). Mauss seeks to follow the long historical movement during which the "idea of 'person,' the idea of the 'self' grew up" (Mauss [1938] 1985: 263). But he does not take either a psychological or a linguistic view: "It is a subject of social history. How, over the centuries, in numerous societies, did there appear, not the sense of the 'self' but the notion, the concept that the men of the various times created of it?" (Mauss [1938] 1985: 265). In other words, to borrow the formula used by Théry in *La distinction de sexe*, how did we come to elaborate "two overarching *normative* conceptions related to rights, religions, customs, social structures and mentalities: the person as a *figure* in societies studied by anthropologists, and the person as '*self*' in modern Western societies" (Théry 2007: 428)?

According to Théry's analysis, "the person as self is contrasted to the person as figure because it is no longer tied to a cosmic, hierarchical religious and all-enveloping totality, but valued as a whole in itself, an independent moral consciousness, which is expressed in the major values of liberty and equality" (2007: 431). However, these two social conceptions of the person must by no means lead us to think that the first is accompanied by the absence of a "sense of self," since as we have already seen for Mauss, "it is clear that there has never been a human being who did not have a sense, not only of his own body, but of his both spiritual and bodily individuality" ([1938] 1985: 265; but see also, for example, Scheper-Hughes and Lock 1987: 14).

This is an important clarification in the context of Oceania, for Leenhardt's writings would tend to suggest the opposite. The diagram in *Do Kamo* of the structure of the person in Melanesia leaves a blank in place of an Ego from which lines should be radiating out to show relations between him and his kin. This blank expresses the Kanak person's supposed ignorance of his body. "He knows himself only by the relationships he maintains with others. He exists only insofar as he acts his role in the course of his relationships" (Leenhardt 1979: 153). Leenhardt has forgotten Mauss' lesson, of which he was aware, and has confused the ordinary use of the word *person*, which designates the concrete agent of human actions that we find in all places and all periods and which moreover is conscious of existing, and the "universal moral and legal ideal advocated by modern Western culture, inherited from Christianity in particular and reconfigured by human rights" (Théry 2007: 422). Louis Dumont, it should be remembered, had spotted the possibility of confusion between these two uses when he emphasized that a distinction must be made between the empirical individual, an indivisible specimen of humanity found everywhere, and the autonomous, rational, free, moral individual as valued in modern ideology, which is the product of a specific Western culture.

In confusing the two levels of apprehension of reality,[3] and in suggesting the Kanak are not conscious of their body and live only through their social

---

3. See on this topic Vincent Descombes' discussion in *Les institutions du sens* ([1996] 2014: 299).

relations, Leenhardt obviously leaves himself open to criticism. Lacking the awareness of self that is possessed by all human beings, might New Caledonians therefore be less human than other humans? At any rate, that is how specialists of this part of the world read the writings of the pastor-anthropologist, and for this reason tend to reject his analyses out of hand. And yet it is now widely accepted that the Melanesian normative conception of the person—in other words, the culturally constructed way of conceiving of personhood—differs from that developed in the West. It is customary to credit M. Strathern with the idea that Melanesians have a relational conception of the person because it is she who took the theoretical reflection on the question by far the furthest, on the basis of a broad sampling of societies in this part of the world. But Leenhardt and another anthropologist, Kenneth Read, had, in a sense, the same intuition.

Read wanted to understand what distinguishes the ethical categories of the Gahuku-Gama, a population living in the Eastern Highlands of Papua New Guinea, from those found in Western culture; to this end, he looked into the conceptions of man and human relations present in the two contexts (1955: 233). First of all, the author attempted to characterize Western representations of the person, which are essentially inherited from Christian culture. According to this thinking, human beings differ from all other living beings by the fact that they have a mind, and the qualities of the mind place them, up to a point, above institutions, in a relation of independence from the social forms in which they live (1955: 249). Owing to their nature as humans, all individuals are regarded as morally equivalent, independently of their social ties and their status (1955: 260). They can be apprehended as creatures endowed with their own objective and intrinsic value and with an individuality distinct from their status, their roles, and the place they occupy in the relational system they live in (1955: 275). The person in the Western world thus has an absolute value, which is not the result of their position in a social network but comes instead from the fact that they are made in the image of God (1955: 250).[4]

For Read, the Gahuku-Gama situation is altogether different: in their conception of man there is no distinction between the individual and their social position. Whereas Christian ethics and morality are universal, in the sense that they are the same for everyone, members of the Gahuku-Gama society do not

---

4.   For all these questions concerning the person in Christianity, see among others, Jérôme Baschet (2008) and Irène Théry (2007: 392–96).

define actions as absolutely bad or good for everyone, but only within a particular group, as is shown by the fact that it is wrong to kill a member of one's own group, but murdering an outsider can sometimes be commendable. For Read, then, this society has no moral rule that can be applied in the same way to everyone, and the value of an individual life is determined by social criteria (1955: 262).

These conceptions stem from different ways of viewing human beings. Gahuku-Gama society lacks the idea that men, as humans, are bound together by an overarching moral tie that subsumes those ties that connect them socially. In other words, humans are figures in a social network before being individuals (1955: 275), and the individual can never be seen separately from the social context in which he or she lives. Their identity is a social rather than an individual matter, which means the ideology of that society is basically sociocentric; that it values society over the individual.

In an effort to better understand Gahuku-Gama ethical categories, Read had sought to identify the differences between this society's conception of the person and Western ideas shaped by Christianity. This approach, which attempts to relate representations found in unfamiliar societies to a system of ideas familiar to the reader, is also that adopted by M. Strathern in *The gender of the gift*.

Before presenting the aspects of the Melanesian theory of the person covered in this work, and which I need for comparison with the Ankave ethnographic material, I would like to review the context in which this theory was produced. It is presented first of all as a critique of the Western approach that poses the problem of gender in terms of individual identity (1988: 59) and views the individual as a being whose existence precedes all social relations.

In Melanesia, gender is not restricted to a question of individual identity; it pervades all aspects of social life (Barraud 2001: 53); it is used to talk about things other than men and women, and it can therefore not be said, a priori, that individual identity is central to whatever is going on (M. Strathern 1988: 59). In an earlier article on gender in Hagen, M. Strathern had already said that gender is a language that provides a means of referring to other qualities and relations (1978: 173). She later expressed this in other terms, writing, "the way of envisaging the sexes was a symbolic vehicle for structuring other values (for instance the hierarchical relation ... between production and circulation)" (1987a: 11). The idea that gender is by no means a "separate" question that might be studied in isolation from everything that goes into the reality and imaginary of sociality is today at the heart of interdisciplinary research that, through its attempts to explore "the gendered dimension of social life," seeks to underscore the fact that gender is more a modality of action than a matter of individual identity or a personal property (Théry and Bonnemère 2008).

It is noteworthy that even feminist anthropologists had not questioned the applicability of the Western conception of individual identity as a personal attribute. They were more or less content to point out the absence or scarcity of research on women and to criticize the work of male ethnographers who held up men's discourse as *the* discourse on society, thereby engendering a *male bias* in the extant literature.[5]

For M. Strathern, the Western view of the person conceives the individual without reference to society. She does not seek to reconstruct the history of this specific conception, but Daniel de Coppet suggests that "it is no doubt in part owing to the Christian promise of salvation and resurrection that the dead are no longer part of society in the West, which, now reduced to the living, finds itself devalued with respect to the precious destiny and awesomeness of each human person" (2001: 392). Irène Théry goes on to say: "This devaluation of society increased with the onset of modernity, which replaced the Christian person . . . by the human person as a *subject*, now creator of itself and whose tie with others is now conceived on the model of the *societas*, the contractual association between consenting individuals" (2007: 423).

Yet, the author of *The gender of the gift* does not retain the notion of society used by anthropologists because it would designate an entity that is too abstract, too separate from people's real social experience. For M. Strathern, we need

5.   In passing, we note that M. Strathern's critical position on the work of feminists led her to clarify the relationship between the field of feminist studies and anthropology, and to defend a somewhat skeptical stance on the possibility of conjoining them entirely owing to their respective positions on the possibility of knowing others. According to what she terms a "radical" view, "feminist theory is 'experiential' in the sense that its first step is consciousness raising" (M. Strathern 1987b: 287). In effect, feminists consider that their research challenges stereotypes presenting an erroneous picture of women's experiences. As she writes: "Because the goal is to restore to subjectivity a self dominated by the Other, there can be no shared experience with persons who stand for the other. Within anthropology, the ethnographer's focus on experience signals an effort to remain open to people's emotional and personal lives" (M. Strathern 1987b: 288). This different relationship with the experience of others and the objectives, in the end distinct, of the feminist view and the anthropological approach may create an irreconcilable tension between the two (see also Bonnemère 2014a: 163–64).

to come back to the concrete character of social relations—which she trans-
lates by the term *sociality*, after Roy Wagner (1974: 104), in other words to "the
relational matrix which constitutes the life of persons" (Gross 1990: 18). The
individual/society contrast running through Western thinking is peculiar to this
part of the world (Scheper-Hughes and Lock 1987: 13–14) and does not seem
to operate in Melanesia, such that she deems it important to attend to the way
the populations themselves view and implement social ties. This is the avenue
she pursues in the book that proposes a theory of the Melanesian person, in the
normative sense I alluded to above.[6]

For M. Strathern, the normative construction of the Melanesian person ex-
hibits a number of distinctive features. First of all, what distinguishes men and
women is not a matter of attributes or properties connected with their sexual
organs but of capacities for acting, modalities of action, and relations with others (1988: 128).[7] She draws this general conclusion from the particularly fine-
grained ethnographic analyses she carried out several years earlier on material
gathered in Hagen. In her Malinowski lecture, published in 1981, which I have
already mentioned, she writes that, contrary to the Trobrianders' skirts, which
are qualified as female goods, in Hagen it is impossible to say that pigs are male
or female because it is not these products of human activity that are gendered
but the activity itself. Pigs are neither male nor female, but their production is
considered to be a female activity and their exchange, a male activity. As for
the shells that also feature in the intergroup transaction known as *moka*,[8] these
belong to the men, just as the netbags are female possessions. But these goods
are exchanged only between persons of the same sex and concern them alone
(1981: 679). As a consequence, they do not come under the rubric of reproduction of the society, as Annette Weiner described in the case of the exchange
of fiber skirts for bundles of banana leaves that Trobriander women organize
for the mortuary rituals ([1976] 1983: 231). In Hagen, it is pigs that circulate
in intersex exchanges: the women who produced them give them to the men,
who present them to their affines; but the product given (the pig) is neither one

---

6.   This is therefore not the concrete individual, "agent of human acts, the one who says
     I/me" (Théry 2007: 448) whom one encounters all the time and everywhere.

7.   This idea has been widely adopted by Melanesianists (see, for example, Eriksen
     2008: 7; Robbins 2012: 125).

8.   *Moka* is the large-scale, competitive exchange network found among the Melpa
     (Hagen), in which Big Men distinguish themselves (A. Strathern 1971).

gender nor the other. M. Strathern calls this an "unsexed" mediator, which, if it had to represent something, would embody the complementarity entailed in exchange and production that lies at the heart of the influence the two sexes exert on each other (1981: 679).

Now, if gender is defined by a capacity to act and not by an attribute, there is no obligatory connection between genitals and gender. This capacity to act in a particular manner is acquired during the course of rituals or exchanges that are, she writes, the occasion to temporarily change one's relational state.[9] If I speak of relational state, an expression M. Strathern does not herself use, it is to express one of the author's original ideas, namely that relations are the true components that make up a person (1988: 131). Over a lifetime, each person's "relational composition" can be reworked in view of a specific goal. It becomes possible to "act like or as," as shown by the Sambia example of the novice ritually engaged in a homosexual relation: assimilated to the wife of his older partner, he acts, according to M. Strathern, as the wife who takes in her husband's semen (1988: 212). It is thus the way of acting and the behavior adopted in a particular situation that "makes the gender" of someone. To be of one gender or the other then becomes a state that varies with the relational situations in which each person finds him- or herself involved at one moment or another in their life and not a permanent state (see also Bonnemère 2014b: 213–14).

Once she has established the premise that gender is not a personal attribute, M. Strathern formulates a set of hypotheses on how the idea of person is constructed in Melanesia; then she tests them over the course of her book, basing her reasoning on numerous ethnographic studies on the region, which she also analyzes. The first of these hypotheses is that, in Melanesia, persons contain a generalized sociality "within." This wording means that they are the plural and composite sites of the relationships that produced them: that between their genitors, of course, but also those between their maternal and paternal kin groups. The singular person can thus be imagined as a "social microcosm" (1988: 13), and their body as the manifest register of their interactions with others (1988: 107).

In accounting for the composite character of persons, M. Strathern uses the terminology proposed by McKim Marriott, who, in a 1976 article on South

---

9.   Note that this expresses, in a way, the idea of the internal character of relations between the persons involved in the ritual, where they enact the change (see also Holbraad 2008: 231–32 and Moutu 2006: 105).

Asian theories of the person, wrote that persons there were not conceived as being "individuals"—in other words, they are not indivisible entities closed in on themselves—as Western social and psychological theory as well as common sense frequently have it. In this part of the world, it instead seems that persons are generally conceived as being "dividual" or divisible.[10] For M. Strathern, in Melanesia too the person is understood not as an individual being but as a "dividual" entity, defined by "relationality" rather than by individuality, to use the expression employed by Andrew Strathern and Pamela Stewart (2000: 63).

A second hypothesis, which flows from the first, affirms that because the person has dual origins, they are differentiated within, and this differentiation operates between same-sex and cross-sex relations. Gender refers not only to relations between persons but also to relations within the parts that make up the persons, and these relations are always of two types: cross-sex and same-sex. According to M. Strathern, in their composite, or plural, state—in other words, when the internal parts are in a cross-sex relation—a person cannot reproduce; for the person to be able to procreate, their gender must first be homogenized in a unitary sexed form, in other words, the internal parts of the person must be in a same-sex relation. In order to achieve this internal state in which all the components are in a same-sex relation with each other, a man must symbolically rid himself of those parts of the body that come from his mother and his maternal kin, and a woman must rid herself of the substances that come from her father and her paternal kin. Again, according to M. Strathern, this hypothesis enables her to explain certain male initiation rituals that involve bloodletting practices, the consequences of which are supposed to be to purge the boys of the blood every child inherits through its mother (M. Strathern 1988: 245).

Over their lifetime, then, persons continually pass from a state in which they are the result of the action of others (M. Strathern 1992b: 194)[11]—and in this case M. Strathern terms them indifferently "complete," "cross-sex," or

---

10. "Correspondingly, persons—single actors—are not thought in South Asia to be 'individual,' that is, 'indivisible, bounded units,' as they are in much of Western social and psychological theory as well as in common sense. Instead, it appears that persons are generally thought by South Asians as 'dividual' or 'divisible'" (Marriott 1976: 111).

11. Contrasting Western and Melanesian ideas about the person, Edward LiPuma writes that in Melanesia, "persons grow transactionally as the beneficiary of other people's actions," while in the West, they "mature biogenetically as a consequence of their inner potential" (2000: 133).

"androgyn"—to another in which they are capable of acting on others, and in this case they take on a gender that Strathern designates as "incomplete," "single-sex," or "same-sex," which is achieved after a process usually initiated in the course of a ritual. As the author writes: "each male or female form may be regarded as containing within it a suppressed composite identity" (1988: 14).

A person termed incomplete—in this event, an adult—and therefore a sexually active and reproductive person, establishes a cross-sex relationship with an equally incomplete, or "single-sex" partner.[12] This relationship manifests itself in the form of its product (food, a child), which becomes, at the same time as its result, a stand-in for the relationship. This product of the relation between same-sex partners takes another form, inasmuch as it embodies within itself a cross-sex relationship. It is complete, androgynous, nonreproductive, inactive. In their exchanges with each other, persons thus alternate between the two states: a "same-sex state" and a "cross-sex state." They embody or objectify social relations by manifesting them in one or the other of their two forms.

According to another of the many hypotheses M. Strathern puts forward in her book, the Melanesian person—conceived here once again as a normative, ideal construct—owing to their multiple, or at least dual, origins, and to their "dividual" character, possesses a propensity for detachability. In their relations with others, they can thus dispose of parts of themselves to be used as gifts or substances (1988: 185). We saw that the ritualized homosexual or bleeding practices were analyzed in this way, as moments when individuals' propensity to detach certain of their component parts was put in play.

Another of the author's major goals, pursued conjointly with the objective of understanding how the person is conceived in Melanesia, is to contrast gift economies, predominant in this part of the world, with the commodity economies present in the West. In gift economies, objects take the form of persons, whereas in commodity economies, objects take the form of things (1988: 177). The author emphasizes that, in Melanesia we find single-sex persons in the form of women's or men's bodies, but also in the form of male or female valuables that circulate between them (M. Strathern 1992a: 97). These objects, she writes, act as persons in relation to one another (1988: 176) and can also be conceptualized

---

12. When discussing differentiation within the person, it is preferable to use the expression *single-sex*, which refers to one of the possible make-ups of the person. Alternatively, when speaking of relations between persons, *same-sex* seems more appropriate.

as parts of persons and be transferred as such from one individual to another. Exchanges of goods (pigs, shells, etc.) create a particular type of relation between persons, which M. Strathern qualifies as "mediated," for they manifest themselves through the mediation of an object. Here, one person's influence on another is carried by the object that circulates between them (1988: 178).

The other relational mode, which she calls "unmediated," was mentioned indirectly above: it brings together persons who do not detach parts of themselves in the course of their relation and in which no object circulates between them. Production and reproduction are the most patent examples of these relationships in which persons have an influence on the minds and bodies of those with whom they have ties. A pregnant woman's capacity to grow the child inside her is of this type. This kind of relation creates an asymmetry between its terms but, according to M. Strathern, it is nevertheless an exchange in the sense that each party is affected by the other; in sum, it is an exchange without gift.

Physical growth is a favorite example of the effect of a relationship of this type, in which the influence between the terms involved is direct. One of the most common ideas found in the literature on male initiations in New Guinea is, as we know, that these rituals make the young boys into adults and, in the past, into warriors capable of defending their group against enemy attacks.[13] According to the classic studies of the 1970s–80s, this male maturation could only take place in a masculine environment and, as it was customary to say, out of the sight of the women, whose action on the little boys, while beneficial during their infancy, had become incompatible with their future status and therefore must be counteracted by the ritual actions set in play by the male community.

M. Strathern raises doubts about this claim—found in Maurice Godelier ([1982] 1986) and Gilbert Herdt (1981), as we have seen, but also in Donald Tuzin (1980) and Gilbert Lewis (1980), to cite only a few—that the purpose of the initiations is to make men: "on neither anthropological nor feminist grounds should we, in fact, be content with the formula that male cults are . . . concerned with making men" (1988: 58). In an article devoted entirely to the subject, she asserts that these rituals make the young boys into "incomplete" beings and therefore capable of reproducing rather than transforming immature beings— the young boys—into adult men, completing them by endowing them with the

---

13. Another frequent idea, as we have seen, is that the initiations are institutions for producing and legitimizing male domination (see for instance Godelier [1982] 1986).

essential attributes of their new status. In other words, M. Strathern says that the male initiations make an androgynous, complete person who is the product of cross-sex relations between his father and his mother into an incomplete single-sex person, potentially active when it comes to procreating with an equally single-sex partner (M. Strathern 1993: 47). This movement is "conceptualised as a replacement of its androgynous body or image with one that is single sex; the child emerges as 'male' or 'female' to encounter its opposite female or male . . . half of a whole becomes one of a pair" (1993: 48).

The reader will have understood that, in this context, the expression "half of a whole" refers to the image of the womb and that of "one of a pair" designates the equally metaphorical state of the separation created by birth, then confirmed by initiation, between a mother and her son, who becomes male but born from an enveloping, by-definition-female womb (Breton 2006: 83).[14]

In Melanesia, male initiations would not consist, as a Western view of socialization might have it, in adding something to little boys, in completing them by a social or cultural additive, but in transforming their body, which is of one specific type, into another—type of—body (1993: 44). This is how the process of growth manifests itself and the transformation between being the product of someone else's action and having the capacity to act for oneself or for someone else—in other words, becoming an agent—is brought about. As M. Strathern writes, "The [ritual] actions make potential parents out of the children" (1993: 46). But the goal is not only a change of social status and accession to the status corresponding to this stage in life but also to change the capacity for action. In this case, we find once again the two notions of "agency" and "care" rapidly mentioned in the Introduction to this volume. Summing up the terms of this recent reflection in anthropology, we could say that, for the Ankave, the male ritual cycle consists in transforming the passive component of a relationship into an element endowed with a capacity for acting, which manifests itself in this culture, not in the form of an autonomous action in which the individual exercises his or her "free will," as the notion of "agency" is often understood, but in the form of an eminently relational action, since it is exercised above all on others. In this respect, Ankave culture combines and endows with particular value a capacity for acting on behalf of others, a sort of "care agency."

---

14. For the Ankave, as we have seen, girls do not need their relation with their mother to be transformed in order to become mothers themselves.

The reader will remember that the analysis of the Ankave *suwangain* ritual presented in earlier chapters produced a finding that differed little from M. Strathern's proposition, in which she apprehends the initiations as an avenue of access to parenthood, since, at the close of the public phase organized at the birth of a man's first child, a new parental couple has come into being. But if the result of the ritual is the same, the modalities of action designed to achieve this outcome differ palpably from those this author reveals in the interpretation of the Sambia initiations she proposes in *The gender of the gift*. For M. Strathern, the final phases of these rituals are linked to the birth of children, for "boys must be grown before they can, in turn, grow a new child" (M. Strathern 1988: 210). But M. Strathern focuses primarily on the flutes, objects used in secret by northern Anga men. She bases her analysis of the symbolism on the ethnographic data presented by Herdt in the numerous works he has devoted to Sambia male rituals. In a 1982 paper, he explains that there are two kinds of flutes: "the longer flutes are referred to as 'male' (*aatmwul*) and metaphorically as penes. The shorter and thinner flute is called a 'female' (*aambelu*) and is sometimes likened to the glans penis. The pairs of flutes, moreover, are said to be married and are called 'spouses' (*kwolu-aambelu*)" (Herdt 1982a: 58).

During the "penis-and-flute ceremony," the flutes were shown to the novices and used in teaching them the practices of fellatio that would soon be performed by the novices on their older but still unmarried sponsors (Herdt 1982a: 61). The novices were first presented with an analogy between the flutes and the penis and told that the flute would enter their mouth and later men would do the same thing with them and they would grow up and have fine skin (Herdt 1982a: 61–62). A little later, an association was made between semen and mother's milk. And the boys were told they had to consume semen regularly in order to grow quickly (1982a: 62). For Herdt, this rite is meant to "transfer boys' attachments to their mothers into homosexual fellatio activities with bachelors." And he added, "a fantasy isomorphism is created between the flute player and maternal figure and between the flute sucker and infant figure." In other words, the flute is a symbolic mother substitute (1982a: 79).

M. Strathern offers a different interpretation of this fellatio-teaching rite. For her, in addition to the fact that a single form (here a flute) can represent nurturing by both males (via semen from the penis) and females (via milk from the mother's breast), it also teaches the boys two things: it teaches them that the (male or female) gender of an organ depends on the person activating it and that the activation itself creates a gender distinction: the relation between the older sponsor and the novice, which substitutes the former relationship between the novice and his mother, is cross-sex, despite the fact that both are male (Jolly 1992: 144).

M. Strathern's analysis of the Sambia flutes illustrates her proposition that gender is not a personal attribute but is determined by the kind of relations established within a specific action. In other words, as Margaret Jolly writes, "the gender of human sexual organs, like the flute, is not fixed" (1992: 144). In this case, the nurturing relation is cross-sex, whether it involves a mother and her son with the mother's milk as its vector, or associates a young boy and an older bachelor, mediated by the older man's semen. It is the relations, then, that are gendered, and not the persons themselves.

What relevance does this model of Melanesian sociality have to the Ankave situation? We have seen that M. Strathern considers the Melanesian person to be "a microcosm of relations," which means that relations are contained within persons (1988: 321). Affirming that persons therefore can be divided and that it is possible to extract or detach parts of them leads, in a sense, to substantializing relations, to making them into material entities. By using this terminology, relations become components of persons.

Yet the Ankave rituals do not seem to be based on such a conception, in which relations are concretely materialized as substances or objects. Allow me to recall briefly the findings of my analysis of these practices. The first two (collective) stages of the rituals act on the boys and transform their relationship with their mother according to a specific modality: the former state of the relationship to be changed is first reiterated, which requires the presence of the two persons involved,[15] who act or behave in a parallel manner in separate places. The mothers and the novices are secluded in different spaces, respectively, where they perform the same gestures, staging the symbiotic relationship that bound them together during the pregnancy and, to a lesser extent, during the boy's early years.

Then, when the ritual has been completed, the nature of the mother-son relationship is shown to have changed. How? By means of a gesture considered to be specific to the new relationship. As we know, when the ritual is over, the boys return to the village and present their mothers with some small game, thereby demonstrating that their relationship has gone from one of a symbiotic

---

15. If the presence of both terms is necessary it is because of the internal nature of the relations involved in and transformed by the ritual (see also pp. 105, 227).

nature to one in which exchange has become possible. In M. Strathern's terminology, their formerly "unmediated" relationship, characterized by asymmetry between the two terms, has become a "mediated" relationship in which objects can circulate.

By requiring the participation of certain persons (mothers, sisters, wives) for the performance and the efficacy of major male life cycle rituals, the Ankave express the idea that the relations binding the boys to the persons involved in the ritual remain external to them.[16] As we saw, to make a little boy into a young man,[17] the first thing that has to be done is to act on his relationship with his mother. But his mere presence is not enough, for—and this is my hypothesis— his body does not contain any material, and especially detachable, trace of this relationship. It is not enough, for example, as may be the case elsewhere, for the novices to go through a bloodletting ritual in order to distance themselves from the maternal relationship preventing them from attaining a new stage in their life. To achieve the same result, the Ankave stage the relationship itself, and therefore bring into play its constituent terms. That is the only way they have of transforming the relationship, and this transformation is the condition of their accession to the status of procreator and father.

Briefly put, I subscribe to M. Strathern's idea that relations are at the heart of the Melanesians normative, ideal conception of the person and the way they apprehend the unfolding of human existence; however, analysis of the Ankave ethnographic materials leads me to cast doubt on the idea that this "Melanesian person" represented by the Ankave man or woman, contains within him- or herself relations that can be detached as objects or substances. This society therefore does not have any practices aimed, properly speaking, at detaching "parts of persons" during the initiations. That being said, when life ceases, when the body has died, things change. When a person dies they are, by definition, no longer able to embody the relations that bind them to others, and even less to activate them. At that time, the person's kinsmen, the maternal kin in particular, receive a piece

---

16. The word *external* is used here by way of contrast with M. Strathern's idea of relations as components of persons. Its use therefore does not call into question the internal character of the relations discussed in this volume.

17. Unlike M. Strathern, I have nothing against the idea that the male initiations "make men," even if I believe they do much more than that. In particular, that is what the Anga—the Ankave, Baruya, and Sambia at any rate—say, and the anthropologist cannot dismiss that.

of eel meat and a small sum of money,[18] which everything tends to indicate are a compensation for the loss these kin experience at the disappearance of the soft parts of a body of which they are the origin. These objects indeed represent a detachable part of the person, but it has become detachable only in death. Life enables the real confrontation of the terms of a relationship,[19] and, in transforming persons, the Ankave privilege this operational mode that works on the relationship by involving its terms. It could then be said that, according to the Ankave, *the person embodies relations but does not contain them.*[20] When the person dies, they no longer have the capacity to embody relations, they can no longer play their role, and only then can the relation be compensated by an object.

In other words, *once the person is no longer capable of acting for him- or herself or for close kin*, once they are no longer a potential agent, they become a dividual entity, and their parts can be substituted by objects (cf. Josephides, Rapport, and Strathern 2015: 194). But as long as the person is alive, they can act as "agents of human acts," as Théry says (2007: 227), and they are therefore called upon as themselves. As the Ankave say, "if the novices' mothers are not present, the male initiations cannot be held for they would not be effective." Such a situation reveals a worldview in which relations, although not contained within persons, nevertheless play a role in defining them—by virtue of their "internal" character already mentioned—since it is by acting on relations that persons are transformed. This analysis may challenge M. Strathern's proposition that "mediated exchange draws on the indigenous image that persons are able to detach parts of themselves in their dealings with others. Its effect is evinced in the 'flow' of items" (1988: 192). Among the Ankave, the gifts that circulate at various key moments in life are not considered as detachable parts of the person: as we saw in chapter 5, they are a mark of the parents' gratitude to the maternal kin for

---

18. In the past shells were given, as we saw on p. 146.

19. When one of the terms of a relationship has died, the system of classificatory kinship allows another term to be found to play the role and literally take the person's place. If the novice has lost his mother, for instance, it is his maternal aunt or his father's new wife who will be secluded in the collective shelter.

20. The importance Melanesian societies assign to relationships in the construction of the person can take a number of forms. For the Orokaiva of New Guinea, each individual accumulates relationships throughout life by participating in rituals, whereby they gradually become a social person. Upon death, the mortuary ritual extinguishes these relationships one by one, transforming the person into an image (Iteanu 1990: 40).

their role in helping the child grow properly (various gifts made during child-hood) and at the same time enable the child to be included in its father's own clan. They compensate the nurturing and education the parents have provided a little girl (*tuage* gifts); and they compensate work the maternals have done to prepare the ornaments for a boy's initiation (*simo'e* gift), et cetera.

The gift that might most resemble a "part of a person" is the compensation paid to the maternal kin of someone who has accidently suffered a loss of blood: for example, an initiate beaten during the passage through the tunnel of branches or a wife during a marital quarrel. In this case, the maternal kin are compensated because they share the same blood with the victim; like the victim, their physical integrity has suffered. This is a gift that is considered to be equivalent to a constitutive part of the person, their blood. Someone who has accidently lost blood is partially assimilated to the state of a corpse, which is the only body whose parts can be compensated because they can be detached owing to decomposition. For the Ankave, "detachability" is thus not a feature of living bodies.

Conclusion

The concept [of the we-I balance] *opens up questions of the relation of individual and society to discussion and investigation that would remain inaccessible as long as one conceived a person, and therefore oneself, as a we-less I.*

—Norbert Elias, *The society of individuals*

What does Ankave ethnography contribute to an anthropology of initiation rituals and the person in Melanesia? By involving the women in their own way in the male initiations, the Ankave, like the other southern Anga population known as Kapau-Kamea, force us to rethink the idea that these rituals are based on the exclusion of female actors. To be sure, women are not present in the forest where the secret phases of the ritual are held, but there can be no transformation of boys into adult men without them. And if this is the case, it is because the Ankave view the development of the male person as the outcome of a series of relational reconfigurations. It is through action, not only on the individual himself but also on his relations with certain close relatives, essentially his mother and his eldest sister, that a boy becomes a husband and father. As Michael Houseman writes: "the 'particular realities' people enact when they participate in rituals are relationships" (2007: 415). The male initiations are therefore not purely institutions for the reproduction of male domination, as the former analyses of Anga male rituals had proposed;[1] they are also, and perhaps above all, times when the community carries out the transformation of relational states. A man cannot become a husband and a father without his relationship with his mother having undergone a radical change. Since this relationship is conceived as symbiotic, it is seen as an obstacle to his entry into a conjugal relation. As for his relationship with his eldest sister, it too must undergo a transformation when his wife becomes pregnant with his first child. By respecting the same prohibition as the couple expecting their first child and by wearing the same kind of bark cape as they do, a woman enables her brother to become a father. By finally becoming a mother herself, his sister allows him to become a maternal uncle and thus to be endowed with a relational capacity that women possess simply by being born female: that of acting for others. For at the heart of the system of representations of the Ankave person is a principle that men and women do not acquire in the same way: that of acting for and on others. There is a great difference here with the Kamea situation, since a man will always, as far as I understand, "lack a woman's containing capacity" (Bamford 1998: 170n9). Elsewhere, Sandra Bamford said that "to be male in the world of Kamea is to be decontained; to be female is to possess the capacity to act as a 'container' oneself" (2007: 114). Among the Ankave, a man comes to possess this capacity at the end of a long ritual itinerary; he exercises it first as the husband of a pregnant woman and then, and especially, as a maternal uncle.

In *The gender of the gift*, Marilyn Strathern posited that the male initiations effected a transformation of the boys by bringing them from a bodily state composed of both maternal and paternal contributions, the state she calls "cross-sex," to a "single-sex" bodily state, which alone allows reproduction. This bodily transformation, she writes, is obtained by a process of extraction. The Ankave ethnography indicates an alternative process: the initiation rituals in this society do not enact a process of extraction, they stage a relational transformation in the presence of the two terms of the relation. The only time the Ankave view the person as a set of components that can be extracted is when the person has become a corpse. These components were constructed from the substances contributed by the father and the mother in the process of conception

---

1.   Although I agree with Bamford that "men do not reproduce men independently of women" (2004: 35), I do not reject altogether the idea that Anga male initiation contributes in some ways—that are difficult to evaluate—in maintaining the male domination that imbues gender relations, although less markedly so than among the Northern Angans (see Bonnemère 1996a: 293–303).

and gestation, and are therefore considered to have come respectively from a person's paternal and maternal kin. But as long as the person is alive, they are conceived not as a composite of substances—a body from which parts might be symbolically extracted—but as one of the two terms of a (internal) relation. To give this person access to a new stage in their existence, those relations in need of transformation must be activated by calling on the persons who are the terms of the relationship. It is only once the person is deceased that objects can be given to compensate the loss of one or another of their body components.

Consequently, what we can deduce from the analysis of the Ankave's ideas and practices is that the person is not constituted of components that might be eliminated in the course of rituals. But there remains the question of whether the set of these components forms what M. Strathern calls "a microcosm of relations" (1988: 131). In other words, are relations, of kinship in this event, inherent in the person or simply added to an individuality closed upon itself? As Janet Carsten writes (2004: 96), "the persuasiveness of Strathern's image of the partible person rests partly on the strong contrast between Westerners, for whom relations are somehow added to the person, and Melanesians, for whom relations are intrinsic, or prior, to personhood." But is that the only alternative?

The analysis of the Ankave ceremonial cycle I have conducted in these pages may point to a way out of this alternative. We find ourselves confronted with a conception of the person in which relations play a crucial role, for it is by transforming these that a man is made capable of entering into a conjugal relationship and becoming a father. We might say that they are so important to the constitution of the person that the person can develop over time only by acting on those relations. Yet relations cannot be extracted, except once the person has become a corpse. As long as they are alive, a person can only act as one of the terms of the relationship, and the other term must be physically present in order for the relationship to undergo a transformation. Therefore, it cannot be said that a person literally contains the relations that have produced him or her, and these relations have not become a sort of substance that can be extracted from the person. They remain external to the person while being components on which the change of status depends (see p. 243n16). The Ankave individual is neither closed upon himself nor constituted of relations hidden under substances or which manifest themselves concretely as substances; he is an entity whose evolution over his lifetime depends on rituals enacting the relations in which he takes part, and this is done in the presence of the two terms that comprise the relation. Once a person is dead, he can no longer be in physical relation with his kin, cannot conduct his relationship on an equal footing, and the person is then conceived in terms of substances.

This issue calls to mind a famous debate in Oceanic anthropology. In the 1970s and 1980s, one of the favorite research topics in the anthropology of New Guinea was the body and the substances that compose it. Dozens of books, special issues of journals and articles were devoted to representations of procreation and female pollution (for example, in chronological order, Langness 1974; J. Weiner 1982; Jorgensen 1983; Meigs 1984; Knauft 1989). Numerous, too, were the publications describing and analyzing the ritual practices entailing the expulsion or the circulation of body fluids (Lewis 1980; Herdt 1982b; Godelier [1982] 1986; Herdt 1984; among others). At the same time in France, New Guinea specialists were at odds on how to apprehend the island's societies and particularly on the place to be given to the representations of the human body these societies had worked out. Some did not feel this was the best way to account for the ethnographic situations they found and developed an anthropology of exchange, where relations between the living and the dead, rather than substances, were regarded as the material more valued by the society (Iteanu 1983; Barraud et al. 1984).

I began my own work with the literature on the Anga groups, I wrote my doctoral thesis under the direction of Maurice Godelier, I attended Françoise Héritier's courses at the Collège de France on the symbolic anthropology of the body and read her work on this topic (for example 1983, 1985, 1987). As such, my own evolution could suggest that I tended at first to place too much importance on what the Ankave said about the human body, conception, people's growth, the body substances produced and excreted, and the plants they used as substitutes for these. Between the time I defended my thesis, in February 1993, and its revision in view of publication, which took place over the year 1994, I made another trip to the Suowi Valley to complete my material on the life cycle exchanges, encouraged by the Anga's own commentaries on these events. It was during an additional three-month stay there, in the fall of 1994, that the Ankave decided to organize a set of male initiations. To observe the women during these rituals and be able to draw a parallel, thanks to Pierre Lemonnier's observations of the men, between the behaviors required of them and the ordeals undergone by the boys and the prohibitions imposed on them helped me change the way I had been looking at these rituals; I came instead to consider that relations, rather than substances, were the material these rituals worked with. That is what the analysis of the first-birth ritual presented here showed.

Does this mean I should disavow the earlier proposition that these collective rituals are the enactment of a new gestation under the responsibility of the first-stage initiates and a rebirth? Clearly not, for two reasons: first because, as I said (see p. 104n7 and 107n15), it is their secret consumption of red pandanus sauce once the wound in their septum has dried that marks the beginning of their progressive differentiation from their mothers. And second, because there is too much concordance between the representation of human growth and the practices surrounding birth on the one hand, and the substances used in the rituals on the other hand, what the Ankave women say about the parallel between their behaviors at these two times in their life and the identity of the actors involved, to regard the comparison as illegitimate. Even Bamford resorts to the image of pregnancy to characterize the link between the boys and their mothers prior to initiations—although she firmly states that it is *not* substance-based (1998: 163–64). During the final phases of the ritual, "women collectively envelop the bodies of others, just as a mother envelops the body of her child throughout gestation" (2007: 111). When we do not opt a priori for one approach or another, the ethnographic materials reveal the existence of two levels of meaning, which are activated at distinct moments or in separate spaces. One, which concerns the highly secret actions performed in the collective initiations, takes the physiology of maternity as the model for growing the young boys; the other, which refers to the ritual behaviors required of the community as a whole, men and women alike, in the forest and in the village, advances the males along their life-path by acting on their relations with certain categories of female relatives. While both levels of meaning are called on in the collective rituals, the *suwangain* rite brings into play only one operational model, that which causes the two persons whose relationship is to be transformed to act—or not act—at the same time.[2] Gestation and death are the only subjects for which the Ankave choose to use the idiom of substances. I posit that this is because these are moments in a person's life when they are not in relation with others: not yet for a fetus and no longer for a corpse.

These remarks lead me to several conclusions: first, there is hardly any reason to oppose an approach in which the body and its substances would provide the

---

2.   As well as being a positive action, the prohibition of a food or a behavior is endowed with efficacy, if only that to offer protection. And as I have shown in chapter 6, when it is respected by two persons acting together, it indicates the existence of a relation between them.

best gateway to interpreting the ethnographic materials collected in Melanesia to one that would place relations alone at the heart of social life and ritual practices, sometimes at the expense of what local people themselves say. Ankave ritual practices are proof that substances and relations can coexist within a single thought system. A second lesson is that the only way to show the coexistence of these two levels of meaning is to take into account the complete series of rituals, considering them as points in a single set and not as separate stages that might mean something in isolation. A final conclusion, quite obvious, is that when taking into account all the actors in a given social practice rather than only a portion of them, the analysis is by definition more complete; and this without even evaluating the intrinsic quality of the proposed analysis.

Consideration of all initiation rituals as a set is, up to a certain point, lacking in the earlier analyses of Anga male rituals. Besides the fact that they focused on the men's activities alone, they also paid too little attention to the ritual accompanying the birth of a man's first child.[3] The Ankave ethnography clearly shows that it is impossible to understand what happens in the collective rituals without taking into consideration the culmination of the entire set, which is the man's access to parenthood and to the position of maternal uncle. The necessary presence of the novice's sister would remain inexplicable if we failed to understand the value this New Guinea society attaches to maternal kin, of whom the mother's brother is the main representative.

Not only does the present volume therefore challenge an idea commonly expressed in analyses of the male initiations found in this region, it also proposes a new approach to the life cycle rituals. It now remains to assess the pertinence of this approach beyond the original culture zone and the male initiations. Mortuary rites would be a good candidate, for we know they are organized with the aim of repelling the spirits of the dead, altering the position the dead occupied during their lifetime, and transforming the relationship the society had with them. We also know that mourning is both a psychological and a social process, during which the place the deceased occupied in the life and mind of those close to him or her gradually changes.

---

3.   I am talking here of the analyses of Northern Angans' rituals only, since from reading Sandra Bamford's and Beatrice Blackwood's ethnographies, it appears that no ritual for the birth of a first child ever existed among the Kapau-Kamea or the Langimar.

But above and beyond the interest this book may have for anthropologists of Oceania and those specializing in rituals, the Ankave conception of social relations, in which the role of others is crucial to the construction of the individual, invites us to take a new look at our own ideas and practices. As it brings us closer to other cultures, anthropology enables us to look differently at ourselves, and to put our own culture into perspective. The ways the Ankave accompany men at important moments in their life, the ways they enable them to become fathers are different from our own, to be sure, but the issues remain the same because they concern universal features of the human condition. In the West, even if the passage from childhood to parenthood is no longer accompanied by socially organized rituals, it is never an innocuous process to leave the woman who brought us into the world to, in turn, become the father or the mother of a child. It is simply no longer ritually staged but has become a private matter. However, this change of scale does not eliminate the questions confronting everyone, and the Ankave's responses should not seem incongruous or unrelated to our own experience.

Today our Western conception of the person and gender are undergoing a major overhaul. This conception, produced by a specific history strongly tied to Christianity, endows the person with a universal value independent of local social forms. This value is considered to be intrinsic and absolute, having nothing to do with the person's roles or status and the place they occupy in the relational system in which they live. It is not conferred by position in a social network but comes instead from the idea that the person is made in the image of God (Read 1955: 250). Gender studies have been marked by this view of the individual. And it has been only very recently, thanks to detailed interdisciplinary studies (anthropology, history, sociology, philosophy), that we have come to understand that, two centuries ago, "our societies made 'gender difference' a separate question, inventing an ultimate origin in a purported simultaneously physical and mental *human nature*" (Théry and Bonnemère 2008: 9).

So-called "exotic" anthropology is perhaps the human science that has least made gender a separate issue, owing to the fact that the members of the societies studied did not conceive of gender difference outside established social relations and even, more broadly, outside relations with all manner of entities in the cosmos. M. Strathern, writing in 1978, saw gender as a generalized operator, a language that provided a means of referring to other qualities and relations (see pp. 233–34). Nevertheless, the discipline of anthropology was long in ridding itself of the Western views of the person and relations between the sexes when thinking about gender. For instance, the conjugal—or potentially sexual—relationship was long used as the standard of all relations that might grow up between persons of opposite sex, which is a good example of the difficulty the Western mind has in conceiving kinship and gender together, or rather in conceiving of individuals caught up in an established social world whose relations are mediated by other relationships; or as a second example, in the West, the person is defined by properties and attributes, with those of men and those of women held to be different.

Studies on the difference between the sexes, even in their most constructivist version, are not going to upset this idea because these studies have often simply "replaced the hypothesis of natural determinism by that of cultural conditioning to explain the respective behaviors of men and women" (Théry and Bonnemère 2008: 10). Recent studies on gender in our societies seem not yet to have measured the historically situated and nonuniversal character of the Western view of the person. Only comparative anthropology can challenge our certainties about the shared character of our own vision of the world and the individual that implicitly and therefore unconsciously underlie these studies.

The tiny Ankave society and their ritually orchestrated way of constructing and escorting persons over their lifetime may provide food for thought for authors from a variety of disciplines working in the area of gender studies—a domain French academia has finally come to recognize. They help us to consider gender not as an attribute of personal identity but as a modality of relations that need to be worked on. The outcome of Ankave male initiations is not simply to transform boys into men, as a strictly gender-oriented view would say; it is to allow them to become fathers and maternal uncles, thus illustrating the fact that gender cannot be isolated from kinship or other relational networks in which people are involved.

Glossary

a'ki' [a'ki'] : *Comensia gigantea.* Plant whose leaves are folded to make receptacles for a large quantity of tubers.

a'ki' abare' [a'ki' aβəxə'] : *Comensia* sp. Plant whose leaves are folded to make serving "bowls" for the tubers eaten in the public phase of the first-birth ritual.

a'ki' kura'te' [a'ki' kura'tə'] : Leaves used to cover the shelter of the first- and second-stage initiates.

a'ki' ore' [a'ki' oxə'] : Leaves used to cover the shelter of the first- and second-stage initiates.

a'ki' pungwen [a'ki' puŋwoẽ] : *Comensia* sp. Plant whose leaves are used to cover the parturiant's hut.

a'menge' [a'mɛŋə'] : Gift of money (formerly shell-money) given the person who carries a corpse, usually a cross-cousin of the deceased, to the burial site.

a'we [a'wə] : An endemic taro (*Colocasia* sp.).

a'we ayonge' [a'wə ajoŋə'] : A taro eaten at the first-birth ritual.

a'we imema'we [a'wə iməma'wə] : A taro eaten at the first-birth ritual.

aamain [aamɛ̃'] : *Pangium edule.* Tree whose fruits contain many seeds. These are roasted to extract the kernels that are poured in a hermetically closed basket that is placed in a pool of water for a month. The kernels turn into a very fragrant sauce, also called *aamain*, which is consumed collectively with tubers.

abare' nengwe' [aβəxə' nəngwə'] : Marriage payment consisting of half a cooked pig and money (formerly lengths of shell-money); literally "money woman."

airo' [ajro'] : *Bixa indica*. Tree whose fruits contain bright-red seeds used as a dye.

ajiare' [aȝiaʁə'] : Mourning ornaments made from ficus bark.

amenge' [aməŋə'] : Term meaning "breast" and "mother's milk." It is also used as a term of address between persons whose maternal grandmothers are—or more often were—sisters.

andiwaye [andiwaje] : An impatiens. Shamans use the leaves in healing.

anga' [aŋə'] : House, village.

aobungwen [aɔbuŋwoẽ] : See *nengiye aobungwen*.

apianga' [apiaŋə'] : Term used by a man to call his wife.

apienge' [apiəŋə'] : Cassowary.

ara' [ara'] : Term designating the category "grasses" and "flowers."

ara' era'a [ara' era'a] : *Asplenium* sp.

ara' kiringi' [ara' kəriɲi'] : *Riedelia*. A Zingiberaceae; its fragrant leaves are used in the male initiations.

ara' kwiape [ara' kwiapə] : Pleasant-smelling leaves.

ara' sorebe [ara' ʃɔrebe] : *Riedelia* (a wild Zingiberaceae).

ara' sijiwi' [ara' siȝiwi'] : Strongly lemon-scented leaves chewed with salt before spitting the mixture onto food to bring out the taste. Its origin features in one of the myths concerning eels and eel trapping.

ara' su'e [ara' ʃu'ɛ] : Fragrant leaves.

ara' temi [ara' temi] : Plant whose origin features in one of the myths concerning the origin of eels and eel trapping.

ara' teperepi [ara' təpərəpi] : Fragrant leaves.

ara' torwamonge' [ara' tɔʁwamoŋə'] : Unidentified plant whose shoots are eaten by cassowaries.

atsi' [atʃi'] : Grandmother (also husband's mother for a female Ego).

ayo'o [ajo'o] : A variety of palm tree (*Heterospathe*).

bwarandac : Baruya term meaning "little girl" and "young cassowary."

<u>daka</u> : Tok Pisin for the *Piper betle*, whose leaves and catkins are consumed with areca nuts.

denge' [dəŋə'] : Term with many meanings; here found in expressions where it means "smell" or "odor" (*meemi denge'* [meemi dəŋə'] : birth odor).

djilu'wa [dȝilu'wɑ] : Gift of pig meat or game made by the parents of a man to those of his wife when they are told she is pregnant with his first child; interpreted by some as a compensation for having threaded the string into the new bark cape of the future father of a first child.

gubare [gubɑxə] : Egg cowry shells (*Ovula ovum*) worn as a pendant or cut into small wedges to make necklaces. See *nepedje*.

igijinge' [igiʒiŋə'] : Visit paid by a young man's family to that of a girl or a young woman he would like to marry; a marriage request; literally "to mark the path with a branch."

ijiare' [iʒiarə'] : Man's bark cape falling down over the buttocks and attached by a string to his neck and his belt.

ika'a [ika'a] : Term designating the category "trees."

ika'a ayonge [ika'a ajɔŋə] : *Cupaniopsis* sp. Tree whose bark is used in making lime.

ika'a denge' [ika'a dəŋə'] : *Scalypha insulana.* Tree with pleasant-smelling leaves.

ika'a erwa [ika'a ɛrwa] : *Ficus hesperidiiformis.* Tree whose bark is used to make netbags.

ika'a i'tugwe [ika'a i'tugwə] : *Cinnamomum* (Lauraceae). Tree whose bark is chewed with salt and spit onto food.

ika'a kwipungwen [ika'a kwipuŋwoẽ] : *Cryptocarya* sp. *Ou Alphitonia ou Litsea* (Lauraceae). Tree from the laurel family whose hard wood is used to build fences, bridges and in carpentry.

ika'a kwi'we [ika'a kwi'wə] : *Gnetum gnemon.* Tree whose bark is used for making capes.

ika'a me'we [ika'a me'wə] : *Cryptocarya* sp. (Lauraceae). Tree whose trunk is used to carry the young mother's ornaments in the first-birth ritual; see also *me'we*.

ika'a onu'wa [ika'a onu'wa] : *Litsea toleiana* (Lauraceae). Tree whose bark is chewed with salt and spit onto food.

ika'a oru'wa [ika'a oru'wa] : *Syzygium* sp.

ika'a relebele [ika'a xələbələ] : *Ficus pungens.* Tree whose bark is used in making lime.

ika'a robe' [ika'a xobə'] : *Lithocarpus celebicus.* Big tree whose fruits resemble acorns.

ika'a rwa'ne [ika'a xwa'nə] : *Schefflera sphenophylla.* Umbrella tree; the juice of its fruits is drunk by certain birds; its origin is recounted in a secret myth.

ika'a saore' [ika'a ʃaoxə'] : *Elaeocarpus sphaericus.* Tree that drops its leaves and at the foot of which the secret male part of the first-birth ceremony is held.

ika'a sipiare' [ika'a ʃipiaxə'] : A *Ficus* whose origin is related in a myth.

ika'a siwire [ika'a siwirə] : *Toona surenii.* Tree whose bark is used in making lime.

ika'a suje' [ika'a suʒə'] : *Castanopsis acuminatissima.* Tree whose fruit is sometimes eaten after being cooked in a bamboo tube.

ika'a tuwi'we' [ika'a tuwi'wə] : Tree used to make digging sticks.

ika'a wawirongwen [ika'a wawiroŋwoẽ] : *Ficus variegata* Bl. Tree whose bark is used to make the *ogidje* cloth.

ime' [imə'] : A croton whose origin is related in a myth.

imoere' [imoerə'] : See *nengiye imoere'.*

inenge' [inəŋə'] : Water.

inge' [iŋə'] : Term designating the category "birds."

inge' agidji'we [iŋə'agidʒi'wə] : Unidentified bird whose blood may be drunk (discreetly) by men when they have no red pandanus juice.

inge' ajine [iŋə' aʒinə] : Unidentified bird the origin of whose red feathers is explained in a secret myth.

inge' newimbere' [iŋə' nəwimbərə'] : *Paradisaea rubra* et *Paradisaea raggiana.* Red Bird of Paradise.

inge' noye' [iŋə' nojə'] : *Paradisaea rudolphi.* Blue Bird of Paradise.

inge' paa [iŋə' paa] : A parrot, the colors of whose feathers is explained in a secret myth.

inge' pitongwen [iŋə' pitoŋwoẽ'] : Unidentified bird, the colors of whose feathers is explained in a secret myth. Men can (discreetly) drink its blood when they have no red pandanus juice.

inge' tenge' [iŋə' təŋə'] : Unidentified bird whose short feathers are explained in a myth.

inge' topa [iŋə' topa] : Unidentified bird considered to be a bad omen and a thief.

inge' tsitsa [iŋə' tsitsa] : Unidentified bird.

inge' yama [iŋə' jama] : Unidentified bird, the origin of whose stubby tail is explained in a myth.

iru'gwa' [iru'gwa'] : Ornaments made from braided orchid stems.

itsema'a [itsəma'a] : Nose-piercing ceremony; first stage of the male initiations.

i'tugwe [i'tugwə] : See *ika'a i'tugwe.*

itu'we'ge [itu'we'gə] : Skirt worn by a woman whose husband has just died; made from the fibers of his bark cape. She will discard it immediately after the burial.

kalave : Baruya term designating fourth-stage initiates.

kama'a [kama'a] : Small cowry shells sewn onto a narrow strip of beaten bark to make a chest band; in the past, used as currency.

kambang : Tok Pisin for lime.

ke'ka'a [kə'ka'a] : a blood clot; the thin layer that covers the cooked fruit of the red pandanus.

kiringi' [kəringi'] : See *ara' kiringi'*.

kina : Tok Pisin for the national currency.

komare yarene [komaxə jarənə] : Tok bokis for "to make lime."

komeye' [komejə'] : Tasty leaves chewed before spitting them onto food.

kukukuku : Motu term formerly used to designate the Anga.

kwi' [kwi'] : *Artocarpus altilis*. Breadfruit tree; breadfuit.

kwininge' [kwiniŋə'] : Leafy vegetable that tastes slightly like licorice.

main' [mɛ̃'] : Juice from the second pressing of the cooked seeds of the red pandanus fruit, which is less thick and red than the *tange'*, or first pressing.

marita : Tok Pisin for the red pandanus (tree and food).

meemi anga' [meemi aŋə'] : Literally "birth house," the parturiant's hut.

meemi denge' [meemi dəŋə'] : See *denge'*.

meemi sare' [meemi sarə'] : Literally "birth salt"; a dish eaten by a new mother a few days after the birth, consisting of a half taro and two foods that were forbidden during her pregnancy: setaria and *yaa*.

meemi tse' [meemi tʃə'] : Birth marsupial.

memia' [memia'] : Pearl-shell worn around the neck; countergift to the *simo'e*.

menenge' menepuwe' [mənəŋə' mənəpuwə'] : Species of frog whose origin figures in a myth.

me'we [me'wə] : Fire lit for the public phase of the first-birth ritual; made with wood from the tree of the same name (*ika'a me'we*).

miaru'wa [miaru'wa] : Gift of pig meat or game made by a man to his wife's eldest brother when his child begins to crawl. This maternal uncle shares the gift with his own brothers.

moka : Hagen term designating the large-scale, intergroup ceremonial exchanges.

moodangu : Sambia term designating the sixth and final stage of their male initiations.

mumu : Tok Pisin for an earth oven and for this mode of cooking.

ndaya'a [ndaja'a] : *Acalypha grandis*. An Euphorbiaceae with red-veined leaves whose origin is related in a myth.

nenge' [nəŋə'] : Plant whose leaves are used by the wives of cassowary hunters to magically lure the cassowary into their husband's traps.

nengiye [nəŋije] : *Areca catechu*. Areca palm, areca nut.

nengiye aobungwen [nəŋije aɔbuŋwoẽ] : A wild areca palm.

nengiye imoere' [nəŋije imoexə'] : A wild areca palm.

nengwo [nəŋwo] : Term used by a male Ego to designate his father-in-law, his father-in-law's brothers, his father-in-law's sisters' husbands, and his mother-in-law's sisters' husbands; term also used by a male and female Ego to designate their sons-in-law.

nepedje [nɛpədʒə] : *gubare* egg cowry shells cut and attached to a strip of beaten bark to form a necklace.

newimbere' [nəwimbərə'] : See *inge' newimbere'*.

nie'wa su'wa [nie'waʃu'wa] : Gift made to a child's maternal grandmother for rubbing it with *omore'* clay; literally "to show the child."

noje nangwen [nojə naŋwoẽ] : Gift of pig meat or game made by a man to his wife's eldest brother once or several times during his child's early years. This maternal uncle shares the gift with his own brothers.

nwabe' [nwaβə'] : Mourning songs.

ogidje [ɔgidʒe] : Large piece of red-colored bark cloth prepared for the first-birth ritual.

oremere' [oxɛjməxə'] : See *wareba oremere'*.

ombo' [ombə'] : Cannibal spirits.

omore' [oməxə'] : See *rwa'a omore'*.

onu'wa [ɔnu'wa] : See *ika'a onu'wa*.

perengen [pərəŋə'] : See *simangain perengen*.

pidzemena'a [pidʒəməna'a] : Shamans' auxiliary spirits.

piipi [piipi] : Small cowry shells cut in little circles and sewn onto a very narrow strip of beaten bark to make a forehead band.

pisingain awo' [pisiŋẽ awo'] : Forest spirits.

pisingain suwe'wa [pisiŋẽ suwɛ'wa] : Unidentified edible insect whose origin figures in a myth.

pisingain tebo'o [pisiŋẽ tebɔ'o] : Literally "stories of the deceased"; accounts handed down from one generation to the next.

pisingain ubrere [pisiŋẽ ubrerə] : Unidentified edible insect whose origin figures in a myth.

pitpit : Tok Pisin for the food *Saccharum edule* as well as the cane from which miniature arrows and nose plugs are made.

potiye' [pɔtije'] : Gift of a live piglet made by a man to his uterine niece. This is a countergift to the gift of meat he received when she was asked for in marriage.

pugwe' [pugwə'] : Unidentified edible insect whose origin figures in a myth.

rarena' [xarena'] : See *ungwen imenegne'*.

renamia' [xənamia'] : Unit formed by a female and her young or a mother and her nursing baby.

renei onanengo' [xenɛj onanəŋo'] : Gift of a marsupial chosen among the "birth marsupials" to the sisters of the new mother; literally "to please his/her maternal aunt."

robere [xobəxə] : Lemon-scented leaves (not identified) used to scrub the new mother.

rodja'a meke [xodʒa'a məkə] : Origin myths; literally "important words," considered locally to recount true events.

roju'wa [xoju'wa] : Digging stick.

rwa'a omore' [xwa'a oməxə'] : The orangish-yellow clay mothers rub on their newborns.

rwa'atungwen [xwa'atuŋwoẽ] : Gift of pig meat or game made by a man to his parents-in-law during the childhood of their grandchildren.

rwonangwen [xwonaŋwoẽ] : A squash forbidden to children because it ripens slowly.

saore' [ʃaoxə'] : See *ika'a saore'*.

semayi'ne [ʃəmaji'nə] : Rubbing with red pandanus seeds; second phase in the male initiations.

senge' [ʃɛngə'] : Gift of smoked eel made to the male and female classificatory cross-cousins of the deceased after the *songain* end-of-mourning ceremony.

sere'pia [ʃəxə' pia] : A variety of bamboo.

sijiwi' [siʒiwi'] : See *ara' sijiwi'*.

simangain [ʃimaŋẽ] : Red pandanus.

simangain perengen [ʃimaŋẽ pərəŋə'] : First red pandanus of the season, of which a myth recounts that it grew there where the blood of the man-with-no name spilled out.

simo'e [ʃimɔ'ɛ] : Gift of a whole raw male pig made by a man to his wife's eldest brother after the initiation of the man's son. This maternal uncle shares it with his own brothers and sisters. It is the final gift connected with children's growth.

sindere' [sindərə'] : See *ungwen imenegne'*.

siru'a [siru'a] : Cassowary quill.

songain [ʃoŋə'] : End-of-mourning ceremony; the hourglass drum beaten during this ceremony.

sonkwo [ʃɔnkwo] : Lime.

sorebe [ʃorebe] : See *ara' sorebe.*

suwangain [ʃuwaŋẽ] : Third and final stage in the Ankave male ritual cycle; also designates the third-stage initiate.

ta'ne' [ta'nə'] : Red pandanus juice from the first pressing.

tange' [taŋə'] : Blood.

temi [temi] : See *ara' temi.*

tewiba [təwiba] : *Plectranthus.* A Labiaeceae with red-veined leaves whose origin is related in a myth.

tok bokis/tok piksa : Tok Pisin for hidden or imaged words. This is a practiced consisting in using one word for another (known by everyone) in specific circumstances.

tse' arma' [tʃə' arma'] : Small marsupial rat. When it is among the product of the hunt that follows a birth, its ashes are mixed with the *omore'* clay rubbed on the baby's body. A fast-growing animal, this is a quality desired for the baby.

tse' rwatse' [tʃə' xwatʃə'] : An echidna whose origin is told in a myth.

tse' pipia'wo [tʃə' pipia'wo] : Small arboreal marsupial known as the glider.

tsindrayé : Baruya term meaning "pubescent girls" and "young cassowaries."

tuage [tuagə] : Marriage gifts in kind made by a man's family to that of his wife.

tuwi'we' [tuwi'wə'] : See *ika'a tuwi'we'.*

unanengwa [unanəŋwə] : A variety of vine.

ungwen [uŋwoẽ] : Sugarcane.

ungwen imenegne' [uŋwoẽ imənəɲe'] : One of the three varieties of sugarcane (with *ungwen rarena'* and *ungwen sindere'*) that can be eaten by the father of a first child three days after the birth.

wareba e'ire' [warəba ə'irə'] : A cordyline with red-veined leaves whose origin is told in a myth.

wareba oareso'we [warəba oaxɛʃo'wə] : A red-leaved cordyline.

wareba oremere' [warəba oxɛjmɔxə'] : A cordyline with red and purple leaves used in initiation rituals. The myth tells that the first specimens grew on the spot where the blood of the man-with-no-name spilled out onto the ground and formed a clot.

wareba yauya'we' [warəba jauja'wə'] : A cordyline with red-veined leaves whose origin is related in a myth.

wawi ore' [wawi oxə'] : A variety of ginger whose origin is related in a myth.

wiamongen [wiamɔŋoẽ] : *Mucuna albertisii.* A nut used in numerous magical practices.

yaa [jaa] : *Rungia klossii.* A leafy vegetable.

ya'me [ja'me] : A squash forbidden to children because of its slow growth.

yo'o erwa'a [jo'o exwa'a] : *Ficus hesperidiiformis.*

yore' [joxə'] : *Setaria palmifolia,* or palmgrass; grown as a vegetable crop, but forbidden to pregnant women.

References

Ahearn, Laura M. 2001. "Language and agency." *Annual Review of Anthropology* 30:109–37.

Alès, Catherine. 2001. "Introduction." In *Sexe absolu ou sexe relatif? De la distinction de sexe dans les sociétés*, edited by Catherine Alès and Cécile Barraud, 9–22. Paris: Éditions de la Maison des Sciences de l'Homme.

Alès, Catherine, and Cécile Barraud, eds. 2001. *Sexe absolu ou sexe relatif? De la distinction de sexe dans les sociétés*. Paris: Éditions de la Maison des Sciences de l'Homme.

Anonymous. (1973) 1993. *La notion de personne en Afrique noire*. Paris: Éditions du CNRS.

Ardener, Edwin. 1967. "Review of *Purity and danger: An analysis of concepts of pollution and taboo*, by Mary Douglas," *Man*, n.s., 2 (1): 139.

Ballard, Christopher, Paula Brown, R. Michael Bourke, and Tracy Harwood. 2005. *The sweet potato in Oceania: A reappraisal*. Sydney: University of Sydney Press.

Bamford, Sandra. 1997. "The containment of gender: Embodied sociality among a South Angan people." PhD diss., University of Virginia.

———. 1998. "To eat for another: Taboo and the elicitation of bodily form among the Kamea of Papua New Guinea." In *Bodies and persons: Comparative perspectives from Africa and Melanesia*, edited by Michael Lambek and Andrew Strathern, 158–71. Cambridge: Cambridge University Press.

———. 2004. "Embodiments of detachment: Engendering agency in the highlands of Papua New Guinea." In *Women as unseen characters: Male ritual in*

Papua New Guinea, edited by Pascale Bonnemère, 34–56. Social Anthropology in Oceania Series. Philadelphia: University of Pennsylvania Press.

———. 2007. *Biology unmoored: Melanesian reflections on life and biotechnology.* Berkeley: University of California Press.

Barker, John. 1991. "Honorary fellow: Kenelm Burridge." *ASAO Newsletter* 78:20–22.

Barlow, Kathleen. 2004. "Critiquing the 'good enough' mother: A perspective based on the Murik of Papua New Guinea." *Ethos* 32 (4): 514–37.

Barnes, John A. 1962. "African models in the New Guinea Highlands." *Man* 62:5–9.

Barraud, Cécile. 2001. "De la distinction de sexe dans les sociétés. Une présentation." In *Sexe absolu ou sexe relatif? De la distinction de sexe dans les sociétés,* edited by Catherine Alès and Cécile Barraud, 23–99. Paris: Éditions de la Maison des Sciences de l'Homme.

Barraud, Cécile, Daniel de Coppet, André Iteanu, and Raymond Jamous. 1984. "Des relations et des morts. Quatre sociétés vues sous l'angle des échanges." In *Différences, valeurs, hiérarchie: Textes offerts à Louis Dumont*, edited by Jean-Claude Galey, 421–520. Paris: Éditions de l'École des Hautes Études en Sciences Sociales.

Baschet, Jérôme. 2008. "Distinction des sexes et dualité de la personne dans les conceptions anthropologiques de l'Occident médiéval." In *Ce que le genre fait aux personnes*, edited by Irène Théry and Pascale Bonnemère, 175–95. Paris: Éditions de l'École des Hautes Études en Sciences Sociales.

Beehler, Bruce M., Thane K. Pratt, and Dale A. Zimmerman. 1986. *Birds of New Guinea*. Princeton: Princeton University Press (Handbook n°9 of the Wau Ecological Institute, P.O. Box 77, Wau, Papua New Guinea).

Belmont, Nicole. 1978. "Conception, grossesse et accouchement dans les sociétés non occidentales." *Confrontations psychiatriques* 16:285–305.

Benveniste, Émile. 1974. *Problèmes de linguistique générale, vols. I et II*. Paris: Gallimard.

Blackwood, Beatrice. 1939. "Folk-stories of a stone-age people in New Guinea." *Folk-Lore* 50 (3): 209–42.

———. 1940. "Use of plants among the Kukukuku of South-East-Central New Guinea." *Proceedings of the Sixth Pacific Science Congress* 1939 (4): 111–26.

———. 1950. *The technology of a modern stone-age people in New Guinea*. Oxford: University of Oxford, Pitt-Rivers Museum.

———. 1978. *The Kukukuku of the Upper Watut*. Edited by Christopher R. Hall-pike. Oxford: Oxprint.

Bonnemère, Pascale. 1990. "Considérations relatives aux représentations des substances corporelles en Nouvelle-Guinée." *L'Homme* 114:101–20.

———. 1994. "Le pandanus rouge dans tous ses états." *Annales Fyssen* 9:21–32.

———. 1996a. *Le pandanus rouge: Corps, différence des sexes et parenté chez les Ankave-Anga, Papouasie Nouvelle-Guinée*. Paris: CNRS Éditions / Éditions de la Maison des Sciences de l'Homme.

———. 1996b. "Aliment de sociabilité, aliment d'échange: Le *Pangium edule* chez les Ankave-Anga (Papouasie-Nouvelle-Guinée)." In *Cuisines: Reflets des sociétés*, edited by Marie-Claire Bataille-Benguigui and Françoise Cousin, 423–34. Paris: Editions Sépia, Musée de l'Homme.

———. 1998. "Quand les hommes répliquent une gestation: Une analyse des représentations et des rites de la croissance et de la maturation des garçons chez les Ankave-Anga (Papouasie Nouvelle-Guinée)." In *La production du corps: Approches anthropologiques et historiques*, edited by Maurice Godelier and Michel Panoff, 81–113. Amsterdam: Editions des Archives Contemporaines.

———. 2001a. "Silence and surprise, noise and terror: Going through the same ritual several times over the years, or the process of being initiated among the Ankave-Anga of Papua New Guinea." Paper presented at the symposium "Emotion, Memorization, and Knowledge Transmission in Ritual Context," Marseille, Maison Asie-Pacifique, September 14–15, 2001.

———. 2001b. "Two forms of masculine ritualized rebirth: The Melanesian body and the Amazonian cosmos." In *Gender in Amazonia and Melanesia: An exploration of the comparative method*, edited by Tom A. Gregor and Donald F. Tuzin, 17–44. Berkeley: University of California Press.

———. 2002. "Eléments pour une étude des représentations de la canne à sucre chez les Ankave-Anga (PNG)." *Journal de la Société des Océanistes* 114–15:181–85.

———. 2004a. "When women enter the picture: Looking at Anga initiations from the mother's angle." In *Women as unseen characters: Male ritual in Papua New Guinea*, edited by Pascale Bonnemère, 57–74. Philadelphia: University of Pennsylvania Press.

———, ed. 2004b. *Women as unseen characters: Male ritual in Papua New Guinea*. Philadelphia: University of Pennsylvania Press.

————. 2005. "Why should everyone have a different name? Clan and gender identity among the Ankave-Anga of Papua New Guinea." In *The changing South Pacific: Identities and transformations*, edited by Serge Tcherkézoff and Françoise Douaire-Marsaudon, 314–34. Translated by Nora Scott. Canberra: Pandanus Books (Translated from the French: *Le Pacifique-Sud aujourd'hui: Identités et transformations culturelles*. Paris: Éditions du CNRS, 1997).

————. 2006. "'Nous sommes tous les rejetons de ce casoar primordial.' Imaginaire et taxonomie chez les Ankave-Anga (PNG)." In *Les Messagers divins: Aspects esthétiques et symboliques des oiseaux en Asie du sud-est*, edited by Pierre Leroux and Bernard Sellato, 357–71. Paris: Editions SevenOrients.

————. 2008. "Du corps au lien: L'implication des mères dans les initiations masculines des Ankave-Anga." In *Ce que le genre fait aux personnes*, edited by Irène Théry and Pascale Bonnemère, 75–90. Paris: Éditions de l'École des Hautes Études en Sciences Sociales.

————. 2010. "Histoire de l'échec d'une conversion: Trente ans d'incursions missionnaires en pays ankave (1972–2002)." In *Les Dynamiques religieuses dans le Pacifique: Formes et figures contemporaines de la spiritualité océanienne*, edited by Françoise Douaire-Marsaudon and Gabriele Weichart, 113–30. Marseille: Pacific-Credo Publications.

————. 2014a. "Petite histoire des études de genre dans l'anthropologie de l'Océanie." In *Les Sciences humaines et sociales dans le Pacifique Sud: Terrains, questions et méthodes*, edited by Laurent Dousset, Barbara Glowczewski and Marie Salaün, 161–79. Marseille: pacific-credo Publications.

————. 2014b. "Marilyn Strathern en Mélanésie: Un regard critique sur le genre, les objets et les rituels." *Tracés: Revue de Sciences humaines* HS 14: 203–31.

————. 2014c. "A relational approach to a Papua New Guinea male ritual cycle." *Journal of the Royal Anthropological Institute* 20 (4): 728–45.

————. 2015a. "Doing it again: Transforming men and relations among the Ankave-Anga of Papua New Guinea." Paper presented at the 10th ESfO Conference, Brussels, June 24–27, 2015.

————. 2015b. "'I suffered when my sister gave birth.' Transformations of the brother-sister bond among the Ankave-Anga of Papua New Guinea." In *Living kinship in the Pacific*, edited by Christina Toren and Simonne Pauwels, 128–42. Pacific Perspectives: Studies of the ESfO Series, vol. 4. New York: Berghahn Books.

———. 2017. "The materiality of relational transformations: Propositions for renewed analyses of life-cycle rituals in Melanesia and Australia." In "Matter(s) of Relations: Transformation and Presence in Melanesian and Australian Life-cycle Rituals," edited by Pascale Bonnemère, James Leach, and Borut Telban, special issue, *Anthropological Forum* 27 (1): 3–17.

———. Forthcoming. "Interpreting initiation in Melanesia: Past and present." In *The Melanesian world*, edited by Eric Hirsch and William Rollason. Oxford: Routledge.

Bonnemère, Pascale, and Pierre Lemonnier. 1992. "Terre et échanges chez les Anga (Papouasie Nouvelle-Guinée)." *Études rurales* 127–28:133–58.

———. 2007. *Les tambours de l'oubli: La vie ordinaire et cérémonielle d'un peuple forestier de Papouasie / Drumming to forget: Ordinary life and ceremonies among a Papua New Guinea group of forest-dwellers.* Translated by Nora Scott. Pirae: Au vent des îles / Paris: Musée du quai Branly.

———. 2009. "A measure of violence: Forty years of 'first contact' among the Ankave-Anga (Papua New Guinea)." In *Oceanic encounters: Exchange, desire, violence*, edited by Margaret Jolly, Serge Tcherkézoff, and Darrell Tryon, 295–333. Canberra: ANU e–Press.

———. 2012. "When social anthropologists become go-betweens in a humanitarian and development project." Report. Port Moresby, Ambassade de France (28 pages).

Breton, Stéphane. 2006. "La matrice masculine." In *Qu'est-ce qu'un corps? Afrique de l'Ouest / Europe occidentale / Nouvelle-Guinée / Amazonie*, edited by Stéphane Breton, 82–147. Paris: Musée du quai Branly/Flammarion.

Broude, Gwen J. 1988. "Rethinking the couvade: Cross-cultural evidence." *American Anthropologist* 90 (4): 902–11.

———. 1989. "A reply to Munroe and Munroe on the couvade." *American Anthropologist* 91 (3): 735–38.

Brunois, Florence. 2007. *Le Jardin du casoar, la forêt des Kasua.* Paris: CNRS Éditions.

Bulmer, Ralph. 1967. "Why is the cassowary not a bird? A problem of zoological taxonomy among the Karam of the New Guinea Highlands." *Man* 2 (1): 5–25.

Burridge, Kenelm O. L. 1957. "The *gagai* in Tangu." *Oceania* 28 (1): 56–72.

———. 1958. "Marriage in Tangu." *Oceania* 29 (1): 44–61.

———. 1959. "Siblings in Tangu." *Oceania* 30 (2): 128–54.

Carsten, Janet. 2004. *After kinship.* Cambridge: Cambridge University Press.

Chalifoux, Jean-Jacques. 1998. "Chamanisme et couvade chez les Galibi de la Guyane française." *Anthropologie et Sociétés* 22 (2): 99–123.

Chernela, Janet M. 1991. "Symbolic inaction in rituals of gender and procreation among the Garifuna (Black Caribs) of Honduras." *Ethos* 19 (1): 52–67.

Clark, Jeffrey. 1991. "Pearlshell symbolism in Highlands Papua New Guinea, with particular reference to the Wiru people of Southern Highlands Province." *Oceania* 61 (4): 309–39.

Clifford, James. 1982. *Person and myth: Maurice Leenhardt in the Melanesian world*. Berkeley: University of California Press.

Conklin, Beth A., and Lynn M. Morgan.1996. "Babies, bodies, and the production of personhood in North America and a Native Amazonian society." *Ethos* 24 (4): 657–94.

Coppet, Daniel de. 2001. "De la dualité des sexes à leur dissymétrie." In *Sexe absolu ou sexe relatif? De la distinction de sexe dans les sociétés*, edited by Catherine Alès and Cécile Barraud, 373–413. Paris: Éditions de la Maison des Sciences de l'Homme.

Cova, Florian. 2010. "Pourquoi se soucier du care?" *nonfiction.fr* http://www.nonfiction.fr/article-3480-pourquoi_se_soucier_du_care_.htm.

Derlon, Brigitte. 2002. "L'intestinal et le matriciel: Aux origines mythiques d'une 'monnaie' mélanésienne (Nouvelle-Irlande, plateau Lelet)." *L'Homme* 162:157–80.

Descola, Philippe. 2010. "Anthropologie de la nature." *L'Annuaire du Collège de France* [En ligne] 109:521–38.

———. 2013. *Beyond nature and culture*. Translated by Janet Lloyd. Chicago: University of Chicago Press (Translated from the French: *Par-delà nature et culture*. Paris: Gallimard, 2005).

Descombes, Vincent. 2003. "Individuation et individualisation." *Revue européenne des sciences sociales* 127:17–35.

———. 2014. *The institutions of meaning: A defense of anthropological holism*. Translated by Stephen Adam Schwartz. Cambridge, MA: Harvard University Press (Translated from the French: *Les Institutions du sens*. Paris: Éditions de Minuit, 1996).

Détrie, Catherine, Paul Siblot, and Bertrand Vérine. 2001. *Termes et concepts pour l'analyse du discours: Une approche praxématique*. Paris: Champion.

De Vos, George A. 1975. "The dangers of pure theory in social anthropology." *Ethos* 3 (1): 77–91.

Doja, Albert. 2005. "Rethinking the couvade." *Anthropological Quarterly* 78 (4): 917–50.

Douglas, Mary. (1966) 1981. *Purity and danger: An analysis of concepts of pollution and taboo.* London: Routledge.

———. 1972. "Self-evidence." *Proceedings of the Royal Anthropological Institute of Great Britain and Ireland* 1972:27–43.

Dubois, Jean. 1974. *Dictionnaire de linguistique.* Paris: Larousse.

Dumont, Louis. 1978. "La conception moderne de l'individu. Notes sur la genèse, en relation avec les conceptions de la politique et de l'État à partir du XIIIe siècle." *Esprit* 2:18–54.

Durkheim, Émile. (1912) 1995. *The elementary forms of religious life.* Translated by Karen Fields. New York: The Free Press (Translated from the French: *Les Formes élémentaires de la vie religieuse.* Paris: Presses Universitaires de France, 1912).

Durkheim, Émile, and Marcel Mauss. (1903) 1969. *Primitive classification.* Translated by Rodney Needham, 2nd ed. London: Cohen & West (Translated from the French: "De quelques formes primitives de classification: Contribution à l'étude des représentations collectives." In *Oeuvres*, 13–89. Paris: Éditions de Minuit, 1974).

Élias, Norbert. (1939) 1991. *The society of individuals.* Translated by Edmund Jephcott. Oxford: Basil Blackwell (Translated from the German: *Die Gesellschaft der Individuen*).

Eriksen, Annelin. 2008. *Gender, Christianity and change in Vanuatu: An analysis of social movements in North Ambrym.* Aldershot Burlington: Ashgate.

Errington, Frederick K., and Deborah B. Gewertz. 1989. "Tourism and anthropology in a post-modern world." *Oceania* 60 (1): 37–54.

Fabre-Vassas, Claudine. 1994. *La Bête singulière: Les juifs, les chrétiens et le cochon.* Paris: Gallimard.

Feld, Steven. 1982. *Sound and sentiment: Birds, weeping, poetics, and song in Kaluli expression.* Philadelphia: University of Pennsylvania Press.

Fessler, Daniel M. T., and Carlos D. Navarrete. 2003. "Meat is good to taboo: Dietary proscriptions as a product of the interaction of psychological mechanisms and social processes." *Journal of Cognition & Culture* 3 (1): 1–40.

Fischer, Hans. 1968. *Negwa: Eine Papua-gruppe im Wandel.* Munich: Klaus Renner Verlag.

Fortes, Meyer. 1966. "Totem and taboo." *Proceedings of the Royal Anthropological Institute of Great Britain and Ireland 1966:5–22.*

Garine, Igor de. 2001. "Views about food prejudice and stereotypes." *Social Science Information* 40 (3): 487–507.

Gell, Alfred. 1979. "Reflections on a cut finger: Taboo in the Umeda conception of the self." In *Fantasy and symbol: Studies in anthropological interpretation [Essays in honor of G. Devereux]*, edited by R. H. Hook, 133–48. New York: Academic Press.

———. 1999. "Strathernograms, or the semiotics of mixed metaphors." In *The art of anthropology: Essays and diagrams*, edited by Eric Hirsch, 29–75. London: Athlone Press.

Gewertz, Deborah B., and Frederick K. Errington. 1991. *Twisted histories, altered contexts: Representing the Chambri in a world system*. Cambridge: Cambridge University Press.

Gillison, Gillian. 2016. "Whatever happened to the mother? A new look at the old problem of the mother's brother in three New Guinea societies: Gimi, Daribi, Iatmul." *Oceania* 86 (1): 2–24.

Godelier, Maurice. (1982) 1986. *The making of great men: Male domination and power among the New Guinea Baruya*. Translated by Rupert Swyer. Cambridge: Cambridge University Press (Translated from the French: *La production des grands hommes: Pouvoir et domination masculine chez les Baruya de Nouvelle-Guinée*. Paris: Fayard, 1982).

———. (1996) 1998. *The enigma of the gift*. Translated by Nora Scott. Chicago: University of Chicago Press; Cambridge, Polity Press (Translated from the French: *L'Enigme du don*. Paris: Fayard, 1996).

———. (2004) 2011. *The Metamorphoses of Kinship*. Translated by Nora Scott. London, New York: Verso (Translated from the French: *Métamorphoses de la parenté*. Paris: Fayard, 2004).

Goody, Esther. 1982. *Parenthood and social reproduction: Fostering and occupational roles in West Africa*. Cambridge: Cambridge University Press.

Gould, Drusilla, and Maria Glowacka. 2004. "Nagotooh(gahni): The bonding between mother and child in Shoshoni tradition." *Ethnology* 43 (2): 185–91.

Gross, Claudia. 1990. "Anthropology and the end of 'society.'" *Anthropology Today* 6 (3): 18–9.

Hallpike, Christopher R., ed. 1978. *The Kukukuku of the Upper Watut*. By Beatrice Blackwood. Oxford: Oxprint.

Healey, Christopher J. 1985. "Pigs, cassowaries, and the gift of the flesh: A symbolic triad in Maring cosmology." *Ethnology* 24 (3): 153–65.

Herdt, Gilbert H. 1981. *Guardians of the flutes: Idioms of masculinity*. New York: McGraw-Hill Book Company.

———. 1982a. "Fetish and fantasy in Sambia initiation." In *Rituals of manhood: Male initiation in Papua New Guinea*, edited by Gilbert H. Herdt, 44–98. Berkeley: University of California Press.

———. 1982b. "Sambia nosebleeding rites and male proximity to women." *Ethos* 10 (3): 189–231.

———. 1984. "Semen transactions in Sambia culture." In *Ritualized homosexuality in Melanesia*, edited by Gilbert H. Herdt, 167–210. Berkeley: University of California Press.

———. 1987. *The Sambia: Ritual and gender in New Guinea*. New York: Holt Rinehart and Winston.

———. 1993. "Introduction to the paperback edition." In *Ritualized homosexuality in Melanesia*, edited by Gilbert H. Herdt, vii–xliv. Berkeley: University of California Press.

Héritier-Augé, Françoise. 1983. "Stérilité, aridité, sécheresse. Quelques invariants de la pensée symbolique." In *Le Sens du mal. Anthropologie, sociologie, histoire de la maladie*, edited by Marc Augé and Catherine Herzlich, 123–54. Paris: Editions des Archives Contemporaines.

———. 1985. "Le sperme et le sang." *Nouvelle Revue de psychanalyse* 32:111–22.

———. 1987. "La mauvaise odeur l'a saisi." *Le Genre humain* 15:7–17.

Héritier, Françoise. 1996. *Masculin/féminin: La pensée de la différence*. Paris: Odile Jacob.

———. 2002. *Masculin/féminin II. Dissoudre la hiérarchie*. Paris: Odile Jacob.

Holbraad, Martin. 2008. "Relationships in motion: Oracular recruitment and ontological definition in Cuban Ifá cults." In "Éprouver l'initiation," edited by Michael Houseman, special issue, *Systèmes de pensée en Afrique noire* 18:219–64.

Houseman, Michael. 2007. "Relationality." In *Theorizing rituals: Issues, topics, approaches, concepts*, edited by Jens Kreinath, Jan Snoek, and Michael Stausberg, 413–28. Leiden: Brill.

Iteanu, André. 1983. *La ronde des échanges: De la circulation aux valeurs chez les Orokaiva*. Paris: Éditions de la Maison des Sciences de l'Homme.

———. 1990. "The concept of the person and the ritual system: An Orokaiva view." *Man* 25 (1): 35–53.

————. 2001. "Hommes et femmes dans le temps." In *Sexe absolu ou sexe relatif?
De la distinction de sexe dans les sociétés*, edited by Catherine Alès and Cécile
Barraud, 325–56. Paris: Éditions de la Maison des Sciences de L'homme.

Jamous, Raymond. (1991) 2003. *Kinship and rituals among the Meo of Northern
India: Locating sibling relationship*. Translated by Nora Scott. Oxford: Oxford University Press (Translated from the French: *La relation frère–soeur:
Parenté et rites chez les Meo de l'Inde du Nord*. Paris: Éditions de l'École des
hautes études en sciences sociales, 1991).

Jeudy-Ballini, Monique. 1995. "Les formes de la coopération chez les Sulka de
Nouvelle-Bretagne." *Anthropologie et sociétés* 19 (1–2): 207–28.

Jolly, Margaret. 1992. "Partible persons and multiple authors." *Pacific Studies* 15
(1): 137–49.

Jorgensen, Dan. 1983. "Introduction: The facts of life, Papua New Guinea style."
Mankind 14 (1): 1–12.

Josephides, Lisette, Nigel Rapport, and Marilyn Strathern. 2015. "Dialogue." In
Knowledge and ethics in anthropology: Obligations and requirements, edited by
Lisette Josephides, 191–229. Bloomsbury: Bloomsbury Academic.

Juillerat, Bernard. (1986) 1996. *The children of the blood*. Translated by Nora
Scott. Oxford: Berg (Translated from the French: *Les Enfants du sang: Société, reproduction et imaginaire en Nouvelle-Guinée*. Paris: Éditions de la maison
des Sciences de l'Homme, 1986).

Keck, Frédéric. 2008. *Lucien Lévy-Bruhl entre philosophie et anthropologie: Contradiction et participation* Paris: CNRS Éditions.

————. n.d. "Le problème de la mentalité primitive: Lévy-Bruhl entre philosophie et anthropologie." http://documents.univ-lille3.fr/files/pub/www/
recherche/theses/keck-frederic/html/these.html.

Knauft, Bruce M. 1989. "Bodily images in Melanesia: Cultural substances and
natural metaphors." In *Fragments for a history of the human body*, Part 3, edited by Michel Feher, Ramona Naddaff, and Nadia Tazi, 199–279. New York:
Urzone.

Kupferer, Harriet J. K. 1965. "Couvade: Ritual or real illness." *American Anthropologist* 67 (1): 99–102.

Lambek, Michael. 1992. "Taboo as cultural practice among Malagasy speakers."
Man 27 (2): 245–66.

Langness, Lewis L. 1974. "Ritual, power, and male dominance." *Ethos* 2 (3):
189–212.

Laugier, Sandra. 2010. "L'éthique du care en trois subversions." *Multitudes* 42:112–25.

Leach, James. 2003. *Creative land: Place and procreation on the Rai Coast of Papua New Guinea*. New York: Berghahn Books.

Leenhardt, Maurice. 1939. "La personne mélanésienne." *Annuaire 1940–1941 and 1941–1942*: 5–36. Paris : École Pratique des Hautes Études, Section des Sciences religieuses.

———. (1947) 1979. *Do Kamo: Person and myth in the Melanesian world*. Translated by Basia Miller Gulati. Chicago: University of Chicago Press (Translated from the French: *Do kamo: La personne et le mythe dans le monde mélanésien*. Paris: Gallimard, 1947).

Lemonnier, Pierre. 1981. "Le commerce inter-tribal des Anga de Nouvelle-Guinée." *Journal de la Société des Océanistes* 37:39–75.

———. 1984a. "La production de sel végétal chez les Anga (Papouasie Nouvelle-Guinée)." *Journal d'agriculture traditionnelle et de botanique appliquée* 31 (1–2): 71–126.

———. 1984b. "L'écorce battue chez les Anga de Nouvelle-Guinée." *Techniques et culture* 4:127–75.

———. 1996. "L'anguille chez les Ankave-Anga: Matérialité et symbolique du piégeage." In *Tropical forests, people and food: Biocultural interactions and applications to development*, edited by Claude-Marcel Hladik, Olga F. Linares, Annette Hladik, Hélène Pagezy, and Alison Semple, 1013–26. Paris: UNESCO / Parthenon Publishing Group.

———. 1999a. "La chasse à l'authentique: Histoire d'un âge de Pierre hors contexte." *Terrain* 33:93–110.

———. 1999b. "Agir de concert. La coopération chez les Anga: De la valeur heuristique d'un concept poussiéreux." In *Dans le sillage des techniques : Hommage à Robert Cresswell*, edited by Jean-Luc Jamard, Annie Montigny and François-René Picon, 349-68. Paris: L'Harmattan.

———. 2004. "The variability of women's 'involvement' in Anga Male Initiations." In *Women as unseen characters: Male ritual in Papua New Guinea*, edited by Pascale Bonnemère, 139–53. Philadelphia: University of Pennsylvania Press.

———. 2005a. "Mipela wan bilas: Identity and sociocultural variability among the Anga of Papua New Guinea." In *The changing South Pacific: Identities and transformations*, edited by Serge Tcherkézoff and Françoise Douaire-Marsaudon, 158–81. Translated by Nora Scott. Canberra: Pandanus Books

(Translated from the French: *Le Pacifique-Sud aujourd'hui: Identités et transformations culturelles*. Paris: Éditions du CNRS, 1997).

———. 2005b. "Objets sacrés sans "style." Circulez, y'a rien à voir?" In *L'Interrogation du style: Anthropologie, technique et esthétique*, edited by Bruno Martinelli, 237–54. Aix-en-Provence: Presses Universitaires de Provence.

———. 2006a. *Le Sabbat des lucioles: Sorcellerie, chamanisme et imaginaire cannibale en Nouvelle-Guinée*. Paris: Stock.

———. 2006b. "Objets sacrés? Chasse et initiations chez les Anga (Papouasie Nouvelle-Guinée)." In *La chasse: Pratiques sociales et symboliques*, edited by Isabelle Sidéra, 205–16. Paris: Éditions de Boccard.

———. 2010. "Mythes et rites chez les Anga." *Journal de la Société des Océanistes* 130–31:209–19.

———. 2016. "Les funérailles joyeuses d'un Caterpillar chez les Ankave-Anga de Papouasie-Nouvelle-Guinée." *Techniques & Culture* 65–66:112–33.

Lenel, Emmanuelle. 2009. "L'approche du care dans le débat féministe." *Les Cahiers jeu & symbolique* 2: 84–86.

Lévi-Strauss, Claude. 1963a. *Structural anthropology*. Translated by Claire Jacobson and Brooke Schoepf. New York: Basic Books (Translated from the French: *Anthropologie structurale*. Paris: Plon, 1958).

———. 1963b. *Totemism*. Translated by Rodney Needham. Boston: Beacon Press (Translated from the French: *Le totémisme aujourd'hui*. Paris: Presses Universitaires de France, 1962).

———. 1966. *The savage mind*. Chicago: University of Chicago Press (Translated from the French: *La pensée sauvage*. Paris: Plon, 1962).

Lewis, Gilbert. 1980. *Day of shining red: An essay on understanding ritual*. Cambridge: Cambridge University Press.

Lindstrom, Lamont. 1987. "Introduction: Relating with drugs." In *Drugs in Western Pacific societies: Relations of substance*, edited by Lamont Lindstrom, 1–12. Lanham, MD: University Press of America.

LiPuma, Edward. 1988. *The gift of kinship*. Cambridge: Cambridge University Press.

———. 2000. *Encompassing others: The magic of modernity in Melanesia*. Ann Arbor: University of Michigan Press.

Lloyd, Richard. 1973. "The Anga language family." In *The linguistic situation in the Gulf District and adjacent areas, Papua New Guinea*, edited by Karl Franklin, 263–77. Canberra: Pacific Linguistics.

Loraux, Nicole. 1989. *Les expériences de Tirésias: Le féminin et l'homme grec*. Paris: Gallimard.

Majnep, Ian, and Ralph Bulmer. 1977. *Birds of my Kalam country*. Auckland: Oxford University Press.

Malinowski, Bronislaw. 1927. *Sex and repression in a savage society*. London: Routledge.

Marriott, McKim. 1976. "Hindu transactions: Diversity without dualism." In *Transaction and meaning: Directions in the anthropology of exchange and symbolic behavior*, edited by Bruce Kapferer, 109–42. Philadelphia: Institute for the Study of Human Issues.

Mauss, Marcel. (1950) 1968. *Sociologie et anthropologie*. Paris: Presses Universitaires de France.

———. (1938) 1985. "A category of the human mind: The notion of person; the notion of self." In *The category of the person: Anthropology, philosophy, history*, edited by Michael Carrithers, Steven Collins, and Steven Lukes, 1–25. Cambridge: Cambridge University Press.

McKnight, David. 1973. "Sexual symbolism of food among the Wik-Mungkan." *Man*, n.s., 8 (2): 194–209.

Meigs, Anna S. 1984. *Food, sex, and pollution: A New Guinea religion*. New Brunswick, NJ: Rutgers University Press.

Menget, Patrick. 1979. "Temps de naître, temps d'être: La couvade." In *La fonction symbolique: Essais d'anthropologie*, edited by Michel Izard and Pierre Smith, 245–64. Paris: Gallimard.

———. 1989. "La couvade, un rite de paternité?" In *Le Père. Métaphore paternelle et fonctions du père: L'interdit, la filiation, la transmission*, 87–103. Paris: Denoël.

Merlan, Francesca, and Jeffrey Heath. 1982. "Dyadic kinship terms." In *Languages of kinship in Aboriginal Australia*, edited by Jeffrey Heath, Francesca Merlan, and Alan Rumsey, 125–40. Sydney: University of Sydney.

Métraux, Alfred. 1963. "The couvade." In *Handbook of South American Indians*. Vol. 5, *The comparative ethnology of South American Indians*, edited by Julian H. Steward, 369–74. New York: Cooper Square Publisher, Inc.

Mimica, Jadran. 1981. "Omalyce: An ethnography of the Iqwaye view of the cosmos." PhD diss., Australian National University.

———. 1988. *Intimations of infinity: The mythopoeia of the Iqwaye counting system and number*. Oxford: Berg.

————. 1991. "The incest passions: An outline of the logic of the Iqwaye social organization (Part 2)." *Oceania* 62 (2): 81–113.

Mintz, Sidney W., and Christine M. Du Bois. 2002. "The anthropology of food and eating." *Annual Review of Anthropology* 31:99–119.

Moisseeff, Marika. 1995. *Un long chemin semé d'objets rituels: Le cycle initiatique aranda.* Paris: Éditions de l'École des Hautes Études en Sciences Sociales.

Moore, Henrietta. 1988. *Feminism and anthropology.* Cambridge: Polity Press.

Morren, George E. B. J. 1986. *The Miyanmin: Human ecology in a Papua New Guinea Society.* Ann Arbor, MI: UMI Research Press.

Moutu, Andrew. 2006. "Collection as a way of being." In *Thinking through things: Theorising artefacts ethnographically,* edited by Amiria Henare, Martin Holbraad, and Sari Wastell, 93–112. London: Routledge.

Munroe, Robert L., and Ruth H. Munroe. 1989. "A response to Broude on the couvade." *American Anthropologist* 91 (3): 730–35.

Munroe, Robert L., Ruth H. Munroe, and John W. M. Whiting. 1973. "The couvade: A psychological analysis." *Ethos* 1:30–74.

Naepels, Michel. 2007. "Notion de personne et dynamique missionnaire." In *Terrains et destins de Maurice Leenhard,* edited by Michel Naepels and Christine Salomon, 69–91. Paris: Éditions de l'École des Hautes Études en Sciences Sociales.

Newman, Lucile. 1966. "The couvade: A reply to Kupferer." *American Anthropologist* 68 (1): 153–56.

Olivier de Sardan, Jean-Pierre. 1998. "Émique." *L'Homme* 147:151–66.

Ortner, Sherry, and Harriet Whitehead, eds. 1981. *Sexual meanings: The cultural construction of gender and sexuality.* Cambridge: Cambridge University Press.

Pitt-Rivers, Julian. 1973. "The kith and the kin." In *The character of kinship,* edited by J. Goody, 89–105. Cambridge: Cambridge University Press.

Poole, Fitz J. P. 1982. "Couvade and clinic in a New Guinea society: Birth among the Bimin-Kuskusmin." In *The use and abuse of medicine,* edited by Martin W. De Vries, Robert L. Berg, and Mack Lipkin, 54–95. New York: Praeger Publishers.

Poser, Anita von. 2017. "Care as Process: A Life-Course Perspective on the Remaking of Ethics and Values of Care in Daiden, Papua New Guinea". *Ethics and Social Welfare* 11 (3): 213–29.

Purdy, Laura M. 1990. "Are pregnant women fetal containers?" *Bioethics* 4 (4): 273–91.

Read, Kenneth. 1952. "Nama Cult of the Central Highlands, New Guinea". *Oceania* 23 (1): 1–25.

———. 1955. "Morality and the concept of the person among the Gahuku-Gama." *Oceania* 25 (4): 233–82.

Revolon, Sandra. 2014. "Les couleurs de la métamorphose. Des interférences lumineuses comme mode d'action sur le monde." In *L'Éclat des ombres. Objets en noir et blanc des Îles Salomon*, edited by Magali Mélandri and Sandra Revolon, 146–51. Paris: Somogy / Musée du quai Branly.

Rival, Laura. 1998. "Androgynous parents and guest children: The Huaorani couvade." *Journal of the Royal Anthropological Institute* 4 (4): 619–42.

Rivière, Peter G. 1974. "The couvade: A problem reborn." *Man* 9 (3): 423–35.

Robbins, Joel. 2004. *Becoming sinners: Christianity and moral torment in a Papua New Guinea Society*. Berkeley: University of California Press.

———. 2012. "Spirit women, church women, and passenger women: Christianity, gender, and cultural change in Melanesia." In "Christianismes en Océanie," edited by Yannick Fer, special issue, *Archives de sciences sociales des religions* 157:113–33.

Ross, Eric B. et al. 1978. "Food taboos, diet, and hunting strategy: The adaptation to animals in Amazon cultural ecology [and Comments and Reply]." *Current Anthropology* 19 (1): 1–36.

Salmon, Gildas. 2008. "Lévy-Bruhl et le problème de la contradiction." http://www. laviedesidees.fr/Levy-Bruhl-et-le-probleme-de-la.html.

Scheffler, Harold W. 1985. "Filiation and affiliation." *Man* 20 (1): 1–21.

Scheper-Hughes, Nancy, and Margaret M. Lock. 1987. "The mindful body: A prolegomenon to future work in medical anthropology." *Medical Anthropology Quarterly* 1 (1): 6–41.

Schneider, Almut. 2017. *La vie qui vient d'ailleurs: Mouvements, échanges et rituels dans les Hautes-Terres de la Papouasie-Nouvelle-Guinée*. Berlin: Lit Verlag.

Simoons, Frederick J. 1994. *Eat not this flesh*. Westport, CT: Greenwood Press.

Sørum, Arve. 1982. "The seeds of power: Patterns in Bedamini male initiation." *Social Analysis* 10:42–63.

———. 2017. "Bedamini male initiation and marriage as transformation sequences." In "Matter(s) of Relations: Transformation and presence in Melanesian and Australian Life-Cycle Rituals," edited by Pascale Bonnemère, James Leach, and Borut Telban, special issue, *Anthropological Forum* 27 (1): 63–76.

Speece, Richard, and Marilyn Speece. 1983. "Angave Anthropology Sketch." Ukarumpa, Unpublished manuscript.

Stasch, Rupert. 2009. *Society of others: Kinship and mourning in a West Papuan place*. Berkeley: University of California Press.

Strathern, Andrew J. 1971. *The rope of Moka: Big-Men and ceremonial exchange in Mount Hagen, New Guinea*. Cambridge: Cambridge University Press.

———. 1975. "Kinship, descent, and locality: Some New Guinea examples." In *The character of kinship*, edited by Jack Goody, 21–33. Cambridge: Cambridge University Press.

Strathern, Andrew, and Pamela Stewart. 2000. *Arrow talk: Transaction, transition, and contradiction in New Guinea highlands history*. Kent, OH: Kent State University Press.

Strathern, Marilyn. 1972. *Women in between: Female roles in a male world (Mount Hagen, New Guinea)*. London: Rowman & Littlefield.

———. 1978. "The achievement of sex: Paradoxes in Hagen gender-thinking." In *Yearbook of symbolic anthropology*, edited by Eric Schwimmer, 171–202. Montréal: McGill-Queen's University Press.

———. 1980. "No nature, no culture: The Hagen case." In *Nature, culture and gender*, edited by Carol P. MacCormack and Marilyn Strathern, 174–222. Cambridge: Cambridge University Press.

———. 1981. "Culture in a netbag: The manufacture of a subdiscipline in anthropology." *Man* 16 (4): 665–88.

———. 1984a. "Subject or object? Women and the circulation of valuables in Highlands New Guinea." In *Women and property, women as property*, edited by Renée Hirschon, 158–75. London: Croom Helm.

———. 1984b. "Domesticity and the denigration of women." In *Rethinking women's roles: Perspectives from the Pacific*, edited by Denise O'Brien and Sharon W. Tiffany, 13–31. Berkeley: University of California Press.

———. 1987a. "L'étude des rapports sociaux de sexe: Évolution personnelle et évolution des théories anthropologiques." *Anthropologie et sociétés* 11 (1): 9–18.

———. 1987b. "An awkward relationship: The case of feminism and anthropology." *Signs* 12 (2): 276–92.

———. 1988. *The gender of the gift: Problems with women and problems with society*. Berkeley: University of California Press.

———. 1992a. *Reproducing the future: Essays on anthropology, kinship, and the new reproductive technologies*. Manchester: Manchester University Press.

———. 1992b. "The mother's brother's child." In *Shooting the sun: Ritual and meaning in West Sepik*, edited by Bernard Juillerat, 191–205. Washington, DC: Smithsonian Institution Press.

———. 1993. "Making incomplete." In *Carved flesh / cast selves: Gendered symbols and social practices*, edited by Vigdis Broch-Due, Ingrid Rudie, and Tone Bleie, 41–51. Oxford: Berg.

———. 2013. "Appendix II: Social relations and the idea of externality." In *Learning to see in Melanesia: Lectures given in the Department of Social Anthropology, Cambridge University, 1993–2008*, by Marilyn Strathern, 179–204. Hau Masterclass Series, Volume 2. Manchester: HAU.

Strauss, Claudia. 2004. "Is Empathy Gendered? And, If So, Why? An Approach from Feminist Psychological Anthropology". *Ethos* 32 (4): 432–57.

Tarot, Camille. 2008. "Problématiques maussiennes de la personne." *Cahiers internationaux de sociologie* 124 (1): 21.

Taylor, Anne-Christine. 2008. "Corps, sexe et parenté: une perspective amazonienne. In *Ce que le genre fait aux personnes*, edited by Irène Théry and Pascale Bonnemère, 91–105. Paris: Éditions de l'École des Hautes Études en Sciences Sociales.

Taylor, Anne-Christine, and Eduardo Viveiros de Castro. 2006. "Un corps fait de regards." In *Qu'est-ce corps? Afrique de l'Ouest / Europe occidentale / Nouvelle-Guinée / Amazonie*, edited by Stéphane Breton, 148–99. Paris: Musée du quai Branly / Flammarion.

Taylor, Douglas. 1950. "The meaning of dietary and occupational restrictions among the Island Carib." *American Anthropologist* 52 (3): 343–49.

Taylor, John P. 2008. *The other side: Ways of being and place in Vanuatu*. Pacific Islands Monograph Series 22. Honolulu: University of Hawai'i Press.

Théry, Irène. 2007. *La distinction de sexe: Une nouvelle approche de l'égalité*. Paris: Odile Jacob.

———. 2010. "Le genre: Identité des personnes ou modalité des relations sociales?" *Revue française de pédagogie* 171:103–117 (Position, débats et controverses).

Théry, Irène, and Pascale Bonnemère, eds. 2008. *Ce que le genre fait aux personnes*. Paris: Éditions de l'École des Hautes Études en Sciences Sociales.

Troy, Aurélie. 2008. "Les pagnes des circoncis : Séparation et émotions dans les rites d'initiation seereer (Hireena, Sénégal)." In "Éprouver l'initiation," edited by Michael Houseman, special issue, *Systèmes de pensée en Afrique noire* 18:41–104.

Tuzin, Donald F. 1980. *The voice of the Tambaran: Truth and religion in Ilahita Arapesh religion*. Berkeley: University of California Press.

van Gennep, Arnold. (1909) 1981. *The rites of passage*. Translated by Monika Vizedom and Gabrielle Caffee. London: Routledge and Kegan Paul (Translated from the French: *Les rites de passage*, Paris: A. et J. Picard, 1909).

Vilaça, Aparecida. 2002. "Making kin out of others in Amazonia." *Journal of the Royal Anthropological Institute* 8 (2): 347–65.

Viveiros de Castro, Eduardo. 1998. "Cosmological deixis and Amerindian perspectivism." *Journal of the Royal Anthropological Institute* 4 (3): 469–88.

Wagner, Roy. 1967. *The curse of Souw: Principles of Daribi clan definition and alliance in New Guinea*. Chicago: University of Chicago Press.

———. 1974. "Are there social groups in the New Guinea Highlands?" In *Frontiers of anthropology*, edited by Murray J. Leaf, 95–120. New York: Van Nostrand Co.

———.1977. "Analogic kinship: A Daribi example." *American Ethnologist* 4 (4): 623–42.

Weiner, Annette B. (1976) 1983. *Women of value, men of renown: New perspectives in Trobriand exchange*. Austin: University of Texas Press.

Weiner, James F. 1982. "Substance, siblingship and exchange: Aspects of social structure in New Guinea." *Social Analysis* 11:3–34.

———. ed. 1995. "'Too many meanings': A critique of the anthropology of aesthetics." *Social Analysis* (special issue) 38:1–111.

Whitehead, Harriet. 2000. *Food rules: Hunting, sharing, and tabooing game in Papua New Guinea*. Ann Arbor: University of Michigan Press.

Wurm, Stephen A. 1982. *Papuan languages of Oceania*. Tübingen: Narr.

Yen, Douglas E. 1974. *The sweet potato and Oceania: An essay in ethnobotany*. Honolulu: Bishop Museum Press.

Index

HAU Books is committed to publishing the most distinguished texts in classic and advanced anthropological theory. The titles aim to situate ethnography as the prime heuristic of anthropology, and return it to the forefront of conceptual developments in the discipline. HAU Books is sponsored by some of the world's most distinguished anthropology departments and research institutions, and releases its titles in both print editions and open-access formats.

www.haubooks.com

Supported by
Hau-N. E. T.
Network of Ethnographic Theory

University of Aarhus – EPICENTER (DK)
University of Amsterdam (NL)
Australian National University – Library (AU)
University of Bergen (NO)
Brown University (US)
California Institute of Integral Studies (US)
University of Campinas (BR)
University of Canterbury (NZ)
University College London (UK)
University of Cologne – The Global South Studies Centre (DE)
and City Library of Cologne (DE)
University of Colorado Boulder Libraries (US)
Cornell University (US)
University of Edinburgh (UK)
The Graduate Institute – Geneva Library (CH)
University of Groningen (NL)
Harvard University (US)
The Higher School of Economics in St. Petersburg (RU)
Humboldt University of Berlin (DE)
Indiana University Library (US)
Johns Hopkins University (US)
University of Kent (UK)
Lafayette College Library (US)
London School of Economics and Political Science (UK)
Institute of Social Sciences of the University of Lisbon (PL)
Ludwig Maximilian University of Munich (DE)
University of Manchester (UK)
The University of Manchester Library (UK)
Max-Planck Institute for the Study of Religious and Ethnic
Diversity at Göttingen (DE)
Musée de Quai Branly (FR)
Museu Nacional – UFRJ (BR)
Norwegian Museum of Cultural History (NO)
University of Oslo (NO)
University of Oslo Library (NO)
Princeton University (US)
University of Rochester (US)
SOAS, University of London (UK)
University of Sydney (AU)
University of Toronto Libraries (CA)

www.haujournal.org/haunet

Lightning Source UK Ltd.
Milton Keynes UK
UKHW01f1403240918
329434UK00003B/5/P